T0243353

Advance Praise for *Weight in the Fingertips*

"In her autobiography *Weight in the Fingertips,* Inna Faliks gives a very personal account of her life, full of vivid, colorful details and written in a very beautiful, rich language. An interesting, informative, and enjoyable reading."—**Evgeny Kissin**, concert pianist

"A moving, exciting artistic journey by an important female voice, told with honesty and immediacy. I couldn't put it down— life's twists can certainly be more surprising than fiction."—**Jane Seymour**, Golden Globe and Emmy Award–winning actress

"Inna Faliks travels the world and becomes a musician of poetry and power. What an inspiring book—and life."—**Tim Page**, winner of the Pulitzer Prize for Criticism

"Inna Faliks's words have the same fluidity and assurance as her piano playing; both are well worth your attention. There are a lot of musician's memoirs out there; this one, about a piano prodigy turned professional, is a standout. Highly recommended."—**Anne Midgette**, American music critic and co-author of *My Nine Lives,* the autobiography of Leon Fleisher

"Of course this is the story of piano virtuoso Inna Faliks from her beginnings as a 'wunderkind' in poverty-stricken Odessa, Ukraine, played out over her musical and romantic adventures throughout Europe, the United States, China, and even Russia. But it is much more than that. It is Inna's *Eroica*: a mirror to Beethoven's towering heroic variations for piano with all its shifts, emotions, and surprises that play a recurring role throughout this endearingly engaging book. As Inna navigates her way through a moving and well-crafted coming-of-age story about a young person determined to unleash everything within her, she is a storytelling Beethoven, communicating via the language that binds us all: music."—**Hershey Felder**, pianist, actor, composer

"Inna Faliks's memoir is a rare and colorful window into the fraught process through which a young, vulnerable talent becomes a virtuoso. Filled with insights and adventures, her recollections—from tentative beginnings in Odessa to eye-opening explorations at cultural centers around the world—reveal the challenges of coming of age in the pressurized atmosphere of an emerging artist. Along the way she allows us to peer into the secrets behind the forging of beautiful sounds. *Weight in the Fingertips* explores the thrills, dangers, frustrations and triumphs of a life in music."—**Stuart Isacoff**, author of *Temperament: How Music Became a Battleground for the Great Minds of Western Civilization*

"Inna Faliks's playing long ago convinced me she had universes inside her. Now, in this memoir, we are shown the thousand rooms of a house spread across years and continents, in a style swift, considered & conspiratorial. One wants to remember one's own life this way."—**Jesse Ball**, author of *Autoportrait* and winner of the Plimpton Award and the Guggenheim Fellowship

"The story of Inna Faliks's life is not your everyday book of a great musician's beginnings. Like life, it is filled with the unexpected, moving from horror to hilarity, despair to hope. I just kept laughing and crying. It is unforgettable and paints a profound portrait of life; what is lost and what is found."—**Stephen Tobolowsky**, actor and author of *The Dangerous Animals Club*

"This is a gorgeously written memoir from an absolutely original voice that braids the book's concerns—music, pride in a difficult identity, immigration, belonging—into a spellbinding vision of the transcendent saving power of art."—**Boris Fishman**, author of *Don't Let My Baby Do Rodeo* and *A Replacement Life*

"A gripping tour-de-force packed with adventure, challenge, survival, heartbreak, love, and above all, the power of music. Inna Faliks is a storyteller to the manner born, who is not afraid of honesty and emotion, yet avoids any trace of self-indulgence. Her generous spirit, her sense of humor and gift for narrative pacing make it difficult to put this book down for a second. In short, here is a great musician and pianist who proves time and again to be equally articulate and communicative away from the keyboard."—**Jed Distler**, composer/pianist, radio host, reviewer for Classicstoday.com and *Gramophone*

WEIGHT IN THE
FINGERTIPS

WEIGHT IN THE
FINGERTIPS

A Musical Odyssey *from*
Soviet Ukraine *to*
the World Stage

INNA FALIKS

Backbeat
Books

Essex, Connecticut

**Backbeat
Books**

An imprint of Globe Pequot, the trade division of
The Rowman & Littlefield Publishing Group, Inc.
4501 Forbes Blvd., Ste. 200
Lanham, MD 20706
www.rowman.com

Distributed by NATIONAL BOOK NETWORK

Copyright © 2023 by Inna Faliks

All rights reserved. No part of this book may be reproduced in any form or
by any electronic or mechanical means, including information storage and
retrieval systems, without written permission from the publisher, except
by a reviewer who may quote passages in a review.

British Library Cataloguing in Publication Information available

Library of Congress Cataloging-in-Publication Data

Names: Faliks, Inna, author.
Title: Weight in the fingertips : a musical odyssey from Soviet Ukraine to the
   world stage / Inna Faliks.
Description: Essex, Connecticut : Backbeat, 2023. | Includes index.
Identifiers: LCCN 2023011041 (print) | LCCN 2023011042 (ebook) | ISBN
   9781493071746 (cloth) | ISBN 9781493071753 (ebook)
Subjects: LCSH: Faliks, Inna. | Pianists—United States—Biography. |
   LCGFT: Autobiographies.
Classification: LCC ML417.F189 A3 2023 (print) | LCC ML417.F189 (ebook)
   | DDC 786.2092 [B]—dc23/eng/20230310
LC record available at https://lccn.loc.gov/2023011041
LC ebook record available at https://lccn.loc.gov/2023011042

♾️™ The paper used in this publication meets the minimum requirements of
American National Standard for Information Sciences—Permanence of Paper
for Printed Library Materials, ANSI/NISO Z39.48-1992.

To my parents, Irene Faliks
(in memoriam, 1954–2021) and Simon Faliks
To Misha, Nathaniel, and Frida

CONTENTS

ACKNOWLEDGMENTS

This book would not exist without all the people appearing in it—however briefly—and I thank all of them for the way they inhabited it. I am grateful to my teachers, to my students, and to audiences that have given my music-making their ears and, thus, become a part of something fleeting yet, hopefully, meaningful and memorable. I have never and will never take a single one of you for granted. And, of course, I am grateful for the music I get to give life to—and for those who created it.

Thanks to my wonderful literary agent, Jud Laghi, for believing in me and in my writing. I think you know how much this means to me.

To my wise and sensitive editor, Chris Chappell: Thank you for making the process of editing as fascinating and engaging as writing. I feel bittersweet as our work comes to an end, and will dearly miss our exchanges. I've come to look forward to them.

To the team (Barbara, Dominique, Laurel) at Backbeat Books and Globe Pequot: Thank you for your support.

Thank you to all those who read, commented, advised, shared, corrected, argued, and otherwise helped over the course of this book's creation, including: Stephen Tobolowsky, Jesse Ball, Dimitri Dover, Daniel Schlosberg, Michael Sheppard, Oni Buchanan, Sandra Beasley, Mari Yoshihara, Inga Kapouler, Perry Gartner, Katherine Shonk, Jun Fujimoto, Inna Barmash,

Ljova Zhurbin, Rob Baker, Jan Baker, Anna Abramzon, David Kaplan, Rosalind Wong, Roberto Prosseda, Yevgeny Kissin, Alexey Steele, Olga Vlasova, Anna and Mark Gurevich, Tim Page, Jane Seymour, Stuart Isacoff, Hershey Felder, Boris Fishman, Anne Midgette, Peter McDowell, Yulya Dukhovny, and Don Osborne.

Thanks to the intrepid Cynthia Comsky who helped create *Polonaise-fantasie: The Story of a Pianist*—the performance piece based on a few chapters from this book—and to Rebecca Mozo and Cameron Watson for helping bring it to life. Thanks to all those who have supported this piece, including but not limited to Bonnie Barrett, Makia Matsumura, Hilary Jansen, and the rest of the Yamaha Artists team in NYC.

To my Mom, Irene Faliks (1954–2021): How I wish you could know this book exists.

To my Dad, Simon Faliks: Thank you for making up stories on the bus when I was four, for speaking in rhymes, for irony and sarcasm without which language is boring, for filling life with books, for giving me the endless love for words and the desire to play with them.

To Nathaniel and Frida: You fill my life with endless joy, whimsy, and adventure, and you make me feel like a kid, not just your Mom. I think that's the only state in which one can write a book.

To Michael Shpigelmacher, a.k.a, Misha, a.k.a, Shpilka: You are my everything. Each day you teach me humility, kindness, patience, and optimism, managing to be brilliant and hilarious at the same time. You fill life with oceans of love. Living with you is like reading a great book—on the edge of your seat, totally immersed, hoping there is no end in sight.

PRELUDE

I tighten my core, like in Pilates, getting ready for my entrance. The orchestra is almost there, the music teetering between a syncopated high F and G, as if unsure where to settle, how to resolve this long, fervent climb, so unabashedly gushing and gorgeous and full of love. This moment—the end of Tchaikovsky's First Piano Concerto—never fails to bring tears to my eyes onstage, but I cannot afford to let them come. This is the last solo piano entrance in the third movement—the famous long-octaves passage that precedes the orchestra and pianist joining forces. I have been playing it all my life. "Don't attack the piano," I tell myself. "Shape the notes in a long line, and they will carry themselves. Stay relaxed, don't forget to breathe, and feel the center in your belly. Power comes from singing, so sing!" And off I go.

We finish the piece, and the audience jumps up. They cannot not do it—the piece is designed that way, its heart on its flailing sleeve at every moment. And now I can cry.

I arrived in Memphis to play the Tchaikovsky Concerto the day after my mom's shiva in Chicago. She would not have wanted me to cancel. She had practiced every note of this piece with me when I learned it many years ago, at twelve. I tell this to the audience: "I lost my mom to brain cancer just a few days ago. She was my first teacher. She is with me as I play, and I am celebrating her. I want to play an encore for you. It won't be a sad one but a fun one."

By then, my mascara is running, but I grin ear to ear. The audience can see this because, for the first time in eighteen months, I am onstage and without a mask. I am savoring my favorite feeling—the plasticity of hands after a concert. The muscles are so warm and alive they can do anything. As a pianist, you feel all-powerful. As a musician, you feel connected to each person in the audience. And you want to give them more.

"La Campanella" ("The Bells") is a concerto by Paganini, transcribed into a piano showpiece by the composer-pianist Franz Liszt, who also happened to be one of the first truly great arrangers. Its many repeated notes and jumps give it a reputation of near impossibility, but I was lucky to learn it in childhood. There is never a better time to play it than as an encore. The key to "Campanella" is that it needs to sound bell-like, and each sound needs to connect to the next in a seamless phrase. It must look and feel easy, natural, and inevitable. In performance, the difficult filigree where the right hand needs to reach, in nanoseconds, the highest register of the piano to bring out the bell-like melody, needs to sound easy, hummed, almost casual. My mom probably heard me play this piece thousands of times. This is the first time I perform my beloved encore without her present in my world. But playing the music connects me and the audience to something eternal, something that will be there long after we are gone. With every note, music—black dots on a page—comes to life and celebrates it.

1

BACH SOUND, SPOON RHYTHM

I knew I was a musician long before I knew I was Jewish, Ukrainian, or Soviet. Red October, our family piano, did not have three legs, though its name suggested the stomping sound of many feet marching, running, storming one ornate, aristocratic building after another. It was an upright and fit neatly against one wall of my parent's room. It was caramel and chocolate in color, like the insides of the cone-shaped candies that were hidden on top of the commode in my great-grandmother's room. I pretended to play this majestic, untouchable thing with grand motions. It was an important member of the household, and I had to treat it accordingly.

My father, Simon, still claims that he was the only Jewish child in Odessa who was not a musical wunderkind. Unlike my dad, my mother, Irene, was a musician. She taught at a music school on the outskirts of town. Coming home from work after taking three buses, exhausted, she'd have a quick peek into the kitchen. Was I drawing, reading with Great-Grandma, or getting into trouble? Then she would quickly change into a housedress. (Every woman in the Soviet Union had one. It was something between a cotton bathrobe and a muumuu of an unidentifiable color and pattern and would have been washed by hand hundreds of times. In its defense, it was made of comfortable, thick cotton and lasted for years.) She would put on the kettle and go to the room she shared with me, Dad, and the piano for a brief practice session. A tall, slender, bushy-haired brunette, Mom was shy and reserved. Never much of a hugger, she treated me in a respectful, collegial manner—with warmth but without cloying baby talk or much cuddling. Her elegance and seriousness could be seen in the way she touched the keys. Her long fingers searched delicately and quickly, as she would move on, a little nervously, from scales to Scriabin. Having to share three rooms with six other family members, she hadn't any place but the piano bench that she could call her own.

Mom and me in Odessa, 1979.

I tried to replicate my mother's ease at Red October, but I hardly ever pressed on the keys for fear of breaking them. After observing me air-play the piano enough times, the family—Mom, Dad, Grandma Rimma, Grandpa Boris, and Great-Grandma Fanni—decided to start me on music lessons.

When I turned four, Mom dressed me in a pink frilly skirt and a slightly worn sweatshirt with a baby bear and the emblazoned letters *UCLA*—most definitely a regift from the relatives who had immigrated to the United States a decade earlier. While I wondered who "Ookla" the bear could possibly be, Mom asked me to vocalize a simple C major arpeggio, "Do Mi Sol Do," which I sang cleanly, and "Solnechnii Krug" ("Sunny Circle"), a Soviet song about peace. She was biting her lips and playing with her thin necklace. When she was seven, she had auditioned for a chorus that appeared in a Soviet film, singing that very song. I sang brightly, but she was somber, sharing with me the seriousness of the moment. She explained that Dad would be taking me to the music school for the first time for a singing audition and that they might even choose which instrument I would play, right then and there. She must have been very nervous, as she didn't want to go with us.

I didn't care about the exam; all I cared about was the tram ride through town, an exciting prospect in theory because there was a soda machine at our tram stop. If ten kopeks were properly dispensed, yellowish sugared water and bubbles would pour from the machine out into a single glass, to be used and reused by reckless customers. The glass was never washed, of course. I asked for this treat over and over again, but alas, it was unhygienic, sugary, and forbidden to me forever.

Tram wires were draped across the city like cobwebs. While we waited for the tram, my father passed the time and distracted me from the soda machine by picking up threads of various stories that we had going. My dad's talent had always been in improvising clever rhymed poetry and stories on random subjects. There was one about a baby dragon who would infuriate his pedantic, proletarian teachers at school with his antics and one about a musician mouse. But my favorite were the spontaneous, surreal incantations he would recite, conjuring the tram to arrive. They always worked—the tram would inevitably roar into the stop after a short while. Because of Dad's curly hair and beard, I thought that we might be related to Pushkin, the king of Russian verse. How else could he make up poetry on the spot? Dad's hair was red, while Pushkin's was pitch-black, and Dad's nose was somewhat potato-shaped, like mine, while Pushkin's was long and slender—but I still believed it. I often wanted to ask Pushkin if this was true. We passed him by on the way to the school, the bronze bust in a little garden, gracing the promenade leading to the Potemkin steps and overlooking the Black Sea. Every Soviet child knew at least one Pushkin poem by heart, learned in the first few years of their life: "A green oak stands by the seabed. There is a golden chain on it, and a learned cat walks round and round. He goes left, and begins a song. Goes right, and speaks a fairy tale . . ."

The tram would arrive, and I would hop on and run for the red seat. The seats were smooth plastic, alternating between scarlet and gray, shaped to accommodate a sizable rump. Unless

I got the red seat, I refused to sit down. This was not so much a patriotic gesture on my part but rather a distasteful association with the color gray after I once overheard my mother saying to my father, "I hope that the children she meets are lively, interesting, with hobbies. I would hate for her to have to spend time with children who are . . . gray."

Gray children sounded terribly depressing—sad, very quiet, maybe living in a room all by themselves. I lived in an apartment that housed seven people, and I loved the noise and ruckus. I didn't know any gray children. I was dark-skinned and black-haired, an Ashkenazi Jew who stuck out among the other children playing in the courtyard at the front of our apartment building. They were blond-haired and blue-eyed and spat the word *Evreika* ("Jew girl") at me. I didn't know what that meant, as I'd never even heard the word *Jewish* yet.

The tram passed Direbasovskaya Prospect, with its cafés, chestnut trees, and painters setting up their canvases on the street, and turned to greet the old Kircha, a cavernous, mostly collapsed church that was covered in soot and pigeon droppings. It alarmed me with its single spire. To me, it was a forlorn, forgotten castle, like the sad, lilting second movement of Mussorgsky's *Pictures at an Exhibition*. It looked like something one might build out of wet sand, releasing dark rivulets onto the ground and making complex, curvy structures. Its darkness drew me in. There was something forbidden dwelling there in the ruins, something that nobody could talk about: ideas and beliefs and ways of being that were thought of as either archaic, dangerous, or both. Whatever people did there for hundreds of years was no longer permissible. As it passed from view, a helpless sadness came over me, as though a large animal was drowning.

Religion in the Soviet Union was, of course, illegal. There were no churches in Odessa, no synagogues that I could identify. I didn't know who God was or what praying meant. Nor did I know that Teofil Richter, father to the great pianist Sviatoslav Ricther, had worked as the church organist in the Kircha. He was killed in 1941—not by the Nazis, but by his own people after being accused of espionage. This is why his son never gave concerts in Odessa.

As I write this, Odessa is caught in the middle of the Russian-Ukrainian war, but it was still ablaze with Communist red in the 1980s. Odessa Jews had once numbered in the hundreds of thousands, but during the late '80s and early '90s, most of the Odessa Jews immigrated to the United States, Israel, Canada, Australia, and other countries. Some were aided by nongovernmental organizations, such as the Hebrew Immigration Aid Society. This was to the great relief of many Soviets. Jews often heard casual proclamations like "Yids, go home to Israel or any place that will take you!"

On my first day at National Music School 4—a yellow, French-style building guarded by a stone statue of Atlas—I was greeted in the lobby by an important-looking man with a belly and beard. He took me by the hand and led me into a room with an upright piano, leaving my father to wait for me. A short-haired lady in a suit waited at the piano.

"This is Valentina Anatolievna, one of our finest piano teachers. And I am Yuri Barsky, director of the school," the bearded man told me.

The lady gestured for me to come toward her. "I will play a tune, and I want you to sing back what you hear." She began to play short melodies—some sad, some joyful. What a fun game! I would sing what I'd heard, and she would ask me about the character of the music. Then she played a waltz, then a march, and asked me what these sounded like. *Is that ringing, bell-like sound a bird or a bear? And is this gentle sound in the middle of the piano a lion or a cat?* Apparently, I did well. They invited my dad into the room and told him I was accepted. I smiled widely but didn't jump up and down or clap. I was going to be a musician, so I had to act accordingly—like a professional. Well-behaved Soviet children didn't jump up and down.

I thought that I would immediately learn to play piano like my mother. Instead, I was handed two red and gold wooden spoons adorned with phoenixes and taken to a room where a Ukrainian folk instrument orchestra for children under five was rehearsing. I was flabbergasted. I was a soloist! I was ready to perform on my own, all the music I had heard my mom practice—Mozart, Bach, Scriabin—and to make up my own pieces. I just needed to figure out how to play the piano! But they didn't understand, and so for my first public appearances, I sang in the chorus and played the spoons.

* * *

What is more important for a child to learn first: sound or rhythm? I suppose this is similar to such questions as "If Sylvester Stallone and Chuck Norris had a fistfight, who would win?" or "If Godzilla took on Swamp Thing, who would come out on top?" The truth is that both hold the key to making music. Rhythm is primordial and ever present: the beating of our heart, our breaths, our steps. I wanted to be able to touch the piano, to make it sing about all the colorful landscapes and characters that traversed my mind. But it's easier for a small child to learn rhythm at the earliest stage possible, so my parents were smart to put me in a rhythmic studies group. The orchestra usually performed publicly during big Communist holidays, like February 23, the Day of the Honoring of the Soviet Army. These were my first moments on a stage, and concert attire consisted of *kokoshniki* (Russian folk headbands, lavishly decorated and shaped like a musical accent) and ruffled, embroidered tops and skirts.

After a few months of listening to me rehearse on the spoons, my mom thought it was time to start me on the violin. She called her friend, a teacher at the music school. Luckily for me, the violin studio was full. That evening, Mom's own piano teacher from the famed Odessa Music Conservatory came over for tea. She took Mom aside and said reproachfully, "With those hands, no piano?" My hands were, in fact, large for a little girl, with a rather square base at my wrists ("bodes well for octaves!") and fingers both thick and long ("will have a solid, deep sound!"), so it had to be the piano.

Most people rightfully assume that professional pianists start early. First, they might be taught how to make rainbows with their arm, landing the second finger on the same note in every octave—moving like a dancer, gracefully, or like a cat, with a soft paw, stealthily. Around the same time, they would learn to add single-digit numbers in preschool. Sometimes pianists start training before they've even learned to hold a spoon, or in notable but rare exceptions, they start much later. For the most part, though, by their late teenage years, a concert pianist has developed an artistic voice. *Artistic voice*: such a lofty term. How can an awkward instrument that looks something like a cross between a three-legged buffalo and a black swan, percussive and hungry looking, be conducive to developing any kind of voice?

But that "voice" is what begins with the note that sounds when you press downward on a key. I suppose that a child in whom musical talent manifests extremely early—naturally, like language—has that voice inside them already, even before they have had a chance to show it to the world as a "prodigy." It is unique to the artist and honed over a lifetime. If you listen to a few different recordings of the same piece—for example, Beethoven's last sonata, the C Minor op. 111 performed by Maria Grinberg, Sviatoslav Richter, Daniel Barenboim, or even yours truly—each will differ profoundly in the pianist's sound and interpretation of the score. Those differences are the hallmarks of the individual artistic voices, speaking the same music in unique ways.

Mrs. Valentina was a respected teacher, known to be kind, tough, and very successful with children. Her students played sensitively and maturely at a young age. She knew that my mom was also a piano teacher, and they agreed that she and the rest of my family would work with me at home, while Valentina would shepherd me at the school. My first lessons with her were about developing the ear—but also about forming the rounded, natural hand position and the physical relationship with the piano that serves as a pianist's foundation. The hand should form a natural dome when the fingers, no longer flat and asleep on the keys, awaken and rise up, giving a spiderlike appearance. The fingertips become focused, resilient—electrically charged, almost—while the hand remains flexible and relaxed. The elbow and shoulder remain free and flexible, with their weight carried into each individual, tiny fingertip, yielding a sound, sweet, deep, delicious.

* * *

Our Odessa apartment, on the second floor of Soviet Army Street 50, was the perfect place to practice. Sometimes, I would escape to the bathroom, lock the door, and read a book, or I could sneak out onto the balcony and watch the goings-on in the courtyard. No child really wants to practice every day—but I knew that if I didn't, I wouldn't be able to play like my mom. I also began to love the feel of the keys, the color of the piano, its chestnut glow and nasal voice. With six adults around me, I was always under somebody's watchful eye, and discipline developed quickly. Most children don't want to practice, and sometimes I would resist, but the pride of doing something consistently, with care and detail, a little bit better each day—this is what practicing is all about at the start. It drew me in quickly and naturally.

The apartment had three rooms: the piano room, where my parents and I lived; the rug room, where my great-grandmother dwelled; and the book room, for my mother's parents. The last was entirely taken over by books on shelves and in stacks, a mosaic of maroon and dusty blue and gray, battered and inviting. Grandma Rimma and Grandpa Boris were both psychiatrists— they had met at a hospital—and there was a frighteningly infor- mative, perpetually open encyclopedia of solemn anatomical diagrams on the writing desk. "Rimma, what is this?" I would ask, pointing at a man's groin, knowing that somehow this was inappropriate and therefore funny. Grandma, a voluptuous, for- tyish woman, was a little bit of a prude and would turn beet red. "This is what the man pees with."

Grandfather Boris was a handsome and refined man, ath- letic, intellectual, and very restrained with words. He died when I was nine, and I recall the sound of his cough: cackling, lengthy as a monologue. He read in the kitchen late into the night. I remember him walking down the street while reading a book, maneuvering the sidewalk masterfully. When he was bedridden with diabetes, an old man at fifty-one, I went to visit him in the book room. I prepared for these visits mentally, as I worshipped him but was a little afraid of him. He always asked me what I was reading and encouraged me to read at least a book a week, and he would be disappointed if what I had read did not meet his standards for world literature. Grandfather's typewriter had seen many underground pages of banned books surreptitiously reproduced, typed somewhere and retyped elsewhere and again retyped by him and passed on to those who loved books. Even Mikhail Bulgakov's *The Master and Margarita*—possibly the most beloved twentieth-century Russian novel and the most personally important book to me—had been retyped by Grandfather Boris, as it was still banned in those days. A lifetime later, reading it for the umpteenth time to my mother, breaking words into syllables together with her as she recovered from a stroke, I would try to remember: Was it then, in Boris's room, that I first met its intoxicating characters, tracing the pictures with my finger? Woland the devil. Margarita the witch. Master the writer.

Walking down Soviet Army Street in Odessa with Grandpa Boris.

The rug room was deemed as such by me for its giant wall rug, a very typical adornment for a cluttered Soviet apartment. The rug had a delirious amount of detail, filled with creatures that ran, played, ate plants, and rode birds that turned into flowers and four-headed monsters. It was all very involved and multilayered, and the creatures seemed to be entangled differently each time I looked. Beneath the rug lived the queen of the household, Great-Grandma Fanni, or Babushka. *Babushka* means *grandmother* in Russian, but everyone called her that, including her daughter Rimma, my actual grandmother. Her eyes and nose were those of a large, wise bird. She practiced piano with me every day when my parents, then in their late twenties, would slip out for a movie or have tea with their friends.

"You must play with a Bach-ian sound," she repeated to me daily. At six, I had no concept of a Bach-ian sound, and I am

At the piano, age six, already working on my hand position.

not sure Babushka did either. But I imagined something holy, sacred, old, and eternal, like the Kircha that we passed on the way to music school. And like Babushka herself.

When she was young, Babushka had studied piano with Gustav Neyhaus, the father of the legendary teacher in the Moscow Conservatory, Heinrich Neyhaus. She was a chemistry professor but, like many Soviet intellectuals, was educated enough in music to feel confident discussing a piano's sound. She must have been just in her seventies then, but she carried herself as a woman much older—moving about slowly, with a cane. She was the matron of the house, and every decision had to be approved by her. Every pot on the stove had to be inspected by her, every porridge and stew approved. You never left a morsel on your plate under her watchful eye. After surviving World War II, she knew the value of bread. You had to finish your share of the loaf Mom had bought after three hours in line, even if you were stuffed and could not swallow another bite. You had to finish the wheat-germ porridge, even if the congealment of the little particles of porridge with a film of milk over them was so unsettling a texture that to this day the thought of it makes you queasy. I never saw her wear outdoor clothes—I never saw her even leave the apartment—just a housedress. Her tempestuous hair, dark with a few veins of silver, was always gathered in a high bun. She stooped when she walked but looked regal whether she was presiding over cooking preparations in the kitchen, reading a newspaper in her battered, old armchair, or next to me by the piano. You had to report to her every detail of your day—if you were eight or twenty-eight or forty-eight.

So, as I practiced during my first year at the piano, Babushka listened and talked about that special sound of Bach. It had nothing to do with historically informed performance practice, or the harpsichord, of course. It was only a reflection of her imagination—and of mine, in time. I imagined a warm, throaty, purplish-blue, serious sound.

From my early introduction to random piano notes (up high on the keys like birds, and down low like elephants and tigers), I learned to build with sound in the same way a calligrapher carefully works with a capricious brush. The hand had to be relaxed and fluid, as if a long line were being drawn from shoulder to fingertips. The pillowy parts of the fingertips landed on the keys, releasing gently after the sound. I learned legato—like drawing a star or a car or a house without lifting the pen from paper; the sounds formed a smooth line with a clear direction like a question or a statement—and staccato: sharp and satisfying, like little hard New Year's candies in shiny wrappers, the fingertip bouncing until there was a tiny callus. In my lessons, Valentina taught me the different roles of the left and right hands, of singer and accompanist, of conductor and chorus, friends going for a walk, a brother and sister fighting or of one voice speaking over another. First, slowly, then faster and faster. First by reading the music, a most stylish and fanciful alphabet, and then from memory. There were songs with lyrics, like the one about the cat and the goat from the "Russian School of Piano Playing"; in the English-language version, it was translated as "Shaggy old pussycat on the lawn walking, / with three steps behind him a horny goat stalking." Then, some short pieces from the Anna Madgelena Bach notebook, written by J. S. Bach for his wife. And then, finally, I was ready to play small, vivid character pieces by composers like Beethoven, Kabalevsky, Schumann, and Tchaikovsky, and Bach's *Inventions* and *Sinfonias*—simple and brilliant puzzles of intertwined voices.

I practiced after school for a few hours a day, while Anastasia, the child next door, chased stray cats, drew maps of imaginary cities in colored chalk, and stuffed caterpillars into jars in the backyard of our old apartment complex. She had five cats and three hamsters at home. The street cats accepted her as their reigning monarch and humored her by running when she chased them for fun. She would leave milk and fish bones for them overnight.

"Playing piano is for sissies!" she would taunt and then shoot spitballs up at our window through a straw. I ignored her because I knew she really just wanted me to go out and explore the innards of our dirty courtyard; collect chestnuts; snoop into the back of the pastry shop, where the warm, sugary fragrance intertwined with the smells of cat urine and garbage, resulting in something intoxicating; and, of course, the cellar—the horrible catacombs that I never dared descend into.

Anastasia was the best friend I inherited generationally—her family lived in the apartment above ours, and her mother, Olga, was best friends with my mother. Her grandma Ada, likewise, was best friends with my grandma Rimma. Anastasia's love for me was almost that of a sibling, in that the meaner she was to me, the more I knew she adored me. This dynamic between us was nothing new: Family legend had it that she fed me cigarettes when I was two and she was three. Our families shared a small summer house a half hour's walk from the Black Sea, where she taught me that worms came out of the showerhead at night and that the treasure buried near the quince trees could only be dug up after midnight and that the Hound of Baskervilles lived and enjoyed the fresh air in our garden. She bestowed on me a morbid fear of jellyfish, which still prevents me from swimming in the most pristine ocean waters today. When I was three, she decided, without my consent, to play catch with me on the beach with the creatures. The clear, flaccid chunks of jellyfish flesh hit my belly and my knees as I stood there, roaring through tears.

At our apartment, I practiced on Red October, but at the house, where practicing was torturous and the summer sun hard to resist, I played on an ancient creature. This piano was a no-name black upright, with wooden flowery patterns, yellowed white keys, graying black keys, and a tromp l'oeil of Mozart on the side. I had to practice after morning trips to the sea for three requisite swims.

My father taught me to swim early, and his methods remain questionable. One day, after many patient hours teaching me balance, arm movement, and how to keep my head above water, he threw me right into the sea. During what I remember to be a tempest of epic proportions, I had to fight for my life (or so I thought) to find my inflatable swimming mattress. How my mother did not hurt him after this, I do not know. But I did learn to swim very fast.

At other times, I would go with him to the beach, where he caught shrimp, and help him get them back to the summer house. We would boil and eat them immediately, peeling the translucent shells and swallowing the sweet flesh greedily, without chewing. On those evening shrimp-catching trips to the sea, we sometimes saw hedgehogs on the road basking in the unobtrusive warmth of the sunset. How I wanted to bring one with us to show Anastasia so that she would know that she was not the only one who had a way with creatures and insects—that I, too, could hold one gingerly on the palm of my hand and watch its small, black nose retreat into its needled forest.

One day, Anastasia and I had run out to the beach after the sea had turned inky and cantankerous in one of its many moods. The tide had carried some seashells onto the sand, and they looked very different from the usual ones we found and played with. There were little wagons with spiral tails, tiny rainbow hats with pom-poms, and miniature ottomans the color of spotted seals. We gathered them into our pails and carried them home, laying them out to dry across the bedrooms and kitchen. Days later, when the smell of rotting flesh from the dying creatures inside them hit our parents' noses, we solemnly buried them.

On one August night, Anastasia and I drew about twenty tickets on slips of paper that proclaimed, "Grand Summer

Night Performance Gala at the Veranda Tonight Only!" This either came from watching some very pompous Soviet-curated pop shows on television or from reading *Adventures of Moomi Trolls* by Tove Jansson. We used dried pits from apricots for our tickets and wrote out programs on leaves. The invited guests—grandmas, grandpas, parents, and a few neighbors—showed up to the veranda to find a stage decorated with colored-paper garlands (made by Anastasia's golden, artistic hands) and me, crooning, in my mother's red gown—stolen from her closet—and a wide-brimmed hat:

> You are so cold, like an iceberg in the ocean.
> And all your sadness is buried under black water.

It was from "Iceberg," an '80s hit by the Soviet pop star Alla Pugacheva. My red dress was a must, as I had recently listened to an LP of *Carmen*, Bizet's operatic paean to fiery women and free love (in Ukrainian, not French, because all operas had to be performed and recorded in Russian or its sister Soviet proletarian languages). On the cover of that album, a dark-eyed gypsy danced in a splendid red gown. I was smitten with the idea of a femme fatale, her wild free spirit, the passion she inspired in everyone around her. I loved how there were melodic themes for everything—for the ill-fated love of Carmen and the soldier Jose, for the menace of death, for jealousy, for missing home, for bullfighting. With just harmony, rhythm, and melody, a whole world of feelings and actions came to life. I practiced being Carmen, with a rose between my teeth, stomping the ground, throwing up my arms into the air, and wailing the famous "Habanera."

As the audience took their seats, my oversized dress crumpled to the ground, and I was left standing in front of them, fake microphone in hand and wearing only white underpants. I decided then that I would prefer to play Mozart's *Fantasie* in D Minor the next time I performed in public and that it would be best to wear concert dresses in my own size.

* * *

I started composing music when I was six. I first improvised the "Forest Tale," a story of savage forest creatures, playing their themes and narrating their actions from the piano. I was not sure where to go from there, so my mother found me a composition teacher who came over to the apartment to give me lessons. Composition allowed me to play games with sound, to take whatever I was reading or thinking and very simply turn it into a musical shape or gesture.

First came small pieces with an A-B-A form—a few symmetrical phrases, like a question paired with its answer, followed by a section in a new key with a different kind of character, and then a return to the original question and answer. Then I set a few poems to music, which came easily. My first chamber music experience, at age five, was performing a song, "Our Beloved Land, with Its Forests and Rivers," with a horn player for a recital. The horn had a certain timbre and character, and the accompaniment a totally different one. Though the song had been extremely silly, it helped me learn how accompaniment and melody fit together.

When I was nine, my piano pieces started to get longer, darker, and more rambling and chromatic. I was also beginning to read more grown-up books. At the music school, my theory teacher, Natalia Lvovna, noticed that I was composing on a daily basis and suggested a larger-scale piece. She had heard the story of my "Forest Tale" and thought I should take the next step. This was how the opera, innocently titled *The Cat's House*, came about.

The libretto was a children's story by Samuil Marshak, in upbeat, rhymed couplets but with a serious proletarian moral behind it: A wealthy Grande Dame of a cat buys a fancy new house and invites her rich friends over for a party. The conceited goat, gossipy hen, and prudent pig all come to have tea in the splendid veranda and to discuss the latest news of the town. An unwelcome visit from the cat's poor relatives, two shabby kittens, elicits various obnoxious responses from the guests, and the mistress of the house shuts the kittens out without giving them any food. During the night, the house burns down. The cat is homeless and has to find shelter. She stops by the homes of her friends, but the hen, the goat, and the pig all shun her. The kittens welcome her into their tiny, ramshackle home, and she promises to be a good aunt to them.

As an operatic libretto, this had everything. The dialogue allowed for plenty of solo arias, vocal duets, trios, quartets, and more. There was dramatic flair—a fire! (Also, who *buys* a house? Nobody we knew, that was for sure. This was fantasy.) There was heartbreak—the kittens, turned away—and there was justice and forgiveness at the end, just like Mozart's *Figaro*! During a recent music theory and history lesson, Natalia Lvovna had explained to her students the nature of a leitmotif—a tune, or a theme, or a fragment of a theme representing a given character or idea. This was an amazing discovery, and I decided to employ the concept. With her help, I set to work.

I was obsessed with opera heroines—my parents had already taken me to see operas by Tchaikovsky and Verdi, and I had that record of *Carmen* that I listened to over and over. I had already been playing in recitals around town, but I wanted to sing in an opera—so much more flamboyant than playing the piano! This was my chance. So, with profound narcissism, I wrote the part for myself. The opening aria began with an octave leap up and was intricate but melodious. That octave leap became the cat's leitmotif. The hen, goat, and pig all had themes that tried to evoke their appearance, character, and demeanor through the melody's shape and the moods suggested by the chords. But most important was the rhythm—plodding in the case of the pig, silly and jumpy in the case of the goat. The best theme of the score was the kittens' sad aria, which somehow got stuck as an earworm for anybody that heard it. My parents hummed it for years.

The opera was never orchestrated but was skillfully accompanied by Natalia Lvovna on the piano. I had written out everything with her and Mom's help, including the piano part, and all the vocal parts and the libretto. The show, in its entirety, was an hour long. The parts were assigned to other music students, and friends and relatives designed the costumes from scraps. I knew that my costume was sent by Aunt Dolly from the United States, including a blue, gauze dress that was like a dream, one that my mother marveled at, floating on its hanger in cloudlike splendor, like a museum piece. The ears were tufts of fur that came from unspecified sources. And my aunt had donated her fur collar, which was sewn onto the dress as the bushy and manicured tail of the wealthy pampered feline. The cat, my star role, was coming to life.

The performance took place at the Odessa Philharmonic Hall, a building that combined Moorish architectural elements with French elegance, as a part of a big festival of children's music, and it was repeated later at my School for the Gifted and Talented. Segments of it were replayed on Ukrainian television. I found my grandfather Boris waiting for me after school the day after the premiere with a copy of the *Odessa News*—my first review! It was only a few lines long and dryly commented on the nine-year-old composer's surprising use of chromatic harmonies. I was not impressed by this, but Grandpa was the most excited I had ever seen him.

After the success of the *The Cat's House*, my mother went over to the apartment of a prominent Odessa composer, the notoriously grumpy and reclusive Jan Freidlin. He taught composition to college students at the famous Stolyarsky School and never accepted children as students. She spent two hours pleading with him. Finally, probably to get rid of her, he agreed to take me on as a student.

So began my weekly trips to his apartment, full of mysterious art, books, scores, and plants, all enveloped by a mossy darkness. At the first lesson, we rang the doorbell and waited for a few awkward minutes—five or even ten. A greasy-haired man in a stained caftan opened the door, quietly stepped aside, and let us in. I was petrified. In my mind, he resembled the master from the Bulgakov novel—severe, sullen, sad—and somehow I felt that we interrupted something. (My intuition was not wrong, as moments later, a long-haired lady in a transparent nightgown passed through his piano room, disappearing into the kitchen like a phantom.)

I played something I composed that week—like "Song of the Lion," set to a poem I wrote about a lion who was depressed because he had never seen the Black Sea. I played and sang, suddenly acutely aware that the song was pedestrian, childish, and clichéd. How could we make it better? Give the bass more importance. Give the left hand a more interesting line. Make the melody less predictable. Here you stay in G major—go into a minor key!

Maestro Freidlin treated me as an adult, never joked or laughed or even cracked a smile, and dismissed my opera as drivel. He was much more impressed with a few of the darker piano pieces that I had written. One of his first projects with me was an analysis of Stravinsky's *Petrushka*, a difficult and groundbreaking work usually covered by composition majors in college.

I learned that to be a composer, you also have to practice every day. Every single day, after I'd done scales, etudes, and piano pieces, Mom would bring me a few lined manuscript pages and a pencil. "What do you want to write today? What character are you thinking of?" By then, it would have been after 5:00 p.m. Anastasia would already be in the yard, calling me. Babushka would respond, from the balcony, "Inna is composing. She cannot come out."

"Ooh, the great composer," Anastasia would tease. I knew that she was jealous of the piano—not because she, too, wanted to play and compose but because it took me away from her. Imagine: A human could be jealous of music!

Perhaps Anastasia already then could see what I couldn't yet recognize because I was living it daily. Music was an invisible yet vital force of love that propelled me forward every day to do things my own way. It was my voice. It gave life to my thoughts and my questions and worries, and it made my world glow.

2

SHPILKA

By age nine, I was an advanced young pianist. Other people sometimes took advantage of this. My mother had enrolled me in ballet; because I lacked grace and coordination, she thought a Monday night with ten little ballerinas, a perpetually inebriated pianist, and a craggy ballet teacher would do me good. One night, Mom came early and entered the classroom to pick me up, only to find me accompanying the class. The pianist was out smoking in the hallway. "How many times did you do this?" she asked. "Oh, every time! I love these Tchaikovsky pieces, and the lady who usually plays always asks me to play them while she smokes outside. She gives me a chocolate candy." No wonder I hadn't learned a single position. Fuming, Mom took me out of ballet forever.

I never questioned why I had to practice—it simply felt as if the sound I sought ran away from me if I did not spend hours at the piano every day. It's the feeling of being in shape—when your musical intentions face no physical obstacles, your fingers very quickly feel warmed up and ready, and the music flows easily. Of course, practicing in the city on school days was easier than during summers. I went to School 119, for the gifted and talented—and for the children of Communist Party leaders who didn't want their child to take an entrance exam but could afford to bribe their way in. A party member only needed to give a modest bribe, in cash or perhaps in chocolate, European clothes, or vodka. This was the way of the land. Girls had to wear bows in our hair that would not look out of style at a British royal wedding. Mine was just about the size of my rather large head. Each classroom had an assigned color of bows, and ours was red.

I had a close-knit circle of friends in the classroom. My best friend, the only kid in school who was shorter than me, was Misha Shpigelmacher (a.k.a., Shpilka). He was a year younger than the rest of us and about fifteen years smarter, judging by his knowledge of history, his caricature drawings, and his impressively developed sense of wit. We were desk-mates, the Soviet grade-school equivalent of roommates. We exchanged blotting paper, ink, and answers on certain exams. He also tickled me and drew manly bits pointed in my direction on my notebook and on the desk, as well. This was more to disgust me than to show any sign of romantic interest, I was sure. He walked me home after school, and on a few occasions, we skipped school entirely to roam the city and visit bookstores and antique stamp stores—quite rebellious for two straight-A students. We also coedited the "wall" newspaper, a newspaper in the form of a large poster that would go up on the back wall of the classroom early on Monday mornings. I was responsible for the poems; he, for the cartoons; and both of us, for the classroom gossip column:

> Pogrebnaya, Svetlana: seen exchanging cheese sandwiches with Podovedov, Andrei from two grades above. Motive: confidential.

Our jokes were usually made at the expense of the more dedicated Young Pioneers, members of the Soviet youth organization. The Jewish intellectuals who gave birth to us did not particularly encourage feelings of respect for them, with their cow-pasture mentality. To our parents, Soviet organizations went hand in hand with anti-Semitism, inbred into the fabric of that society so much that it became an unquestioned constant in our lives.

One day, my dad stomped upstairs. I was in the bathroom, reading *The Count of Monte Cristo*, with no plans to come out any time soon. I overheard him and Babushka; he was furious. "I offered to help Natasha up the stairs, with the groceries. She actually said, 'I don't let your kind touch my things.' And she doesn't let her dumb daughter Olga play with Inna! So much the better, in case idiocy is contagious."

Later that week, I learned, once again from eavesdropping, that Dad's grandpa Izya (short for Izrael, a name nobody wanted in their passport) had been beaten to disfigurement in a dark alley by a group of drunks, simply for his "Jewish nose." Why? Why on earth did it matter? If your passport identified you as Jew by ethnicity (remember, there was no religion in the Soviet Union), then you were marked, as though you were wearing a yellow star. So, my mom told a fib in her passport and, invoking a Latvian relative, identified herself as Latvian. Otherwise, she probably could not have been able to secure a nice job as a piano teacher.

And yet, for me, growing up in the Soviet state was normal. The parades, the red banners, the cries of "Revolution! Proletariat! Equality!" the pomposity of it all, at once invasive and alienating. To our parents, all this meant dreary bread lines, bribes, and crammed communal apartments at best and denouncements, arrests, and the murder of millions at worst. But to me, back then, it all felt quite festive, if a little silly. Lenin was not merely Lenin. He was "Grandpa" Lenin—the beloved, avuncular, bald little man who never learned how to roll his *r*'s and who, according to some short story we read in literature class, never told a lie. Allegedly, he stole a plum one day and was so distraught that he confessed to it immediately. The plum story always comes back to me when I read the poem "This Is Just to Say" by William Carlos Williams. What is it about cold plums and stealing?

Around the time of my opera premiere, a delegation of American teachers came to visit School 119. We had put together an evening of performances for them—short plays and songs. Shpilka and I were cast in a play about a lizard (me) and a bear (him), and for some reason, it was set to the American Civil War

Song "When Johnny Comes Marching Home" by Patrick Gilmore. The words were changed to narrate the story of the lizard and the bear. As ours was an English-speaking school, they were in English and completely nonsensical. More surreally, I had to wear a gigantic lizard outfit; and Shpilka, a full bear costume. It was a far cry from the American blue gauze of my cat dress. After the show, the students asked pointed questions they had been prepped with about living in a capitalist regime. The hot news item in the Soviet Union at the time was a Washington, DC, professor who went on a hunger strike against capitalism. Strangely, the visiting Americans knew nothing about this (possibly fake) news item. They shifted awkwardly in their chairs, trying to field questions from Young Pioneers about the hungry professor. At last, a hand went up with the question, Who do Americans think is cooler: Stallone or Schwarzenegger? What a relief for the teachers and for us.

Whether we liked it or not, we had to join the ranks of the Pioneers, as all ten-year-olds did in the Soviet Union. The Pioneers' initiation ceremony meant standing for hours under the hot sun next to a granite Grandpa Lenin while the district party official expounded on the five-year plan. Then, a teenager with vodka breath—from the Komsomol ranks!—tied red kerchiefs around our necks. Feeling brave and almost heroic, I ran home, my red kerchief breezily fluttering in the warm Odessa wind. Nobody at home was as excited as I was, it seemed, so I just took the hot and sweaty thing off and went to practice piano.

The next morning at school, Shpilka whispered into my ear, "Did you know that both Stalin and Lenin were horrible people?" Grandpa Lenin was commemorated in numerous couplets set in iambic pentameter that we were forced to memorize for years. He and Pushkin were with us every day. I am grateful for the Pushkin poetry that I still know by heart but could do without the Lenin verses. Anyway, hearing that Lenin was not a nice guy was like an American kid learning there is no Santa. But Shpilka was an authority on this stuff as far as I was concerned, and I took what he said at face value. It also made him a tad cooler in my eyes. He was a dissident—a little edgy, somehow dangerous, obnoxiously smart. Did I actually like the guy, that skinny little twerp? He was still placed last in line in gym class, where they would arrange us by height. Maybe I just wanted him to like me?

* * *

Shpilka and I were oddly competitive. Not in music—I was practically treated as the class's Kapellmeister, having to play, perform, accompany, sing, and improvise on all occasions while the actual chorus teacher went outside with her little flask of vodka. (Was she in cahoots with the ballet accompanist?) But he and I competed in other creative endeavors.

Before the release of the very important New Year's edition of the class newspaper, I managed to get pneumonia and stayed home for weeks, receiving shots of penicillin in the behind, reading lots of Jules Verne, and practicing piano at my leisure—a jolly good time. Shpilka asked to come over and work on the newspaper with me. He rang the doorbell just as our family physician, Dr. Filmus, was masterfully dispensing the penicillin shots. As she packed up her briefcase, Shpilka approached the bed. His grin was pitiful, and he was obviously searching for something to say. Then, as words clearly escaped him on this occasion—mind you, we were nine—he bent over and gave me a slap on my rear end, sore from weeks of shots. I wailed in pain as he screamed, "Oh no, sorry!" I was indignant but had to remain steadfastly professional as we began to work on the newspaper, with him seated at a small desk near my bed.

The newspaper was shaped as a giant pine tree, with round ornaments, each one encasing an article or a poem. I wrote a long ode to the departing old year, the year of the snake, and the approaching year of the dragon. (I am still amazed at how the Chinese calendar made its way into everyday life in the Soviet Union. My mother went by it for years, reading up on the animal of the year and instructing me, "It is year of the horse, so on the 31st of December, we must wear silver, brown, and black but absolutely no greens or reds.") On the night before I went back to school, Shpilka was supposed to come over to look over the paper for final edits. For some reason, he didn't show up. His family didn't have a phone, and each time he wanted to call, he had to go use the one his neighbors owned. He could reach me, but I could not reach him. I finished the last details of the paper on my own. It was beautiful, but I was shaking. *How can he stand me up? How can he not call me? Why do I care so much? Who does he think he is?*

I arrived at school with the paper carefully rolled up as a scroll. I unfurled my creation and made my way to the back of the classroom where there was a commotion. I squeezed through the horde of uniformed girls and boys, and hanging before me was . . . Shpigelmacher's own paper!

It was unmistakable: his signature caricatured self-portrait, with a crooked half-smile, big ears, and a little comma of a nose. As I read it, my mouth hanging open, I had to admit that it was a hilarious piece of child journalism. Unlike my dragon, his New Year's ornaments featured caricatures of Mikhail Gorbachev and his wife, Raisa. He had a long, ironic ode to the recent five-year plan in jolly iambic pentameter. He even had off-color, slightly sexy jokes. But it was utterly treacherous. That sneaky bastard! All my work had been for nothing. Did he think his was that much better than what we had done together? I ran out of the room, fuming, and stomped down the stairs, where I ran into him.

"Falka! How I've missed having you here! I brought you these," he said joyfully, handing me a bouquet of ugly yellow flowers. Darkness fell. I took the flowers and hit him in the face with them, their tiny, fragile heads pouring a sad little rain onto the stairs. I slapped him with what felt like the dramatic panache of Carmen, and then I was running. I wanted to look like a wounded tigress—more wounded than I actually felt—and was extremely aware of my every sound and motion, along with the impressions they made.

We still had to share a desk. I ignored him for a few days, and then I pretended like nothing happened. Sitting next to me, he also pretended not to care. He started talking across the classroom to another girl, also named Inna—a philosophical, slightly weird, but not unattractive friend of mine. I found another Misha to flirt with (in our classroom, there were three Mishas, though only one could boast a fabulous last name like Shpigelmacher) and sent him little notes. He didn't get my jokes, though, and I found myself quickly getting bored. I missed Shpilka's drawings and witty comments.

Finally, on day four of not speaking, he accosted me in the hallway. "If you are mad at me—well, then I am mad at you. And if neither of us are mad, let's forget it." That made no sense to me, at all. And yet, I said, somewhat passive-aggressively, "Who says I am mad? I am not mad at all! By the way, those yellow flowers were really ugly." And we picked up where we left off.

* * *

Shpilka and I began to see each other on weekends as part of a literary society for kids, hosted at the Odessa Literature Museum, an elegant building in the city's old town, with manuscripts, rare objects, photos, and editions connected to such figures as Pushkin, Gogol, Babel, Gorky, Bunin, and Adam Mickievitz. The society, an innovative reading, writing, and discussion group for children, was curated by a dark-eyed, beautiful young woman named Elena Borisovna. On Saturday mornings, we read and wrote poetry, and we selected and discussed passages from serious literature, like Gogol's *Evenings on the Farm near Dikanka*. We even studied a few chapters of Bulgakov's *Master and Margarita*. I found myself falling head over heels in love with this layered, insane book—a retelling of *Faust*, a novel within a novel, a romance, a satire on Soviet life. The devil visited Moscow! The Master, a misunderstood artist, created the story of Christ! Margarita also hated yellow flowers, just like me! For the first time, I encountered writing that jumped off the page with wilderness, audacity, excruciating pain, realism, fantasy, and hilarity. The author was talking directly to me!

As Elena read passages from it, we breathed air redolent of the nearby Black Sea, watching the fog envelop old Odessa, a reproduction of the Greek statue of Laocoön and his sons, and the stately columns at the museum's entrance. Gone was Odessa, as if it never existed.

In the society, we created our own magazine, the *Metaphor*. Each child had a nom de plume and a caricature, designed, of course, by Shpilka. What joy it was to make, to slowly copy out each story, poem, and review by hand. I dreamed, then, that this circle of people creating together would never fall apart, that one day we would all live in a big house, writing, talking, and playing. This bohemian paradise would ideally be situated on a lake or the sea, and somehow, it would always be summer.

The museum also had a concert series. One night after the society's meeting, I stayed to hear a piano recital by Irina Berkovich. This was the first time I heard J. S. Bach's *Well-Tempered Klavier* in its entirety. Every young pianist is introduced to Bach in childhood, and he looks over their shoulder throughout their musical life. I had encountered single pieces before but never the whole cycle of twenty-four preludes and fugues. Each prelude and fugue told a different story. I felt like I was in a long, mystical novel, with each chapter unpredictably changing tone and direction, from buzzing and jaunty to searching and pained. It was long and confusing, but I didn't want it to end.

The intertwined voices I had known from the *Inventions* projected so much more authority here. They had long conversations, argued, pontificated, joked, wept, and listened to each other's silences. They resonated through the marble and gold halls, falling, falling so heavily on the parquet floors. The plaintive thirds of the F minor prelude from book two stayed with me for weeks; its proud loneliness made me shiver. In my lesson the next day, I begged Valentina to let me play that prelude and fugue, but she said I wasn't done with the *Inventions* yet and would have to wait. I would eventually play it, just a few years later.

The Bach concert was at once a ritual—the somber sequence of sitting down for two hours to hear music—and a lively, seemingly spontaneous conversation of voices in each piece. My philosophical friend Inna was at the concert with me, and we argued afterward.

"I don't listen," she said. "I let the music take me places that I imagine."

"But you have to listen," I countered. "How else do you recall the music, the themes, the structure, the mood, the feeling?"

"I don't recall those details, but I recall the places the music takes me," she said. This seemed like a deep kind of listening to me.

* * *

I first heard the word *immigration* shortly after my ninth birthday party, at which my mythical Aunt Dolly from "over there" had suddenly appeared. She brought with her an enormous bag of shiny American goodies. My friends and I were crowding around the kitchen table playing Scrabble when a shapely, impossibly chic lady in a tight khaki jacket and strange blue denim pants (must be those famous American jeans!) came up to the table behind me. "Innochka! How big you are!" I had been a newborn baby when she emigrated from Odessa to Chicago, and she was now back for a visit a decade later.

She put a cloth bag on the table, covering our game, and pulled on the ribbon. My mouth fell open in silence because out came the most coveted of treasures. There were pencils of outrageous colors—lavender, sea blue, forest green, cotton-candy pink. There were stickers of exotic animals with sad eyes. There was authentic American bubble gum with Bazooka Joe comics and erasers in the shapes of dolls and cakes with a sweet, stupefying smell. Rounding out this forbidden foreign bounty were pencil cases and notebooks with a sassy version of Minnie Mouse strutting across glossy polyester. This was hard currency that could make you the most admired, envied, and popular kid in school, even at such a school as mine. My friends stared, silent, wide-eyed, and unhappy.

"Lucky," somebody gasped.

The owner of such riches, I suddenly felt envied and disliked, oddly steeped in a material privilege previously unknown to me. We all wore the same brown, scratchy, sweaty uniforms. We all ate buckwheat for breakfast. None of us had our own room. And now, I suddenly was a bourgeois child, with my big, fat, American bag of goodies. Seeing my friends go dumb with

On a cruise to Yalta with my parents. The ship was named Taras Shevchenko, *after the nineteenth-century Ukrainian poet.*

a want for what I had, I was suddenly completely separated from them because of these material things. Through these presents, I was connected to a land of opportunity they had no access to. I locked myself in the bathroom and cried, alone and overwhelmed.

Where had Dolly appeared from? What was this land of cotton candy, erasers, and gum?

I was in fourth grade, and I knew that a few Jewish students had left, one by one. We weren't allowed to talk about where they went. It all began like a faint echo—I heard it during tea with my parents' friends, in the hushed voices of my parents at bedtime, coughed by my great-grandmother, and whispered into my back by our neighbors. Dad had begun to go on trips to Moscow to "secure documents." Great-Grandma sighed heavily. My parents began to take me to supplementary English lessons and one day announced that we would be making a video of my piano playing so that we could use it for auditions later on.

The video was made in the concert hall of my music school with what may have been the only video camera in Odessa. My dad's aunt worked for the Odessa television station (there were a total of three channels, one of which showed a weekly ten-minute cartoon for kids; this was the extent of our televised entertainment), so she must have pulled some strings. The recording was going to have me playing Mozart, Bach, Chopin, Liszt, and some of my own compositions. My parents were especially worried about the centerpiece of the hall, a large portrait of Lenin behind the grand piano. They tried to cover it in various ways, and in the end, it didn't make it into the frame. I now wish that it had, a small memento of history.

I was starting to learn Chopin's *Fantaisie-Impromptu* then, practicing the whirlwind, melodic turns of the right hand slowly, eager to get to the middle section's intoxicating lyrical melody. What passion this music had! I had never until now played anything so rich, so soulful. It would be a while before I could get the piece up to tempo. Meanwhile, I had just been invited again to perform at the Odessa Philharmonic Hall in a televised concert. I probably would not get the Chopin ready in time, so I instead performed Mozart's *Fantasie* in D Minor. Walking onto the stage for my dress rehearsal, I saw that I was about to sit down at a completely different kind of instrument than the one I was used to. This was not the usual upright I practiced and performed on. This was a long, black, majestic concert grand. It looked poised for flight—huge, yet so light. And when you pressed the keys, you could see the hammers sway and the dampers dance. In an upright, the mechanics of a piano remain hidden, so I never thought about them. But here . . . the instrument was a whole symphony of motion, with every small piece of wood, string, and metal arranged together to make a quivering, talking whole. Mister Bechstein, I respectfully called it. How could I ever stay focused on the music I was playing when I was faced with this mechanical wonder?

For the actual performance, I wore the same frilly, blue dress I had worn for my opera as the cat. It was a little tight a year later, but I could still twirl in it. When I started the *Fantasie*, the sound of the D minor arpeggios was so dark, so smooth and inevitable that I wanted to cry. The piece's stormy episodes are capped off by a joyful, lighthearted ending in D major—but even that ending felt dark and dramatic to me in the moment. I loved that large beast of a piano. I hoped I would get to play it again many times.

* * *

One day after school, Shpilka and I wandered into an abandoned skeleton of a four-story building, yellow and parched like a desert in the sun. We saw a drunk guy taking a pee on the floor of one of the abandoned rooms, his back to us. We giggled wildly and ran until we were out of breath, our square backpacks bopping up and down, our brown wool uniforms sticky in the April sun. When we stopped, we were suddenly holding hands.

I looked down at his hands and said, "You know, everybody says you are in love with me, and I think that you are."

"Not at all!" he spat out in visible disgust.

The drunk guy immediately joined the ranks of our characters and was christened Akakiy Akakiyevich, after the character from Gogol's *The Overcoat*. Neither of us would admit to not reading the story, but we loved the sound of the words. In Russian, the name basically sounds like *Poop Poopevich*, so of course, two nine-year-olds found this to be the funniest thing ever.

Shpilka was allowed to take the bus on his own. My parents weren't so lenient, and I was afraid of it. Once, on a bus with my dad, I looked out the window and saw a man swaying back and forth, a vodka bottle in his hand. He then shoved another man, who shoved him back. He fell backward, and I saw a rivulet of thick, red liquid trickle onto the pavement. There was a commotion on the bus, and my dad quickly, without a word, took me to the opposite window. For one of the many editions of Chopin's cycle of twenty-four preludes, the nineteenth-century pianist and editor Hans von Bulow decided to include alongside them his own definitions, images, and stories. For the fourth prelude, he wrote, "Chopin is frustrated with his own composing and hits himself on the head with a hammer. Blood trickles." When I look at von Bulow's edition, I recall the man I saw from the bus, and for me, this powerful, tragic miniature work is his theme.

Another time—and this upset me a lot more—I lost a precious piece of candy. Though I was never allowed any street snacks or the sweet, unhygienic soda, I had persuaded my parents one time to buy me a lollipop rooster. These were sold by a traveling Romani woman in quivering skirts and flamboyant necklaces, and they came in red and green. My mother was sure that they were pure poison, but on one memorable occasion, she could not take my nagging anymore and bought me the burnt-red, sugary bird on a stick. We got on the wobbly bus, and the crowd surged. I fell backward, and the rooster dropped to the floor, immediately squashed by rampaging feet. My screams matched the screech of the traffic but to no avail. I would never taste an Odessa sugar rooster.

Knowing these stories and my parents' protectiveness, Shpilka the gentleman had begun to walk me home from school at the beginning of our friendship, in first grade. He carried my backpack, which, in Soviet grade school, is one step away from an engagement ring. Our classmates laughed at him, but he never said a word about it. In fourth grade, he still did it each day. A few days after our adventure with the drunk guy, Shpilka dropped me off at my apartment complex. He suddenly looked perplexed and a little angry and said, "You know, you asked me something a few days ago and I said no. Well, I meant to say yes." I pretended I didn't understand because the cruel streak in me had to hear him say it.

"What are you talking about?"

"You said I was in love with you, and I said I wasn't. Well, I am."

I hadn't planned a witty response to this, so the words hung there in the air like a cartoon caption from one of his caricature characters, the one with big ears and ruffled bangs and a prominent nose. We mumbled goodbyes, and I ran up to the apartment on the second floor.

Babushka sat in her armchair as always, waiting for me, as I came to her and shouted, "Shpigelmacher just told me he is in love with me!"

"You are ten years old. This is too young to understand such things, Innochka," she responded predictably, with kind, cackling laughter.

Later that evening, though, Babushka cried alone in her room. I heard her through the thin wall and sheepishly entered. "What's wrong?" I asked.

"You are leaving me, Innochka. You are leaving for good."

"No, I am not! Where am I going?" Despite the English lessons and overheard conversations about immigration, I still didn't know (or didn't want to know) that we were leaving. When I asked my dad, he explained to me that we had to—because of anti-Semitism, because he didn't want us to live in a country of lies, a Communist dictatorship, a failed experiment. They were tired of meaningless slogans, of standing in lines. He and Mom wanted me to have a future. I didn't get it, though. I didn't want to leave my friends, my school. I was terrified of leaving my grandmas. (What I didn't know then was they would be able to join us in the States a few years later, after my parents saw them through the immigration process. As far as I

On the eve of our departure, in front of the Theatre. Shpilka and I are second and third from the left.

was concerned, I would never see them again.) And, let's face it, I didn't want to leave Shpilka.

But nonetheless, just a few weeks later, we left. On my last day in Odessa, my friends, their parents, and mine had gone to the city's famous Potemkin stairway. We walked on the seafront promenade with our uniformly dripping ice cream cones and stopped at the Pushkin monument. I gazed up at the glossy, black curls and full lips of the poet and said goodbye. I petted the stone griffon next to a park bench. Then, we all took a photo next to the Odessa Opera House. Shpilka, in tiny shorts, the tiniest child in the photo, stood next to me. I then began to realize that perhaps I'd had my bohemian paradise all along.

The next morning, we left for the rented bus that would take us to Czechoslovakia, the first leg of our long journey to the United States. Anastasia wept with such anger, as though my parents had conspired to take me away from her on purpose. My great-grandmother leaned out the balcony when I turned around to look at her one last time, and I saw that she had let down her hair. I had never seen this before—she always wore it

With my parents before we left, inside the iconic Odessa Opera and Ballet Theatre.

in that bun. Her hair was still black at eighty and long and thrilling like a mermaid's. Her face was wet with tears.

3

DOWN AND OUT IN VIENNA AND ROME

Through the bus's muddy windows, I watched wooden houses with dilapidated roofs, curlicues on the sides, rusty pails chained forever to decaying garden wells, and splotches of birch trees like herds of zebras. One followed the next in a long sequence, as though a well-worn illustrated Russian fairy-tale book had been transported to grainy film. Hours went by or maybe days. I woke up when the bus jolted to a bump and stop. Sunlight illuminated a tall, snowy peak. I imagined Cape Horn to look just like this, a big white tooth sitting upright, as I had seen in a Jules Verne book. I had never seen a mountain up close before.

One of the bus's wheels came off somewhere in the wilderness of the Carpathian Mountains. Yes! A stop! I jumped off the bus and into the grass to stretch and run around a little. The driver's upper half was buried in bus innards. Mom followed me, and we went into the bushes to look for berries. Nobody seemed even a bit concerned.

I knew this was the start of immigration, but I didn't think about the future. Thinking about it made me picture Babushka coughing, saying to me, "You may not see me again. You know this, yes?" I tried hard to take the present and simply respond to it, like one would to dipping their entire head into an ice-cold mountain stream. The mountains were invigorating, and soon I would see Mozart's house in Vienna. I could not let myself

My grandmothers followed us to the United States once we were settled. This is me at age fourteen with Babushka—my great-grandmother Fanni.

imagine Babushka. To make this easier, I wrote picturesque and slightly manic descriptions of what we were seeing in a small oval notebook, ripped out and folded the pages, and hid them in my backpack to send to her when we arrived in Vienna.

After hearing nightmarish stories of border crossings in Moscow and Leningrad, including forced gynecological exams to make sure that no valuables were taken out of the country in any possible crevice, my parents had gathered three families together and paid a small sum to a bus driver to take us and two other families to the border between Czechoslovakia and the Soviet Union, in Uzhgorod. There were five of us traveling: Mom, Dad, myself, and two monstrous brown suitcases nicknamed "vacuum cleaners" because of their ability to hold

enormous quantities of junk. If smuggling me had been necessary, I could have fit into one of them and probably have been
quite comfortable.

If we passed customs, hopefully without any adventure, we
would go to Vienna for the first interview with a consul. From
there, the next stop was Rome, where we would wait for our
interview with a consul from the American embassy and then
for his decision. This could take weeks or even months. My
parents knew Jewish families who could not get permission to
move on, and stayed in Rome for a year or more. Some would
get so tired of waiting that they give up altogether and stayed in
Italy, doing odd jobs. Others would change their plans and go
to Israel or Australia. My family had been promised asylum by
Aunt Dolly, so Chicago was our final destination.

My parents could bring only eighty dollars a head with them.
(The suitcases did not count, unfortunately.) No valuables of any
kind could be transferred—if the border guards discovered any,
they would confiscate—and pocket—them. Because the Faliks
family didn't have any valuables, this was not a problem. Thanks
to my parents' imagination, however, we were able to invest
additional money in seemingly useless accouterments, such as
souvenir wooden spoons (familiar to me from my early musical training days), crudely painted toy chickens, ballpoint pens
with holograms of the Duke de Richelieu on the Potemkin steps,
twenty yellow tassels that looked like they came off Soviet flags,
packets of dry soup, stale chocolates, canned Spam-like meats,
and one ancient photo camera of dubious origins and quality.
They stuffed these tchotchkes in their suitcases to be later sold at
flea markets for pocket money, a much-needed addition to the
tiny stipend given out to Jewish immigrants en route to America.

At the border, a sturdy woman resembling a refrigerator in
shape, voice, and alcohol content asked me to empty my backpack. There were some toys, music books, and three crisp, brand-
new books in it: a science fiction novel by the then-popular Kir
Bulichev, *Guests from the Future*, about a device that could read
people's thoughts; a shiny, brown tome of Greek and Roman
mythology; and, of course, *Master and Margarita*, in a brand-new
edition. The latter had been underground literature for so long

that I was anticipating an interrogation, maybe even torture. To my disappointment, she ignored the books, the music, and the few toys in my bag and moved on to my parents. The whalelike suitcases were flopped on their sides and thrown open.

"What's this?" the refrigerator grunted, lifting some colored papers. My dad explained that those were gouache drawings I had made in school. She then buried her arms up to her elbows in clothes and shuffled them for a few seconds, hoping that some diamond earrings or, at the very least, some furs would manifest. When nothing even remotely resembling precious stones, metals, or animal remains came up, she waved disdainfully, clearly disappointed with us. "No good to keep searching you. You're paupers!"

The bus finally brought us to the Bratislava station. It was dark and dirty and looked like any other dismal station. We were officially out of the Soviet Union, though this felt suspiciously like a Soviet train station. Then my father decided to use the bathroom. He immediately discovered that it cost Czech money. Thinking on his feet, he offered the ancient bathroom attendant lady a bar of Russian chocolate from the Faliks reserve. This seemed to do, and he disappeared behind the door. Sergey, the patriarch of the family traveling with us, also had to go but needed to one-up my dad. His family had brought a similar but slightly more upscale collection of random Soviet food, and he produced a large box of truffles labeled "Evenings in Leningrad." (For some reason, every cake and box of chocolates sold in the Soviet Union bore an opaque title: "Pushkin's Dream" or "Summer in Krasnoyarsk" or "Curly-Haired Black Sea Lover.") The old lady let him in, as well, not terribly moved, however, by this romantic gesture. As I looked on, I wondered why Sergey couldn't just give her a regular chocolate bar. Was there more than one level of prestige, comfort, and luxury in going to the bathroom behind those doors?

The train ride to Vienna was fast and smooth. I sipped my first Coca-Cola through a blue straw, looking at the forests running by. The Iron Curtain was behind us.

* * *

On our first evening walk through Vienna, I saw a tall dragon made entirely out of chocolate bars in the window of a candy store. It was architecturally flawless, each small angle between the bars turned just right, to keep the creature from losing his balance and exploding into dozens of green and gold wrappers all over the display window. I had never seen anything like it and stood there, staring, mesmerized. It's not that I wanted the dragon or any part of it. It intimidated me as something untouchable, impossible. It made me want to go back home.

Other shop windows beckoned with hats and skirts—effortlessly beautiful, like watercolors of lilac and aqua—on perfectly serene plastic models; with rows of leather briefcases, stacked neatly and seriously, perfect building blocks of debonair class; with gleaming steel pens and slender gloves and effervescent handkerchiefs, whose milky whiteness you could almost taste, and flimsy nightgowns with transparent, intricate lace in places that made me look down at my feet, embarrassed. Around us, giant cardboard pictures sparkled and moved and announced things in German. On one of them, a woman was running up the stairs in a short skirt, her lace panties visible, her shapely arm extended behind her, slim cigarette between the fingers. In another, an impossibly beautiful couple was feeding each other round golden discs, laughing at what must have been the funniest thing they had ever heard, crumbs bursting into air around them like beads of golden light. I had never seen a billboard ad or a potato chip. This was life in Technicolor.

We didn't get very far from the apartment where we stayed, stopping to gawk at every sign, every window display, shuffling in place, going in circles. Passersby glanced at us with curiosity and foreign sympathy. Seeing all this at once was too much. Our experiences would have to be measured out carefully, like in a soufflé recipe; otherwise, we would collapse. The old Vienna we had set out to see, its churches, museums, gardens, and fountains, could wait for a day.

On the way back to the apartment, a sweaty man in pants pulled up to just below his nipples came up to us. "First day in the West, huh?" he snorted in Russian.

"Yes, we just arrived," my dad replied.

"Ha, I could tell. You'll get over it. I've been here three days already," he said patronizingly and walked off.

The Hebrew Immigration Aid Society (HIAS) provided us with a room in a two-bedroom apartment and a small stipend for food. Dad read on the HIAS's bulletin board about "Eva's Friends Club," located not too far from our apartment, which was inviting former Soviet citizens to meet and socialize. He correctly deduced—this being Vienna, home of Haydn, Mozart, Beethoven, and Schubert—that there must be some piano-shaped object in the vicinity of the club. Once we arrived there, we were welcomed by Christian Finnish volunteers who helped shell-shocked immigrants like us make baby steps in the West. They smiled tenderly and gave me a bright blue book with pictures of men with brown hair, moustaches, and long beards, in togas, amid mountain settings, surrounded by lions, floods, and winged creatures. A Bible would have been a hot commodity in the godless Soviet Union. I accepted this present, despite my Soviet-bred contempt for religion, as no Faliks would ever turn down a free book—not even *the* book. They also offered us packages of shampoo and clothes. My parents, shy to accept so many gifts at once, asked carefully if, instead of the presents, I could be allowed to play on the little upright piano every once in a while, and they said yes. My fingers were beginning to itch for the feel of a piano. And now I could play in the City of Music.

We continued to explore the city. Mozart's house turned out to be a modest yellow apartment building; I was much more impressed with St. Stephen's Cathedral, where he married Constanze Weber, that lucky girl. (For most of my childhood, I had a crush on Wolfgang Amadeus.) It looked like the healthier, nobler, richer older sibling of the Odessan Kircha, darkly imposing, patina-covered, and stretching up to a sky that was possibly not so godless, according to the Bible I had decided to read.

Here in the West, all sorts of people went in and out of churches, and the buildings commanded respect, not pity like the boarded-up and dilapidated onion-domed churches I had seen back home. In the Soviet Union, saying "I believe in God" was like saying "I am not toilet trained" or "I think the earth is flat"—preposterous, shameful, laughable, or downright scary.

As for a synagogue, I'd never seen one. Being Jewish had been our nationality and race, unrelated to God in any way, and best kept to ourselves, so ingrained, so profound was the anti-Semitism of the "old country."

Once we had gone on a trip to Kaluga, a provincial town near Moscow, and we visited a rarity—an active church—near a cemetery with a monument to the poet Marina Tsvetaeva. I was horrified, having had my brain put through a number of despiritualization laundry cycles at school. I glued my eyes stubbornly to the floor and refused to look around. My dad begged me to look up and see the people burning incense, crossing themselves multiple times and kneeling. "Look, this boy is just about your age—see how devoutly he prays," he whispered. I stole a glance up and saw the boy's back as he faced a wall. In Vienna, I realized that Mozart, too, believed in God.

At the Prater amusement park, I rode the Ferris wheel and ate raspberry-lime ice cream shaped like a gnome impaled on a wooden stick. Its Brothers Grimm–style violence didn't stop me from swallowing it in seconds, green and red goo covering my face in Christmas colors. I had chosen the ice cream from a cardboard poster, a catalogue of wonders that listed dozens of them, with the name of each treat next to a colorful illustration. It stamped itself onto my memory much more successfully than any painting I saw with my parents in Vienna's museums. Depictions of neon animals skewered onto sticks; regal cones with crowns of chocolate and walnuts; and creamy, art nouveau–style swirled peaks still set my heart aflutter.

To keep our ice cream money from dwindling, my father decided to offload some of the Russian junk he had brought. He took the wooden spoons—gold-encrusted, like the city's palaces and fountains and Mozart chocolates—and walked back and forth on a small street that cut a larger street in two, making slices of geographic pie. He made rhythmic clicking sounds timidly, looking pale and out of place, barely glancing up at the passersby. Was this the only time he gave a public musical performance, in that powdered-sugar city of street violinists and singing saws? He didn't know how to sell anything, not even a wooden spoon to wealthy Viennese passersby. My mom and I stood near, and as we watched him humiliate himself, something in me snapped. I started screaming and crying, watching my father trying to do this, asking him to stop. I was hysterical, and he ceased his humiliating back-and-forth dance immediately. He and Mom bought me a colossal hot dog in a bun on a stick. It sprayed scalding, spicy tomato juice when you bit into it. What was it with Western Europe and skewering things on sticks?

* * *

They let us move on quickly, after just a few weeks. We took a train to Rome, and I imagined that our route was like a board game of Europe—we'd roll the dice, take our turn, and then move to a new location and wait again. On the train, I drank another Coca-Cola from a glass bottle through a straw whose joint bent like an accordion. Our train left us, with a large group of other Soviet immigrants, at a train station in the town of Ostia, which was imbued with the homely, nostalgic aroma of cat piss. Big buses took us to a bare spot in Ostia's deep woods, where it would not have been out of the question to find a hut with chicken legs. The area with small wooden huts was divided off from the rest of the forest by barbed wire. The men were instructed to step to one side, the women to another. What was happening?

As it turned out, the men were asked to help with luggage. The barbed wire protected small wooden huts (no chicken legs), our abode for the next few days, from the tusks of wild boar. The Italian morning sun zapped away all sinister thoughts. We happily ate stale rolls with jam and planned our next move.

My mom's best friend, Nadia, happened to be immigrating to Minnesota with her family at roughly the same time. They were ahead of us and had just gotten clearance to move on to the States. This meant that their room in a large apartment in Rome, near Piazza Venezia, was becoming vacant, and we would not have to exchange an arm, a leg, and possibly the sum of our souls for lodgings. We would stay in the center of the Eternal City and not the nearby town of Ladispoli like most immigrants ended up doing. Ladispoli did have the beach and, for this reason, was the waiting place of choice for Odessans. But Rome . . . Well, Rome was Rome.

Nadia's daughter Masha took me by the hand and led me to her corner of the room. All business, she asked, "And I assume you already have a Barbie?"

I had no idea who Barbie was.

"Well, I think you may as well forget living in the United States without a Barbie. Everyone has one over there, and if you don't, it's really not good."

She rummaged in the covers of her bed and produced a lean plastic doll with a small button-like nose, blue eyes, and cascading platinum-blond hair. She looked nothing like the dolls I was used to—no plastic imitations of a cherub, no batting eyelashes and cries of "Mama." No innocence. This was an adult who looked anatomically flawless and really mean.

"Look, her legs bend."

"So what? All dolls' legs bend." I tried to look unimpressed. I'd never played with dolls too much, but this one had a strange pull, something unpleasant and yet magnetic. I didn't like Barbie, and I wanted one very badly right away.

"Ah, but all dolls' legs don't bend at the knees. Check this out." Suddenly, Barbie was squatting, as if she were about to take a pee in the woods. "And look at her clothes."

I knew that my mom, with her long, shapely legs, would have killed for a denim miniskirt outfit like the one Barbie had on. There were also fluffy soft sweaters, jeans, and a pink dress for the doll. Barbie would be mine, eventually, even if I had to nag for months. I wanted one because somebody else had one, because it seemed right somehow, to want one and to have one.

The next day, Nadia and her family took off for the States, and we moved into their room, sharing the three-bedroom apartment with two other immigrant families. The building was in the center of Rome, off the famed Via Trastevere. All roads do lead to Rome but, more specifically, to the huge, white, man-eating typewriter—otherwise known as the Victor Emmanuel II Monument—and Piazza Venezia. Whenever we went to and from the apartment, we inevitably found ourselves there. The apartment building faced a dreary, treeless, circular park with a long concrete path forming a circle. The immigrants called it *skovorodka*—"the frying pan"—and we children loitered in it, frittering away the Roman hours and days of summer.

A lanky thirteen-year-old Barbie look-alike named Annushka played her fancy boombox all day long, and over and over again she would listen to a song by the Russian pop band Tender May. Every day, I heard their macabre song about a young girl whose boyfriend makes out with her one "Rosy Evening" (the song's title). The boyfriend dies a gruesome death, either by knife or by an army supplies truck—I can't remember which. The pubescent nasal voices of the singers narrated this pulpy romance in descending syncopated scales, with only two chords for the entire song. It made me want to drag Annushka by her luscious, curly hair; lock her in a room with a stereo; and force-feed her Beethoven. It's hard to say who was the bigger freak.

In a crusade for classical music, I snuck out to the park benches in the evenings, armed with a black marker. The letters *HMR*—for heavy metal rock—were carved into the benches by Russian immigrant boys with army knives. I colored over the graffiti with the marker, thereby doubly vandalizing the bench. I had never heard of fine bands like Guns n' Roses, Def Leppard, or Kiss. I was sure that HMR was a terrible alien that somehow would chew up Mozart, Beethoven, and Chopin and swallow them into its rattling stomach. To me, it was one kind of music or the other. Not once did I consider, *Can't one like both?*

My crusade couldn't actually extend to making music at that point because there was no piano around. But I did practice. My mother placed a sturdy fold-out table on the balcony of the apartment, and every evening she supervised me for two hours as I played scales, arpeggios, etudes, and some of the pieces that I had begun learning before we left. I was punching out the notes on the imaginary keyboard on the table just to keep the little muscles, the musical memory, and my imagination active. "Legato! Louder! Lift your arm! This is a rest!" This silent music-making made perfect sense to me at the time. It was a win-win situation, as I was both practicing and getting fresh air. I imagined sounds that were glittery and clear for Chopin's

The Maiden's Wish; warm pastel tones for the legato scales and restless lines of Beethoven; and the bubbly, liquid roulades of German composer Moritz Moszkowski.

Yuri Goldman, an older boy whose family had left Odessa on the same bus with us, made fun of me for practicing on the table. He had already dipped his toes into the American dream by making money out of nothing: For hours every single day, for weeks, he walked around very slowly, moving one foot in front of the other with great deliberation, straining his neck to inspect every crack in the Roman pavement. He seemingly cleaned the Eternal City of more than a million lira, including a gold chain, bejeweled single earrings, packs of condoms, and faux-leather buttons. I bet that today he can be found on a beach somewhere with one of those metal detectors. But his parents were proud of his accomplishments and considered me and my parents to be losers and dreamers.

But how does one not become a dreamer when every day begins with an overripe peach from a carton that the grocery next door would throw away, just like that, only because of one spoiled fruit. (Could one bad peach really contaminate the others with its sweet juice, a thick nectar that probably became moonshine overnight in the Roman heat?) How does one not dream when you and your wife, thirty-five years old, walk around with an ever-present ten-year-old dragging her feet between you, the petulant creature who grunts "Shut up" each time one of you open your mouth to sigh with gratitude and delight at a tiny alley leading to a marble fountain, a lopsided square, a dilapidated church, stonework from a thousand years ago, every nun on a bike, every perversely bright tableau thrown your way free of charge? How do you not dream when you catch the kid mapping out her ice cream–eating schedule (the Cornetto this Monday, the Cornetto Grande next Monday, the Magnum the Monday after that, etc.), or when you use the money you made selling junk at the Americana flea market on Sundays for a three-day bus trip to Florence, Venice, and the Republic of San Marino? When you see the gondoliers on the Grand Canal, just like in the Tintoretto reproductions in the Venetian art album we had in Odessa, whose page corners were all mushy from fingers licked to turn

The only photo of my family during immigration: a Polaroid taken in Venice's San Marco Square.

the page? When the ebullient Titian cherubs fly up, up into the gaudily golden altars? When the women and men make love in dark street corners? (You couldn't talk about sex in the Soviet Union or have it very easily, as everyone shared rooms with their parents, but here, it was all over the place.) How do you stay sane when all this is real, not a story or a movie?

My parents never left me at home on their wanderings through Rome. The day began with a breakfast of peaches, bread, and unknown canned meat on the balcony, and then we would begin to roam the city, every corner of it that was free of charge. The Cathedral of St. Peter swallowed us whole. I stayed in front of Michelangelo's *Pieta* for ages. She looked larger than the cathedral, larger than life itself in her sad, peaceful tenderness, the lightness of the body of Christ in her arms. I cried, overwhelmed by beauty, and couldn't look away. Years later, I would return and marvel at how small she really was—like a frail, teenage girl.

In the crypt of the Santa Maria Immacolata Concezione, the gossamer lace flowers and tessellations and baroque garlands on the walls and ceilings were dizzying, the color of dried bone—maybe because they were actually made of old bones, of pelvises and knuckles and ribs and skulls. The Capuchin monk who politely ushered us in—what part of him would grace the walls of these strange rooms?

The Colosseum was a sad giant, lopsided, as if Jupiter had taken a bite, its portholes lit up from within as the evening took over, its age and mildewed coolness slithering over us. Below us we beheld the Forum Romano, a mini universe of geometry and grass. And the mopeds roaring by, the empty bottles flying, the cigarette butts twinkling in the eternal stones. In the distance, the Castello Sant' Angelo sang to me of Tosca, of her last night on earth. We would walk home, down the Via Trastevere, past the giant typewriter, into the *skovorodka* park, up the stairs and to bed and a sweaty, dreamless sleep.

* * *

When not lost in the hot city, my parents tried to make, or at least save, a few lira. They were true Odessa intellectuals—in their eyes, the only type of business was seedy business. Dad had been an electrical engineer, but at heart, he was a poet. He wrote for the joy of it (and today still does through blogging and social media). This didn't stop them from running a smooth operation I called the "Faliks Bus Ticket Scam." The buses in Italy used a system of little paper tickets that had to be purchased prior to the bus ride and stamped while on the bus. Usually, these were not checked and were thrown away immediately. Dozens of them could be seen floating in puddles of oil and grime. My parents quickly realized that buying a ticket every time you rode the bus was a waste. My mother talked (or rather, she pantomimed, adding *-ini* and *-ono* and *-ando* to random Russian words; Russian pronunciation lends itself wonderfully to Italian sounds) to some of the old ladies who sat outside along the Via Trastevere all day, frowning and waiting for Judgment Day. One of the ladies showed her what to buy—a chemical solution akin to bleach and nail polish remover. My parents salvaged the little pieces of paper, dried them on the windows of the apartment, removed the printed stamp by dipping the tickets into chemical solution, and left them overnight in the soapbox so that they smelled clean by morning. This yielded dozens of fresh tickets, and they rode the bus for free for the duration of their time in Rome.

On Sundays, my parents disappeared to the Great Flea Market Americana held behind the Church of San Giovanni. All the junk they had carried through customs was proudly on display here among other tables of junk. The competition was fierce, but finally my father's charm won over many customers, including an elderly Roman gentleman who wasn't willing to live another moment without a dozen packets of powdered Soviet soup and those damn Russian spoons. I did a little dance when I learned that we were rid of the spoons for good.

At first, I insisted on coming with my parents, but it turned out that I was bad for business. I had developed an unattractive affliction: an allergy to the bites of feisty, barely visible Italian mosquitos. They bit my legs, arms, neck—any skin that was available. I scratched the bites into enormous welts, which Mom covered with a pomegranate-colored liquid that supposedly helped cool off the swelling. In reality, it didn't help but made me look like a gruesome, bleeding martyr. On the bus, people stared, and at the market, one compassionate costumer yelled, "This little girl is hurt! Help!" Another costumer looked at me with disgust and dropped the Soviet flag tassel he was about to buy. From then on, I was left at home on Sunday mornings.

Other immigrants in the building were more ambitious. Sharing our apartment was a bald guy named Grisha. He was in his fifties and had a buxom, loudmouthed wife named Olga. He would go out jogging, and one morning, he brought back a stack of old porn magazines that somebody sold him. Olga wailed hysterically and nearly killed him when she saw how he spent their flea market–earned cash. After a sudden break in the screaming, followed by an eerie moment of silence, she cruised into the kitchen and announced that a stellar business opportunity had just presented itself: "We have been lucky to come by these vintage erotic magazines, and I am happy to generously offer them to you at half price. If you send them back to the Soviet Union, you will make a great profit."

Our basic needs were covered through the generous stipend provided by Jewish organizations, which helped us pay for rent, food, and even public transportation while the American embassy reviewed our cases to grant (or refuse) us entrance into the United States. Unfortunately for me, piano practice was not considered a basic need, so I was left with the table until an acquaintance introduced us to a family of Italian Jews who owned one. Renzo Cesano was a flutist in an orchestra, and his wife, Tamar, was a high school teacher. They invited us to their home, communicating with us through a mixture of English, Italian, Yiddish, and gestures. Tamar was from Israel and spoke Hebrew to her children. There were Hebrew books in the house and a mezuzah on the door. They had Shabbat dinner on Friday nights. This was our first introduction to Jewish culture and history as part of family life. It felt foreign, strange, and a little frightening. How could we know so little?

I practiced piano at the Cesanos', and Mom taught piano to their children. A few weeks later, Renzo invited me to play a solo recital in Rome. It was for a Jewish retirement community, Ospedale Israelitico, that had a young-artist recital series.

I was extremely nervous. Most of my practicing until then had been done on the table. I wore a black velvet, long-sleeved dress with green and red bows. (This was clearly a Christmas dress that somebody sent us from America, but we, of course, had no idea.) I played Chopin and Beethoven, as well as some of my own compositions, and I also gave my first newspaper interview.

I still remember the faces of this audience. Looking at them, I was thinking of my great-grandmother: her birdlike nose; her heavy, thick, dark hair; her wise, watery eyes. These were familiar faces, even if I had never seen them before. These were somebody's great-grandmothers. At the end of the concert, they gave me a gift: a handmade clown made of soft silky discs sown together. Each disc was of a different material and a different color. The clown frowned, crying.

* * *

The legend of Santa Maria Maggiore says that in 356 AD, the Virgin Mary appeared to Pope Liberius and asked him to build a basilica on the spot where it snowed. When snow fell on Esquiline Hill that summer, the Basilica of Santa Maria Maggiore was built there. The regal church celebrates the Virgin Mary and is one of the four papal churches of Rome. The square in front of it is the site of a summer holiday, the Festa della Madonna Neve Maria Maggiore.

On one of our last nights in Rome, we found ourselves squashed among hundreds of people on the Piazza Maria Maggiore. The night was sweltering, and Vivaldi's "Winter" movement from *The Four Seasons* blared from large speakers set up on the steps of the giant cathedral. The building was lit up in electric pink, blue, and green, and a line of light traveled over its façade, dancing to the music in zigzags and waves. Lime green, fluorescent pink, and screaming purple flakes of foam snow descended from nowhere, their moistness mixing with our sweat. Amplification distorted the sounds of the baroque orchestra, and then suddenly, a heavy beat began to divide it into leaden measures. The lights danced madly, and the soapy flakes came down in gusts—a wild Vivaldi disco storm on a Roman piazza.

The next day, my father came back from the consulate and told my mother that we had to pack our suitcases. The bus for Aeroporto Roma Fumicino would leave two days later, at 4:00 in the morning; four hours later, we would fly to New York's John F. Kennedy airport and, from there, to O'Hare in Chicago.

The last night of our two months in Rome, I lay in bed, clutching *The Master and Margarita*. In the book, the head of Mikhail Berlioz (the editor of the fictional literary magazine and the namesake of the composer) rolled out from underneath a tram. Meanwhile, on the apartment's black-and-white television, a frizzy, large-breasted redhead threw off her bikini top, as the big-toothed host gave her a thumbs-up. The music played a dippy jingle that ended with the word *Fortuna*. This was the game show *Colpo Grosso*, where women had to take off their tops when they gave a wrong answer. Later, I learned that this was one among many shows, the mark of Silvio Berlusconi's monopoly over Italian television. It was hard to watch the women, apparently overjoyed to reveal themselves to this ridiculously memorable tune.

Between *Colpo Grosso* and *The Master and Margarita*, I dozed off and dreamt of Maria Maggiore in a black-laced bra top, her *Pieta*-like face looking on sadly. She guessed the wrong answer, and the buzzer sounded, but instead of taking off her top, she pointed a laser beam at the host, tracing his bones, one by one, faster and faster, making designs out of them—flowers and animals.

My dad woke me up and told me to take my backpack with my most important possessions: the clown doll from the Ospidale Israelitico, the books, my composition notebook, my toys. The bus was waiting downstairs.

4

WEIGHT IN THE FINGERTIPS

To Mr. D, 1934–2010

My father's aunt and uncle, Dolly and Ilya Kerman, took us in. Dolly was the mysterious American aunt who had visited us in Odessa, and the thought of staying in her house made me nervous. The extravagant gifts she had brought me in Odessa—the bubble gum, the erasers, the blue dress—certainly had to mean that she lived in nothing short of a palace or a museum.

It was not a palace, but I still never imagined that a family could live in a house like theirs. It had large and small rooms, winding staircases, wisteria all around its brick walls, and a blooming garden. It also had a guard—an elderly half-husky, half-Samoyed dog named Sam. He was bigger than I was; followed everybody around with a shuffle; passed gas nonstop; and appraised you with wise, liquid eyes. The Kermans would own many dogs after him, but none, in my opinion, measured up to Sam. Sam was all-knowing.

Ilya had filled the house with slender model ships in glass cases, scowling wooden masks, and stained-glass lamps, all of his own making. (A dedicated hobbyist, he would eventually graduate to making real ships and in 2017 would take his newly crafted boat on a maiden voyage in Bellingham, Washington.) He was our first guide to the particularities of American English and American films. On my first morning in the United States, he shook my hand and inquired, in loud, cheerful English, "Helllllo!! How arrrre you?" He would never lose the rolling *r*'s from his Russian upbringing and retained the thickest accent imaginable. Despite this, everyone could always understand him perfectly.

"I am well, thank you," I replied politely.

"You are well? Have you been sick? You have to answer 'I am fine!'" He accompanied this with upbeat gestures, like a conductor leading an orchestra.

This was the first American expression I learned.

A VCR in 1980s Odessa was a luxury owned by some restaurants and clubs and the occasional well-connected family. I had never met anyone who owned one. The Kermans did have one, and on one of our first evenings in the States, they showed us the Gene Wilder comedy *Frisco Kid*. In this mock-western, an Orthodox Jewish rabbi leaves Poland to bring a torah to a newly founded Jewish community in San Francisco during the Gold Rush. He is robbed by a bunch of hooligans and sets upon a cross-country hike on an incompetent horse. Along the way, he meets the dashing Harrison Ford, a cowboy, and they travel together. Slowly, the rabbi teaches the cowboy the ways of Judaism, and the cowboy toughens up the rabbi, western style.

The film made a lifelong impression on my parents. Soviet Jewish refugees that they were, they'd never witnessed Orthodox Judaism in life or on film and were amazed to see it treated in such a warm, affectionate manner. Rich with images of the Wild West, this film embodied everything they hoped American life would stand for: freedom, adventure, opportunity, friendship between Jews and cowboys, jumping into a chasm while simultaneously yelling "Oi gevalt!" and "Shit!" In 2004, we watched the film together again, and I attempted to criticize its corniness, only to be reprimanded by my father, "You may be right, but can you imagine what a gift this was for us when we just came here?" Embarrassed and clearly in the wrong, I had to retreat. It was just that: a gift.

After a week of resting at Dolly's house, my parents geared up to begin their new life. Driving lessons. Rigorous English studies. Finding work of any kind. Starting me in school. But the first priority for them was finding a piano for me to practice on, as well as a top-notch teacher who would guide me through the classical-music world of our new home country.

I rather enjoyed that extra week off from the piano. Paul and Dima, the Kerman children, both much older than me, showed me a wild game where the player could somehow control a fully operating, beautiful, and lively cartoon on the television! My thumbs became numb from sending Mario over blocks and sewer pipes, hurling fireballs and turtle shells, and fighting a giant monster in a rocky dungeon. Much later, when I was learning Rachmaninoff's *Rhapsody on the Theme of Paganini*, I jokingly referred to the nineteenth variation as the "Super Mario in the dungeon" variation. Take a listen, and you will see why!

The Super Mario championship ended as soon as my first piano arrived. I had never seen a piano like it; it was much shorter than Red October, with a soft, chestnut color and a mild, gentle look. It was a spinet piano, purchased from another family with the little cash my parents had brought with them through immigration. Its arrival was a spectacular parade. Uncle Ilya's enormous station wagon wore it like a hat, with my parents sitting on the roof of the automobile, supporting the wobbling instrument from each side. Ilya waved from the driver's seat, and they made a few attempts to back into the garage, succeeding against all odds and festively unloading the piano. It was a stalwart

The arrival of my first piano in the United States — the long-suffering spinet. I started practicing in the garage!

Me at the spinet, once we moved it inside the house.

instrument. Over the next two years, by age thirteen, I would learn Tchaikovsky's First Concerto, many Beethoven sonatas, and Chopin and Liszt etudes on it. It withstood these trials with dignity. It still resides with the Kermans, reminding me of Sam the dog with its kindly demeanor.

* * *

I spent about a week getting back into shape, practicing my repertoire and scales. Up to this day, the feeling of rusty, unyielding fingers without callus marks (something that only happens when I'm on vacation!) sends me into a downward spiral of discomfort that turns into frustration and then real unhappiness. It is like having to make a toy out of frozen clay—nothing gives. You have to rub the clay for a long time, warming it in your palms, before it can become anything. That week was the very first time I experienced the feeling. The small muscles remember quickly, followed by the big muscles, and soon, making music stops being a mechanical chore. But getting to that state after not playing is a painful process, almost like recovering from an injury. It was only because my mother had me practice on the table almost every day throughout the months of our stay in Rome that I did not completely lost my chops.

Through introductions from friends of friends, we visited a number of Chicago-area music teachers. Everyone recommended Emilio del Rosario. We had heard of this man while still in Odessa. His reputation for teaching children and teenagers, making the highest-level pianists out of them, reached us all the way there. He was known to assign very difficult repertoire, to help students attain technical mastery at a very young age, and to aid them with performance opportunities. A tape of my playing circulated through a few sets of hands before landing in his. And one morning, he phoned Dolly's house and invited us to come and see him at the Music Institute of Chicago, the music school where he had taught for many years. As I later learned, he spent most of his waking hours—and sometimes his sleeping ones—there: late nights, weekends, and even the most sacred of holidays.

I was very nervous, imagining Mr. del Rosario to be a tall man with sharp features, pomaded black hair, and perhaps a few medals. The name had a heroic ring, and the man, a grand reputation. I wanted to impress him. My mom worked with me on preparing Bach's Prelude and Fugues and the Concerto in F Minor, *The Maiden's Wish*—a Chopin-Liszt transcription—and Chopin's *Fantaisie-Impromptu*. I also practiced my own piano compositions. One week later, Dolly took my mother and me to a little redbrick building, situated in one of the most affluent neighborhoods in the entire country: Winnetka, Illinois, home of the title character in *Ferris Bueller's Day Off*. We waited outside the studio, where a couple of nicely dressed children sat on the stairs, to Mom's horror. "They are sitting on the floor! In their concert dresses!"

Finally, the door creaked ajar, and a joyous, rather high, and fizzy voice said laughingly, "Ah, here is my next victim." A short man stepped out, immaculately dressed in a red blazer, black shirt, and perfectly tailored black trousers. I noticed that

With Mom, next to Mr. D's studio at the Music Institute of Chicago.

the shape of his face was very round and his head slightly square. He had dark skin; oodles of smiling wrinkles; intense, luminous, brown eyes; and perfectly shiny, combed, black hair that reminded me of my great-grandmother. He exuded immense kindness. He could have been anywhere between forty-five and sixty-five.

Mr. D had started playing piano in the Philippines and he came to the United States to study at the Peabody Conservatory in Baltimore, where he worked with many well-known teachers, including Mieczyslaw Munz and Leon Fleisher. He had played many concerts in the United States and Asia and spent a great deal of time with singers, coaching and accompanying them in opera and art-song repertoire. When he was in his thirties, he had been invited to teach at the Music Center of the North Shore by Herbert Zipper (he of Zipper Hall in Los Angeles), a renowned musician, philanthropist, maverick, and leader in the art world. Mr. D moved to Chicago, and gradually, his innate talent for teaching and relating to children helped to create one of the strongest precollege piano studios in the world. With just a look, a movement of his hand, and a short humming sound, he was able to pull the best out of any given student—as long as that student was willing and able to fully commit to the piano and to music.

The studio where I would spend my most important hours during the next eight years had two pianos, giant bookcases overfilled with music scores, a small fridge, dozens of clean and stained coffee mugs all over, and a strange painting that would

In a lesson with Mr. D.

always fascinate me—an abstract greenness of triangles, leaves, flowers, and faces. He invited me to the piano, and I launched into my program right away, before I got too nervous. After I finished, he extended his hand to me—a knotty thing, with stubby, hard chunks for fingertips—and said, "Welcome." And thus, I joined the tightly knit group of Mr. D's students.

A child does not yet have a fully developed musical identity. But just as their sense of humor, character, values, and interests are emerging, so, too, is their musical persona. I was fortunate to have a creative upbringing. And now, Emilio del Rosario could take over and nurture everything that was already planted in me, making me a professional pianist and performer.

Immediately after my audition, he took me upstairs to the concert hall, where a student recital was in full swing—this explained the dressed-up kids on the stairs who had so horrified my mother. He asked me to play part of my program, and I had no time to think—I just did it. Most of the school's administration was present, and after I finished playing, they told me I had gotten a scholarship for study with Mr. del Rosario. When Frank Little, the dashing, patrician executive director of the school, found out how much my mother had done to teach and prepare me, he hired her as a faculty member. I was to have two lessons a week, each one and a half hours long. I did not know that Mr. D, as his students affectionately called him, paid for half of these out of his pocket—the other half was covered by the scholarship. It took my family a while to understand that this man lived through and for his students, that his love for them was unconditional, and that they constituted his world.

* * *

We moved to an inexpensive garden-floor apartment in Wilmette, another North Shore suburb that was more upscale than we could imagine. We moved there only because it was a ten-minute drive from the music school. Dolly and Ilya gave us their station wagon, and my father and mother took turns learning to drive it. I started junior high, skipping fifth grade and enrolling in sixth. Our American life was starting to take shape.

On my first day of school, I took with me my pioneer's red scarf and some Soviet coins for show-and-tell. I had no doubt that my story would garner me enormous success in making new friends and that I could easily reestablish the same type of circle that I left in Odessa. I quickly realized that most children at Wilmette Junior High School were, shall we say, privileged. They had an unfamiliar glossiness, a kind of polish that twinkled in their clothes, their perfectly sculpted teeth, their straight and shiny hair, and their shapely jeans. I was the only new student and possibly the first foreigner that any of these children had ever seen.

When asked if Russia was in Canada, I would take out a little notebook with a map and patiently explain where the Soviet Union was located. At lunch, I felt no shame in running to the school office and asking for a lunch card because my father had not yet found a job. When asked, "Where did you buy these jeans?" I saw nothing wrong in truthfully naming a large discount drugstore near our apartment. I couldn't understand why some kids would ask this repeatedly and with glee. Finally, a sympathetic girl took me aside and said, "You better answer, 'The Gap.'"

I had never up to that point had to face malice from other children, taking it as a given that they would be open to somebody new who could teach them something unfamiliar. Gradually, I began to feel the hostility, no longer veiled by roundabout questions about my jeans. The homeroom teacher, Mrs. Jones, chastised me once during free-reading period, "What is this book? What language is this?"

It was a fictionalized biography of Michelangelo, a Russian translation of an English book. She said to me, "I don't want you reading this language in my room ever again."

"Your eyebrows look like Brezhnev's," an especially erudite boy informed me.

That day, I begged my mom to pluck them thin and, while she was at it, to straighten my hair. My mom could not understand this at all. "But it's beautiful! People pay big money to have curly hair and full eyebrows!"

She just didn't get it. I wrote letters to my friends in Odessa and tried to describe the crazy hair-sprayed bangs; the bright makeup; the jeans, folded an inch at the bottom that I saw around me on my eleven-year-old classmates. I was so sure that nobody in Odessa—surely not Shpilka!—would try to look grown-up before they really were.

At first I loved the school bus because it looked like a giant, happy, orange hippo, but that didn't last. The kids kept asking me to open the window, but I didn't know how to do it. The window latches had to be pressed from both sides, and then lifted. I simply couldn't master it. They knew I didn't know how, and it was fun to watch me, the dumb immigrant who'd never been on a school bus, struggle so much. That struggle didn't extend to homework; the classes were very easy. I felt that I had done the sixth-grade math in my second year of school in Odessa. My English got better quickly. I did well in science and was fascinated by the typing class—I had never seen a computer before. None of this helped with popularity. To be popular, I would have needed glossy, straight hair; expensive clothes; and no accent.

I also would have been better off hiding my interest in books and music—at least classical music. My parents bought a VCR and watched the movie *Amadeus* with some out-of-town friends. Until that point, Mozart had been for me one of the gods you learned to play carefully, slowly, one note at a time, the unearthly beauty emerging gradually as you learned the pieces. He was someone you glorified—a saint, a statue with a ponytail, a subject for an ode. And suddenly, there he was, clowning around, chasing girls, gambling, making dirty jokes. And then dying, just like that. I fell asleep that night with the requiem in my head: "*Confutatis maledictis, flammis acribus addictis.*" I watched the movie countless times, and while my peers were cultivating their crushes on Christian Slater, I developed one on Wolfgang Amadeus Mozart. (I was also quite enamored with the acting of F. Murray Abraham, who played Salieri. When asked in school whom I liked—*like* was a word that carried so much weight; it meant finding somebody awesome, hunky, cool—I replied, "F. Murray Abraham," eliciting funny looks and giggles.)

One day in math, a girl named Mindy said to me, out of nowhere, "Why did you come here? Go back to where you came from. We don't want you here."

What can one say to this? Does one whack the other person across the nose? Does one cry and run away? I attempted a witty response about her own ancestors certainly coming from elsewhere because this was America—a country of immigrants. Something garbled came out instead. Four years later, I would win a competition whose prize was a concerto performance with the Chicago Symphony. That performance—I played Tchaikovsky's Concerto 1 in B-flat Minor—was broadcast on public television and radio as part of a popular program about teenage musicians. A few days after my debut, I was in a café with my high school boyfriend, and I saw her, Mindy Lockspear, all blond tresses and whitened teeth, with a big group of friends. I came up to their table and asked if she remembered me.

"Oh my God! Inna Faliks, I think I just saw you on TV," she chirped.

"I think we were in sixth grade together," I said.

"Wow! Do you remember me?"

"Yes, you are the bitch who told me to go back to Russia." The table went silent. I turned around and walked back to my table. In my imagination, my hair swished, and I had the swagger of a model. This probably was not the case. But it felt really, really good. I hated her so much because I had allowed her to make me feel so miserable. And now, because my stock had gone up, I could let her know without fear.

* * *

I didn't tell my parents about my school troubles until much later. I didn't want them to regret bringing me here after all they went through. Plus, I had a separate, wondrous life at the Music Center of the North Shore as part of Mr. D's studio. My very first few lessons with Mr. D rang with cryptic exclamations: "Thumbunder!" "Usedewrist!" "Weightindefingertips!" I could not make out the separate words but somehow knew what he meant. He was teaching me a series of warm-up scales to play each day.

(In fact, I still play them each day—it is like brushing my teeth—and teach them to my own students.) He wanted me to use my wrist when going up or down the keyboard—changing its position to make the phrases more connected and legato—and make sure my thumb did not incorrectly accent notes when I turned it. The scales were to sound like melodies, like a beautiful voice singing on one breath. The slow processional of the upward and downward notes would quicken by two and run up and down, then in contrary motion. "Crescendo!" he would roar. "Now, soft!" He would play along with me in the upper register of the piano while crouched in a large chair next to the instrument. He ornamented my scales with little trills, turns, silly tunes—anything to keep me from getting bored with the exercises.

At our first lesson, he assigned to me a Mozart sonata; a Chopin etude; and the slow, stately and heart-wrenching Scriabin Etude in C-sharp Minor, immortalized in recordings by Horowitz. I also asked for Beethoven's *Pathetique*. I first heard it played live when I was four, by a nine-year-old girl named Anna Bogolyubova, in Odessa and had wanted to play it ever since. I practiced each hand separately, repeating it many times—very slowly, then at medium tempo, then a bit faster, then putting the hands together, all with the dynamics and phrasing the music called for. After this felt natural and easy, the shaping and emotion would come freely, and I could really make music.

Mr. D spent all day at the music school and never took actual lunch breaks. Once in a while, though, a large container of food would emerge from his fridge. "Can I share with you some worm intestines and eel brains?" he would ask. The macabre dishes spanned many exotic varieties, from giraffe snot to hyena livers. In reality, they were mostly Korean food, with slithering glass noodles and colorful vegetables, brought to him by students' parents. I caught on soon and brought him borscht in little Tupperware bowls.

After a few weeks, he felt I was prepared to enter the world of the Mr. D Saturday Night Workshops. The workshops started at 6:00 every Saturday evening and ended after midnight. They were recitals in which Mr. D's students played for each other, their families, and anyone else who wished to stop by the recital hall on a Saturday evening. Once you became a student of Mr. D, the workshops were a non-negotiable part of existence. They meant no other plans, *ever*, on Saturdays.

The recital hall didn't have a stage and was more like a large, airy room with chairs, plenty of light from the floor-to-ceiling windows, and two large pianos—a Steinway and a Yamaha. The students' families came and went throughout the workshops; the younger pianists usually went first and left before the sun went down. One could usually tell the time by what was being played. If you heard some of the lighter repertoire—some easier Debussy pieces, a Bach fantasia, shorter works of Chopin, Mozart sonatas—this meant that the workshop had just started. If you heard some tempestuous rendition of a Beethoven sonata or larger-scale romantic works like a Chopin ballade or Liszt's *Mephisto* waltz, then we were into the 8:00 hour, with the fifteen-year-olds beginning to run through their competition programs. When the school's classrooms, studios, and bathrooms reverberated throughout with the primal sounds of Prokofiev, the fugue from the Barber sonata, Stravinsky's *Petrushka*, Ravel's notorious *Gaspard de la Nuit*, complete Beethoven sonatas—third movements and all—and meat-and-potatoes piano concerti like Rachmaninoff's Second, Liszt's First, Tchaikovsky's First, or Prokofiev's Third, you were hearing conservatory audition pieces and concerto competition repertoire. When needed, Mr. D played the orchestra's part in a piano reduction, providing gutsy, frequently messy, but always inspired accompaniment on the Yamaha that was lovingly nestled to the left of the Steinway, away from the audience. These were the older, precollege kids at work, and the time was nearing midnight.

When it was windy, the tall trees outside beat the windows, crossed fingers, waved, and danced. For the seven years of weekly workshops, I listened to the other students and watched the trees, hypnotized, imagining that they knew the music and moved to it, whether lush and robust in the summer or naked in the winter. After the first year, I allowed my thoughts to wander after hearing the same person play the same repertoire for the thirtieth time in preparation for high-profile auditions or engagements. I would come and go, play downstairs in the practice rooms, laugh with the other students outside, go outside to bring Mr. D his Diet Coke or—once I learned to drive—Starbucks coffee, chat with him a bit between pieces, or make quiet comments on other students' playing. He was a part of me and my emotional world; there was no divide between us. We could laugh and make faces at one another or sigh understandingly when somebody was not playing their best. And then suddenly, he would become a stern teacher, going through my music, his pencil flailing wildly, reminding me who was boss. My mother would come to almost every workshop and sit next to him. At some points, he would gesticulate expressively to her, and at others, he closed his eyes as if he was deep in sleep, seemingly frozen in his chair, his large, crinkly eyes shut, head on his chest, buried between the shoulders of his designer suit. This meant he was listening most intensely, entirely at one with the music he heard.

In my first, shy workshops, I sat behind Mr. D until it was my turn to play and observed his reactions closely, cherishing the respectful distance between him and myself, fearing him a little. The most agitated sound that could come out of his mouth was *tsk*, accompanying a basic sort of imperfection—a wrong note, a missed chord, an out-of-place dynamic, a tiny memory lapse. Mr. D was a perfectionist, and this click was involuntary and frustrated. When we played something in a less-than-perfect manner, he physically revolted against it. His tongue immediately snapped peevishly against the ceiling of his mouth, projecting through the concert hall into the frenzied, adrenaline-packed awareness of the performer. This mannerism became so ingrained into our psyches that we would expect it and even produce it ourselves with the inevitable occurrence of wrong notes. It was not just a reaction to a mistake. It communicated a plethora of ideas about discipline and expectations. In short, it meant, "A musician strives for perfection; music deserves no less. If you can't work for it, don't do it."

When I would hear some of the older kids, I'd be consistently blown away by their technical prowess, their complete control of the instrument, their perfectly sophisticated freedom at the piano. It became clear to me and my parents that being a serious student of Emilio del Rosario meant a certain way of life—coming home early from school; practicing at least five hours a day, if not more; and adopting an edgy, competitive drive that demanded rigorous discipline.

Mr. D's regimen of scales and etudes fostered infallible chops in his students early on, and the workshops trained one to get used to performing weekly and to love it like one might trips to the zoo or the movies or the park. It became routine. As a child, I was taught that technique meant possessing the necessary tools to reach a musical goal. Here, I was suddenly steeped in hard-core virtuoso training. It felt fantastic, like learning how to fly. I had a solid background already and was making fast strides. But as time went on, I felt at odds with the separation of the musical and the technical. The *tsks* bothered me. Even as an eleven-year-old, I thought they focused the mind and ear on something secondary and made technical perfection a goal in and of itself rather than a by-product of focused, deeply considered and felt music making. In my experience so far, the less I thought about occasional wrong notes, the less they appeared. In the grand scheme of things, though, the feeling of ease, the ability to play and learn anything quickly without fixating on its immense difficulty was a gift Mr. D had given us. Every approach has pluses and minuses, but the pluses here were what mattered.

At the first workshop, I became friends with a boy named Matthew Kim. Matthew had fast fingers and chubby hands that helped him produce a warm, effortless forte sound on the piano. He had been born in Korea, and his family moved to the Chicago area when he was a baby. He was gentle, funny, and sharp-witted—qualities that reminded me of Shpilka. On Sunday mornings, our respective parents dropped off the two of us at the Music Center for a day of uninterrupted practice. We quickly learned that Mr. D never got to work before noon on Sundays, so there was nobody around to hear or monitor our playing. We goofed off unapologetically, becoming more creative as we got older. When we were both learning the same Chopin etude, we would first practice it at the same time, very slowly and diligently, and then get faster and faster, pulling apart from one another to make a canon out of it. I would start first, and Matthew would join three or four measures later. The cacophonic result sent us into stitches. Had it been recorded, it could have made for an interesting piece in its own right—two pianos imitating out-of-sync tape recorders. When both of us were thirteen, we made up rude lyrics and silly jingles to some of the great repertoire that we were both learning—the Chopin ballades; the Mendelssohn concerto; the Tchaikovsky First Concerto that I had learned and performed; and Rachmaninoff's Second Concerto, which was Matthew's baby.

One day, we put together whatever money we had in our pockets and took a brisk walk to a nearby deli, where we purchased butter and brownie dough. In the teachers' lounge, which was unlocked for some reason, we managed to find something that resembled a baking pan, buttered it, stuck in the dough, and tried to bake it in the tiny microwave, which was not really meant for baking. The brownies burned immediately, setting off fire alarms. By the time firemen arrived on the scene of the crime, we had disposed of the charred brownie dough, the pan, the butter, and anything else covered with chocolate goo.

Mr. D found all this charming and constantly made fun of us for supposedly being in love. He teased all his students ruthlessly, delving into embarrassing romantic territory by the time they became teenagers and never leaving it alone again, even when the teenagers grew up and had their own teenagers. In his favorite story, a boy's tongue got stuck in a girl's braces, and their parents had to take them to the doctor. But because neither one of us had braces, he had to make do with lame rumors about us: "They held hands so tight that she couldn't do her scales that day at the lesson." We groaned and rolled our eyes.

By age thirteen, in 1991, both of us were entering piano competitions. We would fill out competition application forms from made-up characters with ridiculous names (in the style of Bart Simpson—"Ima Cow," "Anita Laxetif," etc.), background (Berlin Philharmonic, second tuba), and repertoire (the complete piano music of Guns n' Roses). In place of the required photos, we drew horned and mustachioed faces. Matthew's father, a stern statue of a man, took piano competitions more seriously. He saw them as a way to pad Matthew's ever-growing stack of

Ivy League college applications and wanted his son to win at all costs. He regarded me as if I had a bull's-eye on me: I had to be obliterated in competition along with all other girls and boys. Both Matthew and I were scared of him and listened carefully for the jingling of his car keys. The moment we heard the dreaded sound, we would duck into our practice rooms and resume our work as he made his way down the school's single long hallway to check up on his son.

My mother regarded competitions simply as performance opportunities for me, important public appearances that might lead to other concerts. Over the years of watching me enter these bizarre events, she began to view them as antimusical, psychologically unhealthy political events, fascinating at times in their absurdity. In some cases, competitions are a necessary evil, and for child pianists, they were like carrots dangling on a stick in front of a donkey. They made us work at the piano with absolute commitment.

When I first heard the term *competition*, I imagined an event of unbridled majesty. I pictured the International Tchaikovsky Competition, one of the most prestigious piano competitions in history—though, given the Russian-Ukrainian War, this is possibly a thing of the past. When Van Cliburn was the first American to win, in 1958, he came back home a hero, the darling of the media, embodying the hope for an end to the Cold War. So I was overwhelmed with pride when the first competition I entered was the International Tchaikovsky Competition for Young Musicians.

Back when we had immigrated, in 1989, I had slept through my entire first flight to the United States from Rome. My mom had desperately wanted to feed me the chicken served by the flight attendant, which she found uncommonly delicious, probably because she didn't have to take it out of a tin can and because it was free. But I refused to wake up. Once we had landed, O'Hare's futuristic United terminal greeted us with a rainbow of fluorescent lights and twinkling passages of *Rhapsody in Blue*. It gleamed seductively, like perfect teeth.

Only a few years later, the Soviet Union had burst at the seams, and my parents and I boarded a flight on Aeroflot from

Chicago to Moscow, with a Dublin stopover. We were not returning to the Soviet Union but rather to the newly minted Russian Federation. (Apparently, the old country just could not hold itself together without us, remarked Dad with his ever-intact sarcasm.)

I would be performing in the Great Hall of the fabled Moscow Conservatory for the Tchaikovsky competition. To this day, I don't know how Mr. D convinced my parents to go back to the "motherland," even for the short duration of the competition. Perhaps the idea of my presence on that great stage and the collapse of the Soviet Union a couple of months prior to our trip made it seem intriguing. I had been convinced that my father would not set foot there again, and the fact that his own parents were filing their immigration papers meant that he wouldn't have to. And yet, there we were, buckling our seat belts.

The unsmiling flight attendant, tall and rectangular as a coffin, barked short orders at us. It was like being home again. My cup of water had a fly in it. Somebody in the back of the plane was smoking and drinking vodka before takeoff. His name was Uncle Misha, and he had Einstein hair and wore a thousand-year-old sweat suit. He recited Pushkin; sang Soviet anthems at the top of his lungs; and tried to flirt with me and my mom, despite the fact that I was thirteen and she was with my dad. About seven hours into the flight, he became too inebriated to continue this live entertainment and fell asleep on the floor of an empty row. Amazingly, the passengers and the flight crew forgot all about him. The plane landed in Shannon, Ireland, for the stopover, and we got our bags after what seemed like hours. I turned to the window to see two burly males carry him off the plane by the arms and legs. I wondered where they took him.

Our crew changed in Ireland, and the new Russian flight attendant didn't detect Mom's accent in her pleases and thank-yous. Subsequently, we were all treated like dignitaries. My parents had forgotten, in their three years out of the Soviet Union, this small quirky feature of every day Soviet life: Foreigners get treated well. They didn't realize it, but after a few years in the United States, they had started smiling wide, American smiles.

For the 1992 Tchaikovsky Competition, my friend Anastasia came from Odessa to see me. Here we are in the Red Square.

Years after that trip, I would read the novel *Moscow 2042* by Vladimir Voinovich. The narrator's arrival at Sheremetyevo International Airport fifty years in the future matched what we saw in 1992 with uncanny accuracy: grim, unsmiling faces; suspicious glances; pallid stares—a macabre world of the walking dead. It seemed that the name of the country had changed, but life had stayed the same.

We were placed in the historic Moskva hotel, built during the years of Stalin's terror near the Kremlin. Provincial party bosses would stay there when visiting the capital. And now, we poor immigrants, back as sophisticated citizens of the world, were staying in the very heart of this forbidden part of Moscow! We dropped our bags, leaving agape the eager, young translator who met us (he was very disappointed that he had nothing to do because we already spoke Russian), and ran to the Moscow Conservatory so that I could prepare for the competition's first round as soon as possible.

We stepped outside the hotel into Manezhnaya Square and were greeted by a colorful hot-air balloon, prepped for takeoff. This phantasmagoric sight—I'd never seen one before—was just one of many other happenings on the square: marathon runners in what appeared to be gray underpants, jogging in a circle and singing the old Soviet anthem; a military band in full dress uniforms with shiny regalia and a huge banner that proclaimed, "Glory to our Soviet Russia." The ramrod-postured bandleader raised his baton, and we started in shock: Instead of a military march, perhaps "Farewell to Slavianka," the band burst into the jolly Mr. Doolittle tune from *My Fair Lady*. Wouldn't Fellini love this *balagan*?

We arrived at the legendary Moscow Conservatory, and my mother paused meaningfully before crossing its threshold. Whoever would have thought that I, a Jewish girl from Odessa with no connections at all, would make it here, when it was very clear to everyone that, without *blat*—monetary, familial, or political ties—one stayed put? At the introductory meeting and the *zherebyovka* lottery to determine competitors' performance order, I found myself surrounded by girls and boys in frilly, old-fashioned dresses and stiff shirts. I wore jeans and sat on the floor, immediately distinguishing myself as a renegade. Shocked matrons loudly murmured their disapproval: "What do you expect from these Americans? No culture."

Yes, I was already an American, apparently. This strange fact would be commented on in television and radio interviews, where a melodious accent could be detected in my Russian speech. My parents didn't have accents, but apparently, they had become Americanized in a moral sense. Upon his return from the competition office, Dad looked embarrassed: He had forgotten about the obligatory "gifts" expected from participants by the artistic administrators. This country still could not function without bribes. Other parents had come with enormous, wrapped boxes, bottles, or envelopes that presumably contained crisp bills. Apparently, all I could go on was my playing, which would prove to be enough to make the semifinal round but not the final one.

Thus far, in my performance life, nothing could compare to the feeling of stepping on that great stage. I had watched Horowitz take this stage in a worldwide broadcast six years ago, upon his historic return to Russia. I had seen broadcasts of the adult Tchaikovsky competition, featuring the highest order of virtuosi, turning out what seemed like flawless performances, while portraits of Beethoven, Tchaikovsky, and Mozart stared down at them. It was one of the most opulent and famous stages in the world, and here I was, underneath a picture of Pyotr Ilych Tchaikovsky, about to play my thirty-minute solo program. Propelled by immense confidence and enthusiasm, I rattled off my Bach, my Beethoven sonata, and "La Campanella." Later, when watching the TV broadcast, I marveled at the speed of the repeated notes in the Liszt.

I made it to the semifinals and was certain that the finals were not far behind. My pièce de résistance in the semifinals was a solo transcription of Gershwin's *Rhapsody in Blue.* Very self-aware at the piano, I wanted to show my newly American openness by moving around to the music, perhaps more than was called for, more than was organic and natural. When my name was not called for the finals, my parents tried to console me by telling me that it really had nothing to do with my playing. But I had an inkling that I overdid it, that I played like a showman first and musician second, that the way I danced and head-bopped to this most American of tunes had been entertaining but annoying because it looked over the top. Years later, I would come to know that this is done in competitions left and right, and audiences generally love it—just not that audience.

On our last night in the hotel Moskva, our German neighbor, the mother of a young pianist from Berlin, ran out of her room screaming, "Little animals!" Apparently, a battalion of large roaches had marched out of the bathroom in search of food. The screaming lady in her boxy pajamas; the morbid Red Square through the darkened windows of the tourist bus; the pallid, almost automated border control beings; and, most of all, my first career disappointment mark my first trip back. Little did I know that one day, *Rhapsody in Blue* and I would make it back to Russia, together.

The next important competition was the Illinois Young Performers Competition. It played out like a war in the Music Center—especially among the parents. As the February date approached, young pianists, violinists, and cellists spent more and more hours in the practice rooms, working on their concerti. Three people would be picked for each instrument category in the junior (under fifteen) and senior (between fifteen and eighteen) divisions. These lucky three would later compete in the finals, where one from each division was chosen, and the winners would appear in a live-televised broadcast on PBS, performing their concerto with the Chicago Symphony in a program hosted by a national celebrity. When I got to do it, I was fifteen, and the host was Christie Yamaguchi, of Olympic figure-skating vixen fame. I was disappointed. The year before, I didn't get to the finals—and the host had been Neil Patrick Harris (a.k.a., Doogie Howser).

Mr. D enjoyed telling stories of the threatening letters, bribe offers, and pleas he received in conjunction with this event. The parents in the workshops stopped talking to each other and seemed to be taking notes on the other children's performances, noting the obvious flaws and strengths. Dirty looks were exchanged back and forth. The tension could almost be physically felt. When somebody didn't win, a possible reason was "Well, so-and-so had a more effective concerto. You can't compete with Liszt by playing Mozart."

At the televised broadcast, before each young finalist walked onto the stage of Chicago's Orchestra Hall, a short segment about the musician appeared on a giant overhead screen, seen by the live audience and the television viewers. This was filmed in advance and was meant to be a sort of quick summary of their life and personality. The director of my segment wanted to film me in a giant shopping warehouse. The idea was to show the contrast between my childhood in a poor Communist country and my teenage years in a place of bounty. I had to run down the isles with a shopping cart; throw random objects in; and say, with an ecstatic smile, "There are many differences between Odessa and Chicago, and the main one is . . . *shopping*!" I was then filmed eating pizza with girlfriends and doing some other things I never did, such as minigolfing. This reminded me, once again, of how I didn't fit in.

The segment's best few seconds amounted to a conversation with Mr. D. His eyes intense, he said into the camera, "Inna, she is not just a pianist. She is a performer who communicates. She is so emotional, expressive." And then came a quick cut to footage of that year's Olympic gold medalist Oksana Baiul from Ukraine, breaking down in tears on the ice. You see? Ukrainian folks must be emotional by nature.

How important this event seemed to us then! How badly, since the very first month in Mr. D's studio, I wanted to win, and how frustrating it was not to win for a few years in a row. How far-fetched it seems now, as I write this, the notion of a contest like this as an all-encompassing event of great musical importance. Competitions are just a part of a young musician's journey. But they gave us a sense of responsibility, the gravity of solid months-long preparation for a given performance, for coming out onstage at Orchestra Hall and making a beeline for the piano that stands at its center, so elegant and proud, waiting for you to play it.

By the time I finally had my chance to play with the Chicago Symphony, I was fifteen. My parents had recently bought a small townhouse, just a few miles up the road in the city of Skokie. I changed schools in eighth grade and ended up in Niles North High—a much more tolerant place, with a diverse international population. Niles North students were the Vikings, and their color was purple. Every week, somebody won the Viking-of-the-Week distinction for some achievement, like winning a

On stage, performing Tchaikovsky's 1st piano concerto with the Chicago Symphony in my debut, at the 1994 Illinois Young Performers Competition.

debate, scoring the highest in math, or leading the basketball team to victory. The weekend after the competition, I arrived at school to find a certificate and a purple sweatshirt in my locker. On the speaker that morning, I heard it loud and clear: "Inna Faliks is named Viking of the Week for playing with the Chicago Symphony Orchestra this weekend." The certificate identified me as a violinist.

* * *

"What if I marry the person who lets me in?" I thought to myself. I was sixteen, ensconced in a tight bodysuit, jeans low on my hips, eyebrows finally plucked, and outside a birthday party in a fancy suburban neighborhood. Max opened the door. He had dark eyes, a ponytail, an expressive nose with a bump, and an earring, the essence of cool. He was a year older and went to New Trier High School, definitely socially superior to Niles North. "We are just getting the beer out," he said. "Get in." He then turned back to the group of people with whom he was talking about Truffaut and Woody Allen and other people I'd never heard of. I was intrigued. I quickly ran to the bathroom and put on lipstick and blush, trying in vain to cover up an enormous zit on my cheek. What to do? This guy had long black hair and an interesting, angular face with a sensitive Gallic nose; he was smarter than anyone my age whom I'd recently talked to. He was wearing a leather jacket and ripped jeans. I was immediately into him and wanted him to like me. Looking around, I immediately knew how I could score some quick points with Max. There was an upright piano in the corner, and I inched my way over and quietly started playing *Rhapsody in Blue*—if not interrupting the Nirvana album that was playing, then at least joining in as cacophonous backup. It worked like magic—in a few minutes, Max pushed his way over to the piano with two beers.

He called me the next day and asked me out to see some stupid romantic comedy. Mom and Dad were okay with it because his parents were friends of their friends and because it was somewhat reassuring that I was asked out by someone. Their daughter was going out on dates! This pointed to some kind of healthy social life beyond the piano, something I hadn't had or wanted that much, until that time.

Max would lie under the piano, listening to me practice for hours. He introduced me to Pink Floyd and Led Zeppelin and would blast them at top volume in his silver 1984 Corvette with the top down, wailing, "I . . . have become . . . comfortably numb," out of tune. Kaffein, a cafe in Evanston, served free coffee refills, and we would sit there for hours, past curfew. His friends smoked weed, but I quickly realized that when I did, I would not be able to practice the next day. Since then, I've hated marijuana.

We rode down to Lake Michigan on "Cherry," his Yamaha motorcycle, and read poetry under a blanket on the cold beach. We had enormous, epic, bawdy fights. I hated that he was always late picking me up for dates and that he drank. But we both seemed to feed off the drama. My workshop performances only got more dramatic, expressive, even wild. "Are you in love?" Mr. D would tease me.

Max's high school friends admired me because of my piano playing, but otherwise, I didn't fit with their weird, sarcastic, pot-smoking sensibility. Granted, they got me to fall in love with Monty Python, which I still quote—"Every sperm is sacred," "This parrot is no more," "Another mint, monsieur!" and "He's not the Messiah! He is a very naughty boy!"—liberally and often. But I hated pot and what it seemed to do to Max and his friends. They stopped making sense and became lazy and mean, lying back, lazily observing the passage of time—whether late at night in an expensively furnished Wilmette house after their parents went to bed, in their cars, or on the beach of Lake Michigan. His friends smoked a lot and seemed to have very few responsibilities, unlike me. I had to practice at least five hours a day. They barely did their homework and had no discernable hobbies.

All of them were having sex, so Max and I did it, too. It took many drunk attempts, and I cannot actually remember how the first time felt. I was sixteen, he was seventeen, and it was in a hotel room in New York, above a noisy bar in Greenwich Village. We were there because I had won the Chicago Chopin Competition and was invited as a finalist to the follow-up competition in New York City. My parents went, too, and, to my surprise, allowed me to share a room with Max. I think they were lenient because they had gotten married at nineteen and wanted me to find a guy who loved me as soon as possible. After all, since music didn't make me "normal," this did, right?

The next day, we celebrated by going to MOMA and having a champagne lunch afterward. I was late to the competition; I'd barely had enough time in my tiny greenroom at the Kosciuszko Foundation to change out of the baggy jeans and the Pink Floyd T-shirt Max had gotten me and into my long, green, velvet concert dress.

I lost the gold to a thirty-year-old but won the silver medal—no small feat. After the champagne, I'd been mildly tipsy as I played Chopin's Second Sonata and mazurkas in the final round. I didn't care. I was crazy about Max, and as far as I was concerned, this was what an artist's life was all about.

* * *

Max's mom was preoccupied with appearances. She was the very first person I had ever met who had gotten plastic surgery just because she felt like it. She was highly cultured and appreciated me because I had been known in Chicago as a child prodigy and was now one of the city's leading young musicians. At the same time, she thought I was too chubby. When I started staying over at their house, she would give me spirulina smoothies for breakfast and lectured me on how I had not yet reached my beauty potential as a woman. She was like an emotional vampire—each time Max and I had one of our screaming, dramatic fights, her eyes would light up, and she would lecture us individually and together. If there was a peaceful spell for a few weeks, she seemed bored and asked hungrily how we were getting on. If I said, "Great," then she would sulk and lecture me more on how to lose weight.

Max worked at Jiffy Lube and saved up enough money for a trip to Paris for the two of us. His mother made an itinerary—a precise, day-by-day list of all the museums and neighborhoods we should see. We stayed in a tiny hotel near Montmartre and Sacre Coeur. This was the first time I discovered Parisian patisseries—and they made up my diet, three times a day. That certainly was not on Max's mom's list. Max knew his art and his French films. Prior to going, we had watched *Camille Claudel*, *The Return of Martin Guerre*, *Tout les Matins de Monde*, and many other movies with Gerard Depardieu. I had taken French in junior high and before the trip reread *Les Misérables* by Victor Hugo. Max also took me to a French restaurant in downtown Chicago, where we attempted to order in French. We felt adequately prepared.

We gazed at the Notre Dame, the most miraculous building I had ever seen. We got lost in the Louvre, drank in the bars of Place Pigalle, smelled the roses in the Luxembourg Garden, and stared into the rugged faces of the statues in Musée Rodin. We had a makeshift dinner each night while embracing on the left bank of the Seine: a hunk of runny cheese; a baguette; some sausages; and a bottle of wine that, at two euros a bottle, was cheaper than water. On that trip, I lost my beloved stuffed animal, Bobik, a skinny, floppy-eared, red dog given to me by grandmother Rimma when I was two. She had bought him in Kherson when she went there to deliver a lecture on psychiatric medicine of some kind. He had made it through immigration. I have no idea why I took him with me to Paris. Maybe he reminded me of where I came from and who I was, despite all the wild novelty of the romance with Max. He was a reminder of my magical childhood in Odessa. He stayed behind in that tiny Paris hotel room with velvet red walls, and we flew back to Chicago.

Upon our return, I took Max to my senior prom. We had a predance dinner with friends at the Cheesecake Factory, and he arrived drunk on whiskey he had stolen from his stepfather (who very likely was on his way to getting equally drunk that night, as well). My Niles North High girlfriends squealed, "Max is so hot—like a rock star! Where did you get him?" Near the end of dinner, he initiated an epic food fight that ended with a double-fudge-caramel cheesecake going down my cleavage, and eventually, we were thrown out of the restaurant. My dress was ruined, but I didn't feel so bad. It wasn't my mom who paid for my dress, but Max's. I hadn't chosen it; it was an Armani, and I really didn't want it that much. She apparently thought it made me look classy and much skinnier. And now it had caramel and fudge all over the lace bustier.

All my high school friends thought Max was the definition of cool. But I felt like I was in a surreal bad dream. What was the meaning of prom? What was all this nonsense, bad music, ugly dresses, ear-splittingly loud music, awful dancing? They were empty, stupid. I had to practice for college audition tapes, for concerts in Japan, for Mr. D. Why was I with this guy? Maybe because, on some level, he made me feel like I belonged, despite the inexplicably fake social politics of high school in America. It also felt good to be wanted by a man. And I was in love—or maybe in love with the idea of being in love. After all, I had seen Paris for the first time with this guy. That had to count for something, right? Before going to the dance, I cleaned off the cake bits with a piece of brown paper towel from the high school bathroom.

One time, my dad found Max drunk and passed out on the front steps of our town house and took him inside. He still kicks himself for this, thinking he had the opportunity to end the relationship back then. But I convinced him that it was a one-off. I tried to ignore the drinking. We were in love, and Max understood the all-consuming nature of music in my life. And he loved listening to me practice.

* * *

After I turned sixteen, my parents, probably tired from the Tchaikovsky competition, started to allow me to travel to performances on my own. My very first solo trip was to Knoxville, Tennessee. Both then and now, on such trips, I frequently prefer to stay with host families rather than in hotels. It is pleasant, sometimes even moving, to have people who generously take you into their home as if you were family, providing for your needs before a concert appearance. Plus, most of the time, such families have pianos and are tolerant of the artist's last-minute practicing. (A futile effort, for some pianists. As another teacher of mine has said, "Practicing before a concert is like doing breathing exercises before you die.") Staying in a hotel has its own advantages. Sometimes you want to be left alone with your thoughts, your music, and a book. But with a host family, you can feel as though you're home even while away. This can be lovely or very strange.

The host and hostess on that trip were a pleasant couple in their fifties. They told me that their children had moved out many years ago but that they loved hosting and were excited to have a sixteen-year-old pianist in their home. I could practice all I wanted on one of their three full-size Steinways and should feel free to roam the house, play with the parakeets, cook—whatever I was in the mood for. Aside from the burned brownies, I had no cooking experience, but roaming around this three-story mansion of bronze statues, marble lions, and paintings of pale maidens and flowers was appealing. In the library, two life-size knights in full armor guarded each side of the fireplace, atop which was a shelf of books with colorful, intricately decorated spines. I gingerly took a copy of *Jane Eyre* and discovered that it was a fake—a spine with no pages. The rest of the titles on display were fake, as well. I was scandalized. My love for books, not just as reading material but as tactile objects with textures and smells, simply wouldn't allow me to believe that these were, in fact, just empty shells with pretty sleeves. My host pointed out the one real book on the shelf: *Mein Kampf*.

I was frightened. Did they know what this book was, or had it been as innocuous to them as the empty books? Did they know I was Jewish? Were they anti-Semites, neo-Nazis? Or had they no idea what this book represented?

I was taken to my bedroom, located in a former carriage house. I fell asleep, a little cold and wishing for more blankets, and woke up very early, chilled to the bone. I opted for a hot shower only to learn that there was no hot water or heat at all in the guesthouse. It was early March, and a thin layer of white frost covered the sprawling fields that surrounded the property. I threw on a sweater and made my way over to the main house. It was unlocked and empty.

The copy of *Jane Eyre* might have been fake, but here I was, left alone in an enormous, abandoned mansion, surrounded by mires and bogs (well, it really was just grass, but it was wet from the melting frost), pretending to be lost in a gothic novel. I hoped to find some breakfast in the enormous kitchen and discovered a note: "We left for the entire day on a cultural trip with friends to a neighboring town. We are sorry to miss your concert. You will find English muffins in the freezer and a Yellow Pages on the countertop so you can order food." Clearly, this couple had never hosted anyone before.

I ate a frozen English muffin, afraid to use an unfamiliar oven. I practiced until the afternoon, making sure that I went over every note of my concert program in a slow, concentrated manner. If my mind wandered, I would start the piece anew. Practicing this way is like watching a film in slow motion: All the detail, emotion, and intent are there but at a drastically reduced rate. This way, the performer's awareness of every detail is secured within their muscles so that the details spring to life in performance. Mr. D insisted on slow practice, and thanks to that, my performances gained clarity and solidity.

I decided to order Chinese food delivery—surely, they would have that somewhere around Knoxville. But because the concert organizers had driven me to the house late at night, straight from the airport, I didn't know where I was. I saw a great field, and a number on the house, but didn't know the street or the name of the small town we were in. I couldn't find any piece of mail lying around that might have had the address, and so I had to make do with carrots and more frozen English muffins, until it was time to be picked up by the concert presenter and head to the performance.

I played in a golden-domed museum. Evidently, a very persistent printer was going haywire a few floors below the concert stage. This was a glass building with wide staircases and no doors, so sound traveled beautifully. The printer's rhythmic screech resonated throughout the space, accompanying Chopin's Nocturne in D-flat with a nagging ostinato. During intermission, I saw that the paper that came out of the dot matrix printer had borders with perfectly spaced tiny holes. For a souvenir, I separated the borders from the dozens of pages the printer spewed out and made a small keychain out of them, to carry with me on trips, and I managed to hold on to this token for a few years before losing it.

* * *

Shortly after the Knoxville concert, Mr. D announced to my mother during a lesson that he wanted to take me and Matthew to Japan. He explained that we would receive professional fees for performances in multiple cities in the province of Matsuoka and would probably have a little time to travel around. Of course, my mother let me go. What followed was an outlandish sequence of flights—O'Hare to Detroit, Detroit to LA, LA to Seoul, and finally Seoul to Osaka. While in the air, Matthew and I didn't let poor Mr. D catch any sleep, laughing constantly and telling him dirty jokes. We forced him to watch *The Brady*

Bunch, a raunchy film parody of the TV show; stole his sushi; hid his brand-new Hugo Boss briefcase; and, in general, lovingly abused him. During the stopover in Korea, I had to look after him as if he was a child. He was hopelessly, pathologically addicted to shopping and would make for the duty-free shops with a determined gait. Five pairs of designer sunglasses and ties later, we almost missed the last leg of our journey.

When we landed in Japan, we were greeted with a somber ceremony of bows. A group of clean-cut Japanese men was headed by Mr. Ninomiya, our translator. He drove us for many hours to Matsuoka, where the first concert would take place. When we arrived, it seemed to be sometime in the morning. We didn't have any concept of time anymore, and exhaustion had caught up with us. We hoped to go to sleep immediately, but Mr. D, impeccable, smelling of aftershave, and clad in a new suit, came to our rooms and told us to focus: Our first performance was about to begin. He had no mercy. Perhaps this was revenge for our obnoxious behavior on the flight. We moaned and groaned, but a gig is a gig.

I changed into a modest concert outfit, a dark skirt and top. The first performance was not a big evening concert but a morning excursion to an all-girls school, where we were to meet the students and the administration and then each play a thirty-minute program. We came into a beautiful office of light- and dark-brown colors and very little furniture, with stark flower arrangements. We sat in uncomfortable, elegant chairs as a delegation processed in front of us, one by one, each person bowing and greeting us eloquently. By then I was in a faraway, jet-lag world, and I kept thinking I heard Russian swear words. (Later, I learned that many words in Japanese do, in fact, resemble impolite Russian expressions.) There can be a hard, guttural quality to the Japanese language, as if one were cracking a nut, but also a singing, expressive, melodic aspect. As I listened carefully, I became more and more intrigued. After this trip, I would start investigating Japanese cinema and become a die-hard fan.

Amazingly, each person who came to meet us—the mayor of the town, the director of the school, the vice director of the school, the headmaster of the school, the three main teachers, the music teacher, the substitute teacher, the top students—had gifts for us. Each presented a precious, lovingly wrapped box with bows made of fine bamboo leaves. They contained small, frowning dolls; embroidered handkerchiefs; lacquered chopsticks, delicate teacups. I felt the same rush of excitement as when my Aunt Dolly gave me a goodie bag for my ninth birthday—minus the guilt.

Matthew and I both played better than expected, under the circumstances. The young women who listened to us were a wide-eyed, sincere audience that seemed genuinely thankful for our arrival. My part of the concert consisted of Beethoven's *Appassionata*. From that morning on, we seemed to move nonstop. On long drives between towns, the clouds looked like taffy, stretched out long and thin, with ringlets and coils propelling them along—exactly like the reproductions of Hokusai paintings I had seen. We were driven by Mr. Ninomiya, probably enraging him with our goofy behavior and our sad attempts at conversational Japanese. *Kitchiguy* means *crazy*, and that would be Mr. D in the front seat: he who makes too many puns. I was his disciple, and therefore a *kitchigirl*.

Matthew and I went crazy for the udon noodles at every truck stop and for the revolving sushi bars, where we would grab lovingly painted little plates with morsels on them without regard for their actual contents or their price. The sushi melted under the tongue. In one of the towns, we met a group of Mr. Ninomiya's friends for a Kobe steak dinner and karaoke. I suffered through the dinner. Sitting on my knees for three hours caused such pain that I ignored the delicious, perfectly cooked slivers of meat in front of me. I remember the karaoke far better than the Kobe steak—prim, graceful ladies and gentlemen suddenly loosening their ties and hair clips and wildly rocking to '80s pop Americana.

Our big concert at the University of Fukui was sold out. By that time, both of us had played our programs at least four times each, so this performance felt like a culmination. Having performed the program over and over again, I experienced the wondrous state of total freedom onstage. I was completely confident and at ease from the very first notes. Usually, at the start of a recital, it may take a pianist anywhere from a few minutes to an entire half of a program to really get warmed up and comfortable. Here, I could take risks and try new ways of shaping and coloring this music from the start. I played the *Appassionata* and Chopin's Second Sonata. Mr. D never gave big compliments to his students. Following the Fukui performance, he simply said, "Good," so I knew he was pleased.

After the big night came the treats. We were first taken to a beach house for an overnight stay on the Yellow Sea. A traditional tea ceremony, like slow-motion theater, lulled us into a hypnotic presleep, and we fell asleep on the tatami mats to the sound of the waves outside. I woke up at 5:00 and went out for a walk on the wide, empty beach. A lonely surfer was catching waves close to the shore. The clouds moved like long-finned, soft-boned fish. Large, deep-brown snails were scattered across the sand. When I returned to have breakfast with Mr. D and Matthew, I was disturbed to encounter the very same snails in the breakfast bento boxes. They looked perfectly healthy and

With Mr. D in Kyoto, on our tour of Japan.
WTTW Chicago / Courtesy Mark Vitali

alive, as if they had wandered in from the beach like me. I could not eat a single one, but Mr. D seemed to have no trouble at all. I thought of the way he used to tease me with his lunches of monkey brains and worm doodoo.

Our last stop on that trip was the magnificent city of Kyoto. Before this visit, I thought of a temple as a single building. Here, I learned that a temple could be a small, peaceful city containing water, tall pine trees, and bamboo. In one such temple, I tasted the most intricate and elusive green tea and immediately asked Mr. Ninomiya to help me find a box to take home. Unfortunately, when I got home, my family didn't understand the tea and insisted it was soup. They cooked it and served it with spinach and cabbage, as a sort of green borscht.

* * *

Mr. D was enormously helpful with securing these early professional engagements. He was often asked to recommend young performers and had great knowledge of the international musical community. He rarely performed himself during the years I knew him, but he loved music with a childlike and contagious sense of wonder. In his teaching, he followed his intuition and simply taught what he heard and felt naturally, without philosophizing or theorizing. Whole books have been written on the intricacies of producing quality sound on the piano. Mr. D would simply close his eyes, hold out his hand arrestingly, and say, "Like a great singer." Later, when I started teaching, I wondered whether it might be more effective in some cases to delve deeper into the details. Mr. D would advise us to "Relax!" but how does one relax if the technique does not come naturally? How does one learn to make their hands soft and malleable like a jellyfish, free and flexible but also somehow capable of concentrated, almost rigid strength and focus? But he worked more instinctively, and perhaps, for that age of student, this approach was the most sensible one. The way my sound, my hands, and my posture were set in Odessa was the way I would play into my early twenties. He helped me develop it into a natural, confident, flexible style.

Mr. D's own physicality at the piano was highly unusual, in part because, as he told me, he had started studying much later than he would have liked. His gnarly fingers gathered themselves under a rather high wrist like an ominous-looking spider pulling prey into its web. His hands didn't sink deeply into the piano from the shoulders, as I later began to do with my own hands. It seemed that his stayed on the surface, extending his fingertips as feelers, drawing a focused, clear, vocal sound out of the keys. His flawless ears told him what to do and how to do it. As a performer, he was best at Mozart. His simplicity and directness in playing the sonatas could leave no listener dry-eyed. He related to the music so strongly that each time he played, it felt as if he told an inevitable truth. From my very first days at the Music Center, I tried to walk by his studio as much as possible during his few practice hours. There are four or five Mozart sonatas that make the hair on my arms stand up—the ones he warmed up with during the years I studied with him. I have played and taught some of them and of course listened to many performances, but everything pales when compared to the ideal of these pieces that he imprinted into my musical memory.

He never ceased to be thrilled by music. In the beginning, he wanted to make sure that I heard all the recordings he loved and familiarized myself with the singers, operas, and chamber music that moved him. On Sundays, he would sometimes take me to Orchestra Hall for the afternoon concerts. He drove his sports car crazily fast, past Lake Michigan on our left, into the forest of the Chicago skyline ahead and to our right, munching sugarless chocolate while his CD player blasted Mozart operas. He would take me to hear great pianists like Brendel, Lupu, and Argerich. I relished sharing the velvety box seat with him and arguing about what I heard.

Max proposed to me one night after a deep-dish pizza dinner at Gino's East, downtown. We were eighteen and had been together for two years. I said yes, and soon after, we got married in a little synagogue in Skokie. By then, I knew he had a habit of psychologically undermining me—a little bit at a time, at first. He was half-Jewish and would say things like "*Mein Kampf* is a great book," just to provoke me. "Kate Moss is exactly my type," he often said, knowing that I looked nothing like the waifish British model. Somewhere deep inside, I felt inadequate and a bit unattractive, just like I had when I first moved to this country.

Despite Max's mild anti-Semitism, I insisted that a rabbi marry us. My mom and dad were my witnesses. I wore a long skirt and a peasant shirt, and he showed up in a vintage, purple three-piece suit, a provocative costume just to bug me and my parents. Like them, I had married young—and, hopefully, was now taken care of for life! Mom had tears in her eyes, but I was more cynical. In the back of my mind, a little voice said, "How fun. You're getting married at eighteen. You can just get divorced if it doesn't work." I shushed the little voice, and we went to London for our honeymoon with the money I had won in a piano competition.

After I had left Chicago, I still came back to the Music Center during vacations and practiced in my mother's studio, next door to Mr. D's. He was always willing to hear me and give me a lesson. Sometimes, he would knock on the door and tell me, "Enough practice! Don't you want to go out for some ice cream?" I would try to protest but in the end always followed him to his Jaguar. He would have some new recording with him, which he popped into the player during the ten-minute drive— "Listen to this! Cecilia Bartoli's new recording! Absolutely fantastic!" Sometimes we would sit in the parking lot until the recording finished playing and then discuss it over sugar-free ice cream. Over the years, his posture grew more stooped, his eyesight weaker, his scales messier, but his Mozart remained pure and beautiful.

Interlude

CLARA WIECK-SCHUMANN, CONCERTO IN A MINOR AND SONATA IN G MINOR

"I once believed I had creative talent, but I have given up this idea; a woman must not wish to compose—there was never one able to do it. Am I intended to be the one?" asks Clara Schumann in her diary. Presumably, her husband, composer Robert Schumann, never answered her clearly. "It would be arrogant to believe that . . . May Robert always create, that must always make me happy."

An actress in a maroon dress intoned these excerpts from the diary dramatically, hair piled up in a cakelike arrangement of braids and buns in the style of the midnineteenth century. I also wore a maroon dress, of crushed velvet. Seated at the piano onstage at Orchestra Hall, I waited for her to finish reading. Guest conductor Keith Lockhart lifted his baton, and the Chicago Symphony launched into the impetuous A Minor Concerto, written by Clara when she was just sixteen.

I was also sixteen, and by then, I'd given up composing—not because I was a woman, but because it gradually took a back seat to piano playing. I didn't have thoughts like Clara; in fact, up to that point, I'd never recognized music and gender as belonging in the same sentence. But clearly, according to Clara and the producers of this concert, it was something to consider.

It was a great gig. I was asked to play a movement of the concerto with the Chicago Symphony and learned it in just a few weeks. But it seemed to be on the program only in order to show that women can write music, too—just like men! There was something precious and patronizing about the program that bothered me. Why did it have to say "women composers"? We don't say "men composers," do we? I had never even thought about this before. But it was true—all the music I had played until then, other than my own, was written by men.

Around that same time, Mr. D was practicing Robert Schumann's *Carnaval* at the Music Institute of Chicago. As he worked on it, I heard the piece's magical characters emerge from his studio, day after day. I became obsessed with the most unpredictable, whimsical, openhearted musical language I had ever encountered. I had to learn this piece! The obsession never left. Many of Robert Schumann's large-scale piano works would become staples of my core repertoire. But what about Clara?

* * *

In 2017, I am in the back of a large summer concert tent, in a long maxi dress that's not mine and Ugg clogs that are two sizes too big. This time, I get to play Clara's entire piano concerto. The work is very tricky—how did I manage to learn that first movement in two weeks as a teenager? The music is not the problem, though. I am on top of a mountain in Wintergreen, Virginia, but my suitcase is in the maw of the baggage claim in Reagan Airport. I have absolutely no plans to be there any time soon but am flying from Dulles Airport to Europe in just a few hours for three weeks of music festivals. That's the problem.

Erin Freeman conducts the festival orchestra. She is a bright, energetic conductor who happens to wear the same size as me. She usually performs in pantsuits, but she wore a paisley, summery dress for a performance of Mahler's Fourth Symphony the night before, and she has lent it to me for the concerto. (The odds of this lucky coincidence are small: Only 14 percent of conductors in this country are women.) After two days of performing the concerto, Erin stuffs me in a cab to Dulles, while her friend Philip, a Washington, DC, limo driver, manages to rescue my luggage from Reagan, armed with just a picture of my passport, and meets me at Dulles before my flight. He stands in front of the departure gate, and a rainbow unfolds above him. I make my flight, barely, and as I sink into my window seat, the breathless short slurs of the concerto's last movement replay on a loop in my head. I am going to miss Erin and Clara.

* * *

During the first months of the coronavirus pandemic, I assign Clara's complete piano works to my UCLA students, and they play them on Zoom in a marathon concert attended by people from all over the world. The checkered screen looks like a board game. All the little Zoom squares but Mindy's go dark, and a proud, joyful mazurka pours out of the speakers. This is the very piece Robert Schumann "borrowed" for his great *Davidsbundler-tanze*. He and Clara often shared ideas and inspiration—but he didn't credit her for this theme, in one of his greatest works. The mazurka is followed by Clara's dark and probing *Variations on a Theme by Robert Schumann*. My student Lukasz learned them quickly, and his passionate, lyrical playing is a good match for the piece, made all the more poignant by the fact that his internet connection is unstable. The small cracks and pauses in sound make us lean in and listen more intently.

My Clara Schumann journey continues after the marathon: I've received special permission to be on campus, in our recording studio, to record her G Minor Piano Sonata for a forthcoming CD. Never mind that I play in a mask and the recording engineer is also on Zoom one floor below me. I am making music again! Clara composed the sonata in 1841, at age twenty-two.

"I tried to compose something for Robert, and lo and behold, it worked! I was blissful at having really completed a first and a second sonata movement, which did not fail to produce an effect—namely, they took my dear husband quite by surprise," she wrote. The work was not taken seriously again until 1991, when it was finally published. The main theme is at once lyrical, pained, and elegant, eventually turning to giddy joy. The piece propels forward with passionate momentum that is hard to capture in a recording studio, without the natural adrenaline that comes with live concert performance. In contrast, the adagio second movement contains some of the most profound writing in the sonata, full of assured wisdom, extremely specific directions in the score, and concise eloquence. I play it again and again, laying down endless takes to choose from—faster, slower, with varied voicings, a deeper legato, more transparent textures, almost completely straightforward and then filled to the brim with operatic rubato. Picking a version will take many hours, but that's the all-consuming nature of a recording.

* * *

Clara stopped writing music completely when she was thirty-six years old. Her compositional voice, while perhaps not developed to its full extent, speaks with individuality and brilliance. She composed sixty-six pieces—and there is no telling how far she would have gone had she been active today.

In more than one way, though, Clara was a product of her time. "I found myself among a lot of Jews, which makes me really uncomfortable, though one hardly notices the Meyers' Jewishness," she wrote to Robert. How incredibly sad it is that someone as gifted as her still failed to rise above the prejudices of her era. Likewise, her sentiments about the weakness of female composers are refuted by her own works. Playing and recording Clara's achingly beautiful, bold, original music fills me with sadness. Not all great artists have the opportunity, the capability, the historical circumstances to see past the assumptions of their time, as much as we'd like to view them as perfect heroes.

But while Clara's words may have fallen short, she needn't have worried. Her music speaks for her, cutting through the centuries as only a true composer's musical voice is able to do.

5

PINK FLAMINGOES

"Ms. Schein, look at the new edition of the Chopin ballades I just bought! It makes all the difference! Oh my gosh, and the fingerings!"

"Ms. Schein, I listened to your teacher Artur Rubinstein. Wow. Nobody is better at Chopin—I mean, besides you!"

"I started Ravel's *Sonatine* after I heard you play it. I am, like, so excited."

I had just finished playing at my very first class in the piano studio of Ann Schein, the great pianist and my new teacher at the Peabody Conservatory. I had moved to Baltimore with Max, who was starting his undergraduate degree at Johns Hopkins. With our parents' help, we splurged on a rental in the Charles Towers downtown—$450 a month!—and embarked on a cohabitation with absolutely no idea about what being in an adult relationship, let alone a marriage, might entail. What had begun as an impetuous love story would quickly turn into a disaster. In a way, I had wanted this love story to feed my artistic impulses, its drama to translate into my interpretations of Brahms, Chopin, Corigliano, Beethoven, and Rachmaninoff.

The conservatory studio class was similar to the Music Center workshops—except that I was new, and nobody here cared at all that I had been considered a wunderkind, the pride of Chicago, and the apple of Mr. D's eye. I wanted to make my mark, so I banged out a caffeinated performance of *Scarbo*, Ravel's diabolical knuckle buster, galumphing through the repeated notes and almost falling off the bench at the fleeting ending. Whatever impression my performance made seemed short-lived; my fellow students were a lot more eager to flutter around our teacher than talk to the new girl. Ann Schein sat in the middle of the room in an old armchair, simply dressed in a navy blue cardigan and slacks but regal, her small, finely sculpted features birdlike and a little reminiscent of Babushka. She had dark, calm eyes that radiated a luminous energy.

"Ms. Schein, look what I got." I lifted up my tight T-shirt, almost up to my bra, to reveal a puffy, red, infected belly button. It was newly pierced with a beaded hoop—courtesy of Max, a gift for my birthday. (I hadn't wanted a piercing, but he wanted me to get one, and so I agreed to do it in a smoky Fells Point joint, the second day after we moved to Baltimore.) I couldn't decide if I wanted my image to be the hot-shot badass pianist with a belly button ring who is married or to leave the married part out of it, and in the end, I didn't mention it. Her dark eyebrows shot up, and she guffawed, "Oh my goodness!" She seemed to enjoy this display, perhaps more than my *Scarbo*. Her florid handwriting in my beat-up old score of the piece still cautions me to this day: "Pedal—Off! C-sharp is important here! Too much pedal! Clarity of rhythm and pulse needed here!"

I came specifically to Peabody to study with Ann Schein. Her playing, always noble, with a clear sound that cut straight to the heart, and her posture at the piano—proud, as if atop a horse, looking far ahead—reminded me of her teacher Artur Rubinstein and also of Napoleon a little bit. Behind her sweet, ladylike demeanor was enormous physical and emotional strength. She could see straight through the egocentric façade, the "I am hot shit" attitude that I had when I arrived at the conservatory fresh from Mr. D's studio, ready to take over the music world. In fact, it was Mr. D who had called her from the hallway pay phone in the Music Center. He knew her from their childhood studies at Peabody, and he felt our personalities would be a great match. She had been a fiery performer from an early age, and as a mentor, she had the generosity to care, the wisdom to develop one's individuality, and the grace to forgive. That grace would be tested again and again.

The faded beauty of the city's Mount Vernon neighborhood was only a few blocks away. I quickly settled into a routine—running to Peabody as early as possible, securing a practice room, getting in two hours of scales, sight-reading new works, etudes, then on to classes, then back to the practice room until the day was done. The pianos at Peabody had seen better days but they did the job. (When I'm on the road and need a piano to practice, I am usually satisfied with any PSO—a piano-shaped object. After all, it's just the medium.)

One day I was waiting outside to get into a larger classroom that had a less beat-up Steinway than the other practice rooms. Next to me sat a curly-haired guy with glasses and a Henle score of a Brahms piece. Henle editions were and are nearly unaffordable for students; only those who were interested in seeing an unspoiled, original score would prioritize and spend hard-earned dollars on it. This kid was clearly an intellectual.

"Who do you study with?" he asked.

"Ann Schein."

"Me too. What are you working on?"

"Paganini-Brahms *Variations* and Bach's *Chromatic Fantasy and Fugue*. By the way, your Ravel was amazing the other day." He said this almost without any expression, but his eyes twinkled, and he reddened in the face. I'd just met Daniel Schlosberg, born one week before me and destined to be the dude of honor at my "real" second wedding years later. He was both reserved and generous, clearly an old soul. "Hey, Fleisher is doing one of his master classes tonight. Did Ms. Schein put you in? You should play."

The only way to impress anyone at Peabody was to tell them you studied with Leon Fleisher. That automatically meant you'd gotten into the world's most exclusive piano studio. Did it actually mean you were better? Not necessarily. It was just the Fleisher mystique working its magic. Mr. D had studied with Fleisher at Peabody as one of his very first students. I couldn't wait to meet this man.

Meanwhile, my lessons with Ann Schein progressed on another level from any lessons I'd been used to. While they could frequently be hands-on—including dissections of the score and the composer's intentions, with particular focus on harmonic structure, fingerings, and phrasing—they also were conversations about my history with Mr. D, books I loved to read, my life with Max, and my knowledge of music and art in general. Each lesson would be drastically different from the next—as vitally alive and unpredictable as a musical performance. When I brought her Chopin mazurkas, we spent the lesson studying the polyphonic web of voices in op. 59, no. 3, the F-sharp minor. I'd already captured its tempestuous character but wasn't voicing chords or hearing individual lines as well as I could have been. The noble mazurka rhythm didn't quite dance, as I bent it forward and back with overly free rubato. But she loved my sound and got me to play with greater rhythmic simplicity and bring more harmonic awareness to my phrasing. Her notes in scores were famous among her students—big, cursive letters across the bars, with chunks of ideas and incomplete sentences, as if, in writing one thought, she was already on the next. "G-sharp here most crucial!" "What about the pedal?" "More ping!" "Needs to be beguiling." "Bell-like?" And, most cryptically, "Pas de tout, said Marguerite Long," in my score of Gaspard de la Nuit.

One evening, she played Schumann's mysterious *Humoresque* in a faculty recital, and I cried the entire time. There was something in her sound—it was her voice, heroic, tender, heartfelt, speaking to us on her and Schumann's own terms. I knew that this great artist was the right teacher for me. I also had a voice, and I wanted to wield it wisely and hoped that she would point the way.

When I first entered her studio, I was obsessed with submitting as many applications as possible. As a student of Mr. D, I'd become used to being invited to play concerts, thanks to his interloping managerial skills. Everyone knew Mr. D, and everyone loved a prodigy (and I fit that definition quite neatly, ever since I first started performing and wrote my opera). Now, I knew I had to try to advance on my own somehow. I vowed that each day I would fill out an application for a competition or audition or make an uncomfortable phone call to somebody running a concert series, an orchestra, or a festival and ask them to invite me to play. Doing so was embarrassing, but I thought it was necessary. I kept at it for at least my first two years at Peabody. I once called Hilda Goodwin; she ran the Baltimore Hebrew Congregation Series, which had recently featured the violinist Hilary Hahn. When I suggested that I'd like to play a Chopin program for her the following season, she shrieked, "What chutzpah!" But after listening to my tape, she invited me to play the recital and became a long-time supporter, referring to me subsequently as "Ms. Chutzpah."

At Peabody, the pianists were required to take chorus with the choir director, Ed Polochick, who also conducted the Concert Artists of Baltimore, a stellar local orchestra. Chorus usually ends up being the large-ensemble class required for piano majors because they cannot join an orchestra like the string and wind majors. At my first chorus rehearsal, I told Ed that I had to practice piano more than most people (ha!) and that I'd like to be excused from choir practice. He just laughed. Ed was one of Peabody's most beloved teachers and imparted lessons I'd never forget. Projection was a big one. Ann Schein talked a lot about projecting a "stage whisper" in a big hall with a piano that "speaks" and "sings." Ed talked instead about projecting consonants. In Schubert's Mass in G Major, he instructed us to sing "Claudi-Hah" instead of "Gloria," which the audience would hear as correct. I found this to be pure magic and tell this story when my own students try to get out of choir in the same way I had.

Ed was a great conductor and a friend of Ann Schein's. In my third year at Peabody, he invited me to perform Concerto in G Minor by Camille Saint-Saëns with the Concert Artists of Baltimore. A week before this concert, Ann Schein gave me a stately blue gown that she used to wear for concerto performances in her twenties. We went to the seamstress together and had it altered. I still wear it—most recently for a performance of Chopin's First Piano Concerto—with a yellow belt and necklace in support of Ukraine during its war with Russia.

Ms. Schein tried to tell me that competitions had nothing to do with artistry or the reality of the music world. Out with me and my mom for chocolate mousse cake and tea, she told us,

"Competitions are tunnel vision, but I see Inna's life in music as broad, far reaching. Competitions are limiting and don't reflect reality. They're great for focus, but she already has focus." My mom and I had been so used to me practicing to prepare for contests that we couldn't see the truth behind what she was saying. How else could one make way in the music world? I hadn't realized yet that a musician's path was long, and competitions were but one short-lived chapter in a career. Under Ann Schein's guidance, my confidence grew, and my playing became more mature, clear-headed, rhythmically and musically cohesive. I entered two big competitions my first year and won them both—the Hilton Head International and National Federation of Music Clubs.

For the Federation competition, held in St. Louis, my friend and fellow pianist Michael Sheppard and I both ended up in the finals. I played Rachmaninoff's *Rhapsody on a Theme of Paganini*, and he, Beethoven's *Emperor Concerto*. Michael was an uncanny talent who could read anything, from a Bruckner symphonic score to an insanely difficult transcription of a Chopin etude by Leopold Godowsky. He had rehearsed the Rachmaninoff, with me accompanying him on a second piano. At the competition, I realized that the accompanist provided for me was not comfortable with their part, and for the finals, I asked Michael to play with me instead. Despite being in competition with me, he agreed. When I won, I thanked him profusely, but at the time, I didn't truly realize what a rare, selfless thing he had done for me—and how few people, in our small music world, would have done what he did.

The Federation sent me on interesting tours, including a trip through Arkansas, where I played six recitals in seven days across the state. Some were cities with big universities, libraries, restaurants, and museums, whereas others were villages where road signs were handwritten and misspelled. At the end of the tour, I would be presented with a framed certificate, confirming that I was an official "Arkansas Traveler."

On tour, a book is your main companion. I was reading the autobiography of Salvador Dali. I was so engrossed that I found myself thinking socially awkward, Daliesque thoughts and considered actually voicing them out loud to people: "Excuse me, sir? Can you please take the potatoes off my plate? I can only eat things that are green and round in shape. I am here to play a concert, and this would really help." With my Dali book under my arm, I finished my lunch and strolled around a bust of Bill Clinton in the middle of a roundabout in Little Rock, losing track of time. My recital started any moment, and there was no time to warm up and inspect the piano. The program started with Ravel's *Ondine*, a piece whose seductive aura relies on careful pedal work, but as my foot reached underneath the piano, it found emptiness. I would have to play the recital "dry": The piano had no pedals.

The next day, I played at Ouachita Baptist University in Arkadelphia, Arkansas and got my reward for putting up with the pedal-less instrument on the previous day. Everything just flowed—like oil, Mozart liked to say—and I thought I'd never have to practice again. This was the first instrument that the Italian manufacturer Paolo Fazioli had sold in the United States. Little did I know that years later, I would have a thirty-year-old Fazioli piano in my studio at UCLA and that Paolo himself would stop in to look after it.

On a different night at a Baptist church elsewhere in the state, I was preparing to play Beethoven's last Sonata in C Minor. I was breathing deeply and slowly in the corner of my dressing room, searching for the physical and mental centeredness necessary for the performance of the piece. Much has been written about this sonata, from Thomas Mann's *Doctor Faustus* to my colleague Bill Kinderman's books on Beethoven to Jeremy Denk's memoir *Every Good Boy Does Fine*. I had loved the piece since my teenage years and had brought it to Ann Schein a few months before the tour; after I finished the "Arietta" movement, I saw she had tears in her eyes. There is a certain stigma attached to playing the sonata before the age of seventy. I find this to be ridiculous. The earlier somebody learns a work like this, the longer it lives inside them, changing and accumulating layers of experience. It's one of those "lifetime" pieces, as Ann Schein would say. We carry it with us not only for the public and for performances but also for ourselves, for our own growth and love of music.

When I was first learning the second movement—the "Arietta," which features luminous, curlicue triplets at the top of the register that should sound like starlight, or an alternate soundtrack to *2001: A Space Odyssey*—Daniel waltzed into my room in an impromptu interpretive dance. He slowly pirouetted while holding a fork reverently, as though it was the baby Jesus, turning it in his hands above his head, his eyes fixed on it in exalted ecstasy. I lost concentration and cracked up. He always took the sacred and untouchable and made it funny. Now, whenever I get to this part while practicing, I cannot help but recall the image.

The knock on my door came about five minutes earlier than I had anticipated. "We are almost ready for you." Before a performance, the "almost ready" and the "ready" are worlds apart. One needs those extra five minutes to go to the bathroom, eat a banana, maybe do a few stretches—but definitely not have a religious conversation like the one I was about to be dragged into. The concert organizer who was going to introduce me went on: "You are one of the first chosen people I've ever met. I am just curious—have you found time on your travels to let Jesus into your life?" At that moment I was no longer thinking of the grave opening of the Beethoven, but I *was* suddenly aware that I was wearing the blue, sleeveless dress that Ann Schein had given me, and I had forgotten to shave my armpits. "I don't speak English so well. I am sorry!" I walked out to the stage, trying not to swing my arms too wide.

* * *

It was hard to be married and have a social life at Peabody. My gang was a tight one—Michael, Daniel, and other musicians who had come from all over the United States, as well as China, France, Russia, Spain, and the United Kingdom. I'd have them over at the apartment on Charles Street, cooking a barrel of pasta, into which I would put a brick of cream cheese and a pound of tomatoes from the farmers market. Or we would stay up late at Michael's, watching movies and listening to new recordings.

With Daniel Schlosberg, at one of our many dinners during the Peabody days.

"Oh my god, have you heard of this dude Marc Andre Hamelin? Godowsky transcriptions? That piece based on the Nokia ringtone? That guy has three hands."

"Who cares about that stuff? Have you heard the new Brendel recording?"

"Who gives a shit? That's so boring. I got this amazing Furtwangler recording of the *Ring* cycle. Want to hear it?"

I would go dancing with my fellow pianists Christie Julien and Jill Lawson; Christie was the life of the party, with outrageous outfits, huge green eyes, and an irresistible French accent. Daniel and I were inseparable. Together, we became obsessed with Wayne Conor, the great tenor who taught a class on Wagner's *Ring* cycle at Peabody. Wagner geeks, we listened to and compared recordings of the epic operas. We'd hang out at a nearby record shop, wired on coffee from Donna's, everyone's go-to café, and splurge on recordings of it.

I was so busy that I almost forgot I had a husband. Max always hung out late with a few drinking buddies, but as I had my own friends, I was fine with it. On Valentine's Day, I made tuna melts and lit candles and asked Max to bring home a romantic comedy from the neighborhood video store. Max showed up two hours late with *Pink Flamingoes*. We always rented experimental art films—it was through Max that I became familiar with Greenaway, Jarmusch, Jarman, and Godard. But that night I'd hoped we could watch something cozy and nice. He clearly rented John Waters's raunchy film to provoke and offend; doing so in a subtle, calculated manner was a favorite pastime of his. This was quite unsubtle, though, even for him—he knew that I just wanted to relax and didn't want to see anything gross or kinky. We had an epic screaming match; I threatened to leave but then calmed down. The next morning, I had a rehearsal of Shostakovich's Second Piano Trio and could just focus the wrath inside me toward the shattering climax of the trio's last movement, the "Dance of Death." I made Max sleep on the couch.

When not fighting, Max and I explored the cobblestone streets of Baltimore, took the Chinatown bus to New York for day trips, went to classical recitals and to heavy-metal rock shows with bands I tried to but couldn't love. We shared moments of discovery and excitement that made us co-conspirators in a bohemian-tinted world only we were privy to, so the dark moments didn't bother me at first; I knew that instances of whimsical intimacy would follow. Returning home after classes and practicing, I would routinely find him passed out with an empty bottle of hard liquor. I was a young musician, and the drama felt like part of the ritual of becoming a true artist, but addiction was an unfamiliar, menacing monster. This wasn't regular college drinking but something else, an unstoppable pull, an illness I didn't know how to manage. I could not live with the idea that stupefying and mind-numbing drinking could be more interesting than our little life together, than my music, than his classes. Perhaps I had closed my eyes to the fact that he had a real problem. Had I really known how to love and support him, I would have taken him to get the help he so badly needed months before. But I was twenty years old, a self-centered star of the Peabody piano world. I put every ounce of my energy into music, and when drama arose, I internalized it and used it for my playing. I didn't want to or know how to deal with substance abuse. I wanted somebody to look up to, somebody to be inspired by, to learn from—not somebody to mother. We didn't see each other very much during the day, but we fought at night, more and more frequently, and I would lose sleep regularly.

My nerves on edge, I couldn't understand why Scriabin's Fifth Sonata wasn't coming to me as easily as I thought it should. Its mad, impulsive opening and inebriated harmonies should have been easy for me, but I could not make sense of them—the architecture of the piece simply didn't hold when I would play it through. I had my junior recital coming up and managed to have a fight with Ann Schein. While working with me on the Scriabin during one lesson, she suggested a fingering that I told her didn't work: "But this is physically impossible! Have you played this piece?"

The pencil flew out of her hand—whether voluntarily or not, I will never know. Quietly and calmly she said, "Do you want a lesson?"

I didn't. The following week, I didn't come in, as though it was her fault that I was an obnoxious brat. I stayed at home and repeatedly listened to Richter's live recording from 1958 in Sofia, Bulgaria. How did he do it? How did he make this maddening piece so coherent, so logically flawless?

The following week, I played Scriabin for her again. Seemingly hurt, she asked whether I had been working on it with someone else. I was baffled. I hadn't realized how my behavior had affected her: She, too, was vulnerable, deeply sensitive. "I just listened to Richter. I have not played it for anyone," I told her. The Scriabin worked now, and somehow, we made peace. Thank you, Ms. Schein, for not throwing me out of the studio. I would have thrown me out. I hadn't told you then that my relationship had turned abusive. I hadn't known it myself. Max's psychological games made me doubt everything, from my attractiveness to my sanity. If I refused drugs or alcohol, then I was boring. If I ate a bagel, then I was fat. If I wore no heels, then people could see my crooked legs. If I expected him to meet me where and when he promised, then I was needy. If I didn't want to sleep with him, then I was cold. If I didn't want to play sexual games, then I was frigid. If I preferred Daniel's company to Max's friends, then I was nerdy. There was just one thing that I didn't question or doubt yet—my talent. He had no power over it.

Of course, nobody at school was surprised when Max and I got divorced at twenty, with as much drama and noise and tawdriness as expected. Max never showed up on time anywhere, and if he promised to meet me, then I could bet that he probably would not be there. Walking alone in Baltimore didn't always feel safe in 1999. Halfway between school and our apartment, I discovered, a flasher had chosen a hiding spot between the art deco palaces and dilapidated town houses. The first time I came across him, he took his pants off in broad daylight, and I shrieked and ran all the way home. I called the police, who chuckled and told me that during the day, I should be okay. The second time, I walked by quickly. The time after that, I just smiled and kept walking at the same pace.

One night, however, I stayed at Peabody until past 2:00 in the morning, making a tape for the National Chopin Competition. Max had said he would wait for me by the entrance, but of course, he wasn't there. I sprinted home past the flasher, who, as always, waited in his spot. This time, he decided to follow me. I heard his heavy breathing and ran faster, leaving the Xeroxed Chopin score splayed in a puddle behind me. I reached for the key card to my building. Of course, the doorman was asleep, and nobody was around. I ran to the elevator without looking back. I might have lost the flasher blocks behind me, but I was too nervous to turn and see.

Walking into my apartment, I expected—actually, really wanted—to find Max with a girl. That would be soapy and dramatic; I could throw his clothes out the window or something. But instead, I found him in the bathtub, passed out amid vomit and empty bottles. A guy named Ed was hanging out in the living room, drinking vodka from the bottle and banging on my baby grand piano, which had more booze on top of it. I turned around and went to sleep at the home of my friend Xenia, a guitarist, a few blocks away. She was on break from her violinist boyfriend, Sasha, and I was sure she'd be okay with it.

The next morning, Max showed up at Xenia's and demonstratively returned to me his apartment keys and wedding ring. He said he was already with somebody else—she was thirty-three to my twenty, and she had dated Ray Liotta—so I could do whatever I wanted. We were officially done. Later that night, I saw him as I was leaving Peabody. He was walking into the foyer of a tony apartment building, his arm around a tall blonde. The Corvette was parked outside the building.

So what he had told me was true. He really was sleeping this older woman. I hadn't believed it that morning. Well, clearly Ray Liotta's ex-girlfriend was much more interesting than me. I later learned from our common Chicago friends that she supplied him with cocaine, which I had always adamantly refused. When had this started? Who knew? I had been too busy practicing to notice.

After they entered the building, I keyed his beloved Corvette with a confident, expansive arm gesture, just like the one I had used moments earlier, practicing the last glissando in Ravel's *Ondine*.

A few days later, I found a gun he'd hidden in my underwear drawer. He had bought it with the money I won in the National Federation of Music Clubs piano competition. Clearly, I needed to check my bank account every once in a while! The gun appeared to be loaded—an unlikely reward for my performance of *Rhapsody on the Theme of Paganini*. I brought it down to the apartment building lobby in a lunch bag, gingerly holding it with two fingers, when he came by for his remaining stuff.

Max and his Corvette eventually found their way to New York City. That was when I realized just how attached to him I had been. I had trouble separating my tastes and thoughts from his. For a while, I would not wear short dresses because he had told me too many times that my legs were crooked. Inwardly, I asked him what to read, watch, and eat. It took a few years to forget the pain of this teenage marriage. I could have considered therapy, but instead, I had my piano.

I was only beginning to realize that the piano could be approached in other ways than those Mr. D had taught me.

How the arm was used, the body was centered, the shoulders lined up—all changed the sound and the expressive intent. In a performance, musical simplicity and directness were more moving than fanciful, histrionic pyrotechnics, giving sense of continuity and inevitability. I had been trained as a virtuoso—and Ann Schein was helping me use this technical confidence to channel the elegance and depth of the music. She was showing me that the sound I could coax from the piano was specifically mine—like my own voice. The voice had to speak honestly, naturally. It also needed to be nurtured with confidence and care. That was her gift: to make a young pianist understand and value their own musical individuality. I'd lost Max, but my sense of self, expressed through my playing, remained strong and articulate.

Interlude

MAURICE RAVEL, *SCARBO*; BILLY CHILDS, *PURSUIT*

I place the microphone a few feet from my piano and launch into *Pursuit*, Billy Childs's new piece. He is on Zoom, eyes on the score and fingers drumming out rhythms. "Inna, second line, second bar. You are missing some notes."

"Are you kidding me, Billy? That part's impossible! You've got to rewrite it!"

"That's weird. I sort of played it slowly and thought it worked."

Billy has written *Pursuit* for me as a response to Ravel's *Scarbo*, creating a sort of metasymmetry, as Ravel's was itself in response to a poem by Aloyisius Bertrand, bringing to life Bertrand's description of an eerie, nightmarish imp. It's the third piece in his triptych *Gaspard de la Nuit* and, by some accounts, one of the hardest pieces for the piano.

I first met Billy when he played at the Blue Whale Jazz Club in LA, and we bonded over our love of poetry and Ravel. Over a bottle of chardonnay, we came up with the idea that Billy would write a piece for me that responds to Ravel, creating a bridge between then and now. This wasn't intended to be a remake of a classic but rather taking a compositional idea, a cell, an image, and responding to it in a personal way. I hadn't known then just how poignant the timing of this new piece would be.

I first encountered *Scarbo* much earlier, when Mr. D assigned it to me. Mom seemed terrified: "Should Inna really play this? It's the hardest thing written for the piano!" I looked at the shiny, new Dover edition of the score. Lots of busy pedal markings and repeated notes, a gazillion sharps and flats, and wild dynamics, from whole pages of *ppp* (pianississimo: really, really soft) to *fff* (fortississimo: really, really loud). Some pages looked like black-and-white abstract paintings because of the sheer volume of notes. It would take forever to learn, but I loved a challenge. "She can do it," Mr. D said. "Let me just write in some fingerings." Mr. D's fingerings could solve many a technical conundrum. This is the piece that I performed at all my conservatory auditions and the first piece Ann Schein heard me play.

Scarbo, along with *Ondine* and *Le Gibet,* is one-third of Ravel's 1908 triptych *Gaspard de la Nuit*—one of the great impressionist masterpieces of music and one of the most notoriously unplayable piano suites ever written. Each of the three pieces depicts a nightmarish, ghoulish character. Scarbo is an imp who hides under your bed; frightens you at night; and, like a candle, is extinguished before morning. The piece opens with an ominous repeated note, played very quickly. Some pianists choose to play it with one finger—I change between thumb and second finger, alternating at breakneck speed, like a trill on one note. The effect is an eerie, otherworldly vibrato. The piece can be played like the insane bravura storm that it is, but I think it's crucial to think of Scarbo as an actual character, with thoughts and feelings. Who is he? Is he evil? Is he lonely? Is he, perhaps, sad?

Scarbo's motif is one of the saddest melodies Ravel wrote. Paying attention to this might reveal that Scarbo is despised, misunderstood, and lonely. Approaching the work with sympathy for him makes for a very different performance than just playing the notes cleanly and quickly, with wrath and virtuosity. The momentum of the piece, with its jazzy harmonies, macabre dances, and Spanish rhythmic underpinnings (Ravel was part Basque), culminates in two massive climaxes, gigantic chords crashing and obliterating all that came before. From the echoing remains of these chords, the repeated note quivers begin again, until it is snuffed out.

COVID-19 had already begun to swallow the world whole when the brutal murder of George Floyd in Minneapolis sent shock waves through the nation. In the meantime, my mom had suffered a massive stroke, though we didn't yet know about the brain cancer that caused it, which was missed by the pathologist. It felt as though life hung on a precipice, and much new music was created in the key of pain.

Pursuit imagines a Black man running from the police. Like *Scarbo*, it begins with a nerve-racking repeating figure and frantic passagework up and down the piano, before transforming into a melody of such raw pain and pathos that I can barely contain my own emotions. Billy, perhaps unknowingly (he is at once sharply direct and very humble), has created one of the most swooningly beautiful, tragic tunes possible. It might echo Ravel in its harmonies, but it's entirely Billy's language.

"Inna, see, you play this really romantically. Your sound is voluptuous. And you kind of pedal it. It's flowing, but I just want it to be straight, like 'duh-duh-duh bah, bah-duh TA DUM.' That's the Herbie Hancock quote, you know?" (Herbie teaches in my department, though we've never met.)

"I know, Billy. It's so hard for me not to play this like Ravel or Scriabin."

I need to restrain my impulses to shape, to bend time and lyrically taper the ends of phrases here, despite the fact that the harmonic rhythm begs me to do it. But if this last year has taught me anything, it's how to restrain an inner scream and soldier on. So I need to rein in my emotions and play it straight.

Maybe by the premiere, I'll get it.

6

THE INEVITABILITY
OF LEON

In the 1970s, Leon Fleisher was christened Obi-Wan Kenobi by a gang of devoted Peabody piano students. If the actual Obi-Wan had been played by the smoldering Sean Connery instead of Alec Guinness, then this would have made even more sense. Mr. Fleisher reminded me of the minotaurs from Picasso's drawings. One of his most prominent features were his expressive nostrils. They were rhombic, pitch-black, and totally three-dimensional; they moved elastically when we played. His nose was always saddled by black, square glasses. When Fleisher spoke, he would close his eyes, push up the glasses to his forehead, and hold the bridge of his nose between his thumb and index finger.

The thing about him was his magnetism. The man could read a phone book, and you would listen, enraptured. Studying with somebody like this is not only difficult, but it also can be dangerous. At twenty, I had no idea, and the exclusive world of his studio had an intense pull. He taught at Peabody and the Curtis Institute of Music in Philadelphia, and getting into his studio was next to impossible.

I loved Ann Schein, but she was going on sabbatical, during which she had arranged for me to be the only student to come to her house on a weekly basis. It was my last year of undergraduate studies, and I was getting ready for my master's auditions. I was practicing the Liszt sonata, getting it ready for her, when

Daniel called me one day: "A little birdie told me that Fleisher has an opening in his studio."

I threw the phone down; called Fleisher's secretary, Kitty Allen; and demanded an audition.

* * *

I should say here that to ask for an audition from Fleisher was ridiculous. He had already heard me play many times. I had, for three years, been one of a group of the school's top pianists who were not in his studio but who were given the chance to play for him in a series of evening master classes. These master classes were bewitching. A group of fourteen or so would gather in his large studio at the end of the hallway on the fourth floor, right next to Ann Schein's studio. The two pianists chosen to play that evening sat on the edges of their chairs, pale, biting the skin off their fingers. The door would creak. The master would come in, usually wearing a cerulean shirt with a gold pen in the pocket, dapper and bearlike at once. We were ready to hang onto every word.

And words, there were many. Poetic, revelatory in their truth about the art, about the physics of music. Fleisher described the way a phrase had to fall if it had risen—"like the Otis elevator!" The inevitability of timing and rhythm, like blood pumping from the heart. The way playing Schubert was like joining a river that always flowed. The way the late music of Beethoven seemed to rotate through space, full of mystical light; images from the Hubble telescope surrounded us. We were drunk on Fleisher, hooked on him and the music he illuminated for us.

And then he would demonstrate—his poor, crippled right hand tightly grasping a pencil and conducting, while his over-used left hand played, sculpting a phrase simply and inexorably, impossible to imitate without resorting to copying or mannerisms.

Yet imitate we did. That was the pitfall of studying with a force like Fleisher.

"There are three . . . kinds . . . of musics. There is French, sensuous. There is Russian, the big *I*—everybody, how deeply

I feel this! How I suffer! And then, then there is German. That music answers the bigger question. Why are we here? What does it all mean?"

This revealed a certain distaste for the music of Tchaikovsky, Shostakovich, even Rachmaninoff—despite Fleisher's brilliant recording of Rachmaninoff's *Rhapsody* made in his younger days. Many pianists born and trained in Eastern Europe who were accepted into the Fleisher studio had virtuosic technique and total technical freedom at the piano, but many met opposition from Fleisher to their musical and pianistic sensibility, which favored a rich, full sound and an indulgent approach to rhythmic timing. This was ironic, as Fleisher's own family had come from Odessa. Studying with Artur Schnabel had been revelatory for him at a young age. At a time when many highly regarded pianists would charm audiences with the force of their personalities, perhaps taking many liberties with the score, Schnabel taught the idea of "supporting the composer," analyzing the score judiciously, and putting rhythmic integrity first (even if his idea of rhythmic integrity could be viewed as highly subjective!). Schnabel was a direct link to Beethoven, as Schnabel's teacher Leschetizky had studied with Czerny, a student of Beethoven. Fleisher's students found themselves in a sort of rhythmic straitjacket that would permit no liberties for the sake of spontaneous emoting, sentimental mannerisms, basking in the beauty of sound or color—anything that could prevent the direction and flow of the music and possibly detract from the composer's intent. This could nonetheless be, in a sense, mind-blowingly liberating. Suddenly, timing was the most important thing in music, and the placement of a beat could start to feel like the life force itself, with the inevitability of a steady pulse. Of course, this idea could be taken too far and become an artificial parody of itself. Many students would imitate Fleisher's approach, only to suffocate in the stylistic limbo they found themselves in. For a while, I would be no exception.

* * *

Later that day, I received a phone call. Kitty Allen's alto boomed, "Inna? Mr. Fleisher has thought about it. He says yes."

I threw the phone down and screamed. I called Daniel first and then my family and some friends and some friends of friends. The one difficult call I had put off for a while was to Ann Schein. Mr. D was never too excited about me studying with Fleisher, despite the fact that he himself had been one of Fleisher's first students at Peabody. (They were approximately six years apart in age.) Mr. D knew that there needs to be a match between a student and teacher—and I refused to see it.

I didn't consider that, in taking this sudden turn, I would not only be opening myself up to years of artistic difficulty, questioning, uncertainty, and pain but also that I might hurt a mentor who, like any great teacher, gave a piece of her own heart in every lesson. At that moment, I took for granted my phone calls with Ann Schein, our coffee dates, the extra lessons above and beyond what was required of her, the blue dress. I had forgotten that I shared with her all the details of my divorce with Max, all my dating disasters, all my struggles and doubts. I hadn't just cast aside a teacher. I cast aside a friend who had treated me like her own child. I would never forget what Ann Schein had taught me, but as time went on, I came to believe that I had hurt her thoughtlessly. It didn't enter into my mind that, despite how I handled it, she might also have been pleased or proud to see a beloved student join Leon's exclusive studio next door. Such was her generosity of spirit, her collegiality and grace.

When I entered the Fleisher studio, I had recently won some competitions, had professional management, and was planning a number of concerts. It was Fleisher's philosophy that a student was to play a work for him only once, and for this reason, he expected his students—many of whom were, like me, in demand as performers—to drop their performance engagements. Bringing in new repertoire constantly meant that you had to be learning new works at an intense pace, not really internalizing and finishing repertoire and putting aside preparation for professional engagements. During the one time Fleisher heard a student play a given piece of music, he proceeded to teach the student everything he knew about it. He wasn't there to adapt to

The ever-gracious Ann Schein with me at my graduation from Peabody.

the student's interpretation, to try to understand their individual process and voice, but rather to present a clear-cut, objective picture of what the music needed to be. In my previous experiences, a teacher was always there to support the pianist as a new work changed and grew along with them. I had to get used to this new philosophy. His other rule was that everybody had to be present during each others' lessons. This made practicing impossible on some days. He insisted that one does not always need to practice, if one thinks and listens—the opposite of Mr. D, who didn't think I could practice less than six hours a day as a teenager, given the volume of repertoire and concerts I was working on. It would take me years to reconcile these points of view into a cohesive whole. (Ideally, though, one should think, listen, *and* practice.)

As a pianist, I always had a sound that could speak clearly, regardless of the acoustics, to the very back of the hall. It was a sound that felt three-dimensional when I was creating it, something I could sculpt spontaneously, deep in the keyboard bed. It made my fingers feel warm and connected, as though I was sinking them into warm earth or kneading yeasty, fragrant dough. It was the result of countless hours of practicing and listening from a very early age and also of my particular background, pianistic history, and imagination. In other words, the sound was the extension of me. It is something that can be more easily experienced in a live performance; with today's recording and production technology, any sound and reverberation can be manufactured and altered and played with. In the golden age of the piano, however, it could not be, so this type of very personal sound at the piano was much more common than it is today.

Nonetheless, Fleisher said, "Put your talent in the drawer. Focus on the composer's voice, not your own." Only later would I realize the importance of these words; I speak them to my own students sometimes. Fleisher wanted us to forgo our egos in expressing ourselves through the music. He wanted us to focus first on understanding the text precisely and deeply, respecting each detail a composer provided, and treating the score as the script with all the clues needed to interpret it. He was against sloppiness, bad taste, exaggerations, rhythmic distortion for the sake of emoting, and historically inaccurate interpretations. His musicianship, pure and patrician, was the stuff of legend.

However, his technical ideas—such as treating the fingers like spokes in a wheel and making a thrusting wrist motion for a louder, leaner sound—simply did not work for me, a pianist who connected to the instrument through relaxed, rounded, flexible wrists, a sense of the warm depth of the keyboard, a coaxing of sound through weight in the fingertips. His own tragic history (he lost the use of his right hand to focal dystonia, a neurological disorder, for almost the entire duration of his illustrious career) had forced him to find his own ways to make his muscles work at the piano. I believe that he honestly wished to prevent the same horrible ailment from happening to his students, but his methods created psychological roadblocks for me during that period. He might have been the perfect match for some. I would certainly learn a great deal from him, and I mentally make a hat tip to him almost daily, when I teach my own students at UCLA. However, during those few years, I felt like a centipede that thought so hard about which leg to move that she forgot how to walk.

On one of my trips back to Chicago, I played a recital of Liszt's massive B Minor Sonata at the Music Center of the North Shore. The strangest sensation was playing it note-perfect, with total control of its difficult architecture, but without the sense that I made a single sound. It was as if I had mouthed the words to a song without singing it out loud. Everyone congratulated me on how I had matured as a performer, but I wasn't convinced. My mind was working overtime, but my heart was unengaged and my confidence, therefore, was at an all-time low. Mr. D was in the audience and took me aside, patting my back comfortingly. "It takes time to understand Leon," he said. "You are just searching." Later, though, I overheard him speaking to one of his students at the reception: "What happened to our Inna?" It was both complicated and simple. I used to play from the heart; now, I was playing strictly from the head.

Only those who knew me really well could tell the difference. My sound was thin. I suddenly hated the playing of many pianists I used to love, finding their interpretations indulgent. I learned more quickly than ever—because I had to bring new works to class every week—but was stiffer, less excited to play. Something constantly felt unsaid in my performances. I had blown a few big auditions for major conductors, not because I didn't play solidly and well, but because I suddenly didn't know how to project that special something I'd always had. Sound no longer filled the hall naturally and effortlessly. It just sat there like stagnant water, ponderous and murky, without catching the reverberation of the strings. I again stopped sleeping well because my most natural form of expression felt stifled.

To compensate for my misery, I was partying with my Peabody friends harder than before. On weekends, we went salsa dancing until 4:00 in the morning. On weekdays, we took turns cooking pasta and watching movies until late, drinking wine and talking about music. But it wasn't the same as when Daniel had been at Peabody (he had gone on to study at Stony Brook by then), and the recordings we listened to didn't move me.

Live concerts didn't, either. One night, we took the train to Washington, DC, to hear Martha Argerich and Misha Maisky in a piano-cello program. I don't remember the recital, but I do remember missing the train back to Baltimore. None of us wanted to spend money on a night in a hotel. "Inna, weren't you dating somebody in DC?" somebody asked. I looked through my notebook. Indeed, there was a computer programmer I had gone out with in Chicago who had moved there. I'd forgotten all about him but now decided to call him. "Hi, Bill," I cooed sweetly. "It's been a while. Listen, I am stranded here for the night. Would you mind if I come over?" Bill did not mind, and then I said, "I may have a friend with me. A couple of friends." When the five of us showed up tipsy at his expensive minimalist condo, I asked him whether there was somewhere we could all go dancing. He ended up sharing a bed with two of my girlfriends—they were actually a couple and completely uninterested in him—while I and two other friends slept on the couch.

The next afternoon, I arrived at Fleisher's class, less than minty fresh. I had to play Schubert's *Wanderer Fantasie*—a stressful piece to play for Fleisher, knowing his fraught history with it. He had recorded it spectacularly in his youth, but he also told us that it was one of the pieces he had overpracticed relentlessly, right before focal dystonia set in. The piece has four movements connected by one theme. I got through the rambunctious first movement and the grief-filled masterpiece of the second without adventure. I had just begun the third, a buoyant scherzo, when he stopped me. "This needs to sound like a German milkmaid," he said. I tried again. "Hm, why are you such a good German milkmaid?" He looked coy. Was this a compliment on how quickly I could internalize a character, or was he having a bit of fun? Or both?

My discipline was slipping. I thought nothing of going one day, then two, then three without practicing very much. This may not seem like a lot, but for me, it was unheard of until that point. The Ukrainian-born pianist and teacher Heinrich Neuhaus once had said, "If you miss one day, you know it. Two days, your friends know it. Three days, your public knows it."

My concerts remained technically solid, and the public perhaps couldn't tell. I tried practicing in my head. Sometimes, it worked wonders: Things felt fresh after a few days away from the piano, and I was able to focus on each note and hear exactly how it would come out before it actually did, leading the parade of notes from within, by the workings of what Fleisher called the inner ear. But then, in a lesson, those notes would come out messier, without the trust and conviction I had attained in the practice room. And then I had to start the cycle all over with another piece.

Fleisher treated me ironically, with a deep detachment. For one lesson, I'd brought him Shostakovich's First Concerto, which I was preparing for a performance with an orchestra in Colorado. "Why do you bring me this garbage?" he asked. I was shocked. How could this great artist, this immense musical mind, a teacher who had influenced thousands, disdain music that meant so much to so many? In the same lesson, I needed a signature for my Artist Diploma audition, a tuition-free graduate performance program at Peabody. As my two-year master's degree was coming to an end, I wasn't sure what to do, so this felt like the natural next step. But he didn't want to recommend me for it because he probably felt a discomfort between him and me. "I don't think you should audition, even though you do play one hell of a 'Campanella.'"

That hurt. Didn't he see me as an artist? More than anything, I wanted to please him and show him that I could take the ideas that still seemed to me inevitable and beautiful and translate them into clear yet deeply felt music making.

I had been bringing back Beethoven's *Eroica Variations* into my fingers. I had first learned the piece at seventeen and hadn't played it in a few years. It would be one of the last pieces I brought to Fleisher, and an aha moment for both of us. After listening to Toscanini's recording of the *Eroica Symphony*, I felt that I was beginning to relate to Fleisher's ideas about rhythm. I had actually been listening to two recordings of the symphony over and over again: the one conducted by Furtwangler was expansive and breathy, and the one by Toscanini, rapier-sharp, fast, sleek. The idea of quick notes needing to be played more quickly, slightly exaggerating the phrase's shape, and of long notes held longer, with the rests becoming miniature worlds of silent anticipation—all these maxims of Fleisher's came to life under Toscanini's baton and made their way into my own work on the *Variations*. Consistently adding that tiny extra bit of time between long notes suddenly felt just right, as did moving the goofy sixteenths across bar lines, as though the measures weren't there to divide music into vertical, wooden building blocks. One of my favorite sayings by Fleisher has always been "Music should be printed on toilet paper. Then, it's just rolled out and goes on and on. No bar lines!" He inherited a magisterial, uncanny sense of timing in his playing from studying with Schnabel, and it was starting to make sense to me, if still more intellectually than organically.

If ideas like this are merely imitated, then they are bound to sound like caricatures, which is what happened to many of Fleisher's students. One might internalize them and adapt them to their own style, but this, of course, takes years. I wanted immediate results I could show him right away and gain his approval—but I didn't want to sound distorted, either. He would tell us to play the fast notes faster, hold the long notes longer, hear the silences, but if this was exaggerated ever so slightly, then the result was mannered.

Yes, we can sculpt rhythm precisely, conforming perfectly to the physics of sound and the forward momentum of the music, just like an actor might deliberately speed up certain lines and wait longer during the breaks between others—but why? Maybe thinking like a conductor instead of a pianist makes you feel the rhythmic inevitability of Mozart, Schubert, Beethoven—the very same inevitability that makes all music so irresistible?

When I brought the *Eroica Variations* to Fleisher, it was a 9:00 a.m. lesson, and the other students were late. It turned out to be one of only two lessons I would ever have just with him, one on one. I played, emphasizing the hilarity of the long notes in the opening, the lilt of the theme, and the increasingly mad rush of the variations. Halfway through, he stopped me and looked at me without saying anything for a few minutes. "Something changed," he said. "You sound different. It sounds really good."

I couldn't believe it. Then Fleisher's teaching assistant came into the studio, huffing and puffing. He had thought the lesson started at 10:00. "Enrico," Fleisher said, "listen to Inna. Inna, play that again!" But somehow, the second time, it was all wrong.

* * *

One night, at the end of my master's, the Russian poet Yevgeny Yevtushenko came to Baltimore for a performance of Shosta-kovich's Thirteenth Symphony, *Babi Yar*, with the Baltimore Symphony, directed by Yuri Temirkanov. Yevtushenko read his heroic, shattering poem of the same name about the murder of 33,000 Jews in 1941 near Kyiv. This was followed by an epic per-formance of the symphony, in which Shostakovich set the poem to music for an enormous chorus. How brave both the composer and poet had been; neither was Jewish but found the tragedy so devastating that they had to speak out through poetry and music, risking their livelihoods in the Soviet State. For the first time in months, words and music made me cry.

After the concert, I met Yevtushenko, who was drinking with some orchestra musicians in the Owl Bar, a local favorite that was a little classier than the rest of Baltimore's drinking establishments. Seated next to him at the bar, I told him how important his poem had been to me and how much I loved poetry. I showed him the little green notebook of my childhood poems that I had carried in my backpack during immigration. It was one of my most personal treasures. He lifted his pen with gusto, all set to autograph the first page, but first gave me a sug-gestive once-over with his eyes. At the last moment, I withdrew the book and left the bar.

I'd realized I could appreciate Yevtushenko from afar. "No more gurus for me," I thought. I needed to find my voice again, and it was time to leave both Fleisher and Baltimore.

My last lesson with Fleisher was on Beethoven's Fourth Concerto, one of his favorite pieces. He closed his eyes and played the opening—the boldest beginning of all concerti composed thus far. Breaking with tradition, the piano begins the piece, not the orchestra. A tender question in G major, answered—surprise!—in B major by the orchestra, beginning a celestial journey where groups of notes are rays of light. Afterward, I told him I had to leave the studio.

And soon, the sound I searched for began to come back anew.

7

RHAPSODY IN BLUE, RUSSIAN STYLE

Explaining to an average American where I come from is no easy task. The Soviet Union collapsed in 1991, two years after we left, so explaining to *myself* where I am from is not easy either. My first language is Russian. Despite thinking mostly in English, I can still speak, write, and read in Russian. Given this, people assume I am from Russia. Even Mr. D would say, in one of his many terrible puns, "Don't rush this etude, just because you are Russian." *Good Night Little Ones*, one of the few cartoon shows available to children in Soviet Ukraine and hosted by the disheveled bunny Stepasha and his partners, Philya the dog and Hrusha the pig, reached us from Moscow, the center of the universe we lived in—and, of course, it was in Russian. It had been the national language of the Soviet Union, and I've always been proud to speak the language of Pushkin.

And yet, my Odessa-tinged pronunciation—softer consonants, *ah*'s that sounded like *eh*'s, arched phrases that lilt upward in the back of the throat—is still a brew, with notes of Ukrainian and Yiddish. Russian in Moscow sounded different. It had harder consonants and extended vowels, as well as an ironic, somewhat imperious intonation. Muscovites spoke as if from a different planet. Their jokes were overstuffed with *mat*—cursing—but at least, in my experience as a ten-year-old, they were not that funny. After all, Odessa was the capital of humor.

Our main holiday was April Fool's Day, and our city's main festival was Humorina, the gathering of the finest comedians in the Soviet Union.

I was born in Ukraine, though. Unfortunately, I know less Ukrainian than the average tourist. Tasty aphorisms like "На городі бузина, а в Києві дядько" ("A huckleberry grows in the garden, but your uncle lives in Kyiv"—said when something is beside the point) circulated in our kitchen for as long as I can remember, irreverent, sharp, colorful turns of phrase that caused Mom to crack up with delight. Much of the Ukrainian my mom knew came from her grandmother Lyolya, a famous obstetrician in Kherson, as well as her generational friendship with our upstairs neighbors—Anastasia's mother and grandmother, who proudly spoke Ukrainian. Besides a few poems by Taras Shevchenko and a Soviet nationalist poem by Natalya Zabila (the Russian *zabila* in English means *I forgot*, an apt reference to the real estate most of this poetry used to occupy in my brain), all the poetry we memorized was in Russian.

I am also Jewish. In the Soviet Union, this was not a cultural and religious identification but a deeply undesirable ethnicity. So it turns out that I am geographically Ukrainian, culturally Russian, and ethnically Jewish. That's a mouthful, but more important than naming identity is feeling it, and my feelings seesawed. Sometimes, I felt close to people who shared a similar past to mine: Jewish immigrants from Ukraine and Russia. I was comfortable with those who spoke Russian. I envied those who spoke Hebrew and celebrated Jewish holidays. But most of all, I felt at home with those like me, who, regardless of where they came from, spoke the common language of music.

I had finished my studies at Peabody. Soon after, the conductor Jason Love invited me to be the soloist for a tour of Estonia and Russia with the Greater Baltimore Youth Orchestra, which was comprised of players aged sixteen to eighteen. At twenty-three, I would be the most experienced performer and traveler among them. I hadn't been back to Russia since the Tchaikovsky Competition. How would it feel to go there now? I had stupidly agreed to be the group's unofficial translator. (Translating for a sixty-piece children's orchestra and their parents? How hard could that be?) Yet I was secretly wondering if the Russian I knew would still work over there. So much had changed. Would it still feel like I was back in the Soviet Union?

A few sets of parents decided to join the tour, to their kids' wild disappointment. Having seen James Bond films and read John le Carré and other Cold War novelists, the parents were scared out of their wits. All they wanted was to get back alive. We had three concerts planned: Rakvere and Talinn in Estonia and St. Petersburg in Russia. I was to play *Rhapsody in Blue*, one of the most patriotic, hopeful, and joyfully American pieces and the same work that had gotten me kicked out of the Tchaikovsky Competition. I was about to play it in Paris of the North, the city of three names (St. Petersburg, Petrograd, Leningrad, and finally St. Petersburg again), which had been home to my idols Anna Akhmatova and Dmitri Shostakovich, the city of the Hermitage, and the site of my parents' honeymoon, among other things. We were coming during the summer of the city's three-hundredth anniversary, when nobody slept during White Nights, when the sun was out until almost midnight.

Boarding the Aeroflot plane to Moscow, I glanced about, looking for Uncle Misha, the drunk in the back of the airplane. Aeroflot service had not changed much in ten years. My water was still tepid, and the flight attendant, her hair in a tight, blond bun, disdainfully slammed it on my fold-out table. While watching a surreal film about Peter the Great starring the Russian Bob Dylan, Vladimir Visotsky, I fell into a sleepy trance, dreaming of tall ships, the burnished ice of the River Neva, and a sardonic music score by Alfred Schnittke.

* * *

Three days later, I sat in a large Jacuzzi wearing a bathing suit two sizes too big, shot glass in hand. Raul Soot, an Estonian jazz saxophonist, poured me some more vodka. Two of his friends had already polished off a bottle and were whipping one another with birch branches, something one does when going to a sauna. The water was scalding, the vodka cold. I wondered how *Rhapsody in Blue* would go the next morning.

Earlier that day, I had been practicing in a dark church on Talinn's main square, the Raekola Plats. The city was a Disney-like fantasy, all pink and violet and yellow, with gingerbread houses and steeples, cozy cafés, winding streets and cobblestones. My wrists prickled from the heavy action of the Estonia brand grand piano, a beautiful instrument that's hard to find in the States. I had planned to get to the suburban hotel where we were all staying; study the score; and, in commemoration of my Italian immigration days, practice a bit more on a tabletop.

"*Privet*, Inna!" A skinny guy with a buzz cut waved at me from a nearby café table. Raul was a rising-star jazz artist who went to Peabody. We had recently spent a whole day together, hanging out in the Baltimore harbor, drinking beer, and commiserating over failed love affairs—mine with a poet, his with a cellist. I knew he was Estonian, but I'd forgotten to tell him about the upcoming trip. And now, here he was, in the square, basking in the sun. It was summer solstice—the longest summer evening, celebrated by partying in the street and then drinking in the sauna. Raul's Russian was careful, clear, and measured, the words geometrically crisp as they rolled off his tongue—in contrast to mine, which mushed together and tripped over each other. Estonian and Ukrainian accents mingled in a long exchange of "Chto *ti* tut delayesh?" "Nyet, chto *ti* tut delayesh?" ("What are *you* doing here?" "No, what are *you* doing here?")

If you see two young musicians talking on the street, it's very likely that they are having the following conversation:

"Come on. You sound great. You don't need to practice."

"But I really need to. I can't. No, I really can't. I have to."

And then you see them walking off together into a café.

Which is what we did. We drank anise and bitter tea and ate tiny, round, chocolate-covered honey cakes. We roamed the streets and jammed together, improvising a florid piano-sax duet in a tiny, garbage-filled courtyard on a discarded blue upright. When evening set in but the sun showed no sign of setting, he announced, "And now, *banya*." I figured, it's solstice. And, when in Rome . . .

So that's how I found myself in a communal *banya*, just a few doors down from where I'd practiced earlier. Raul's friends passed around an unmarked bottle of clear liquid with a bit of pulp on the bottom. "Papa made this at home!" one of them announced proudly. Conversation consisted mainly of grunts and slaps on the back. Everyone looked alert and not at all drunk. "I am so glad you could join us, Inna," Raul said. "It is very special occasion for Estonian people. And I am glad I had my mother's bathing suit in my backpack."

"Raul, you have to get me back to the hotel. My group can't see me like this. What can we do?"

A cab took us to the outskirts of town, to the hotel where my orchestra group was staying. It was far past midnight, yet when we entered the lobby, Gershwin blasted from the nearby meeting room. Jason Love came running up to me. "Inna! We've been trying to find you all day! We're having a rehearsal. Yes, right now."

"But . . ."

"No buts. There's a small piano here, not tuned, but we need to do it. Everyone just got back from dinner. The parents have been asleep for hours already, and one of the kids bought like a half-pound of weed for thirty-five cents across the street; they're out of control. But I need to get them in playing mode. We lost a rehearsal because our flight was late."

Jason seemed nonplussed by the fact that I was wearing a bikini top with size D falsies sopping wet with *banya* water and a large orange towel. I was barefoot and had my clothes in a plastic bag. "Say hi to Raul. He plays sax."

"Hi, Raul. Wasn't I your TA in Music Theory at Peabody? What are you doing here? Oh, never mind. Come double the horns. We will completely lose them; they tried vodka for the first time in their lives. You've got to play. Oh, also, Inna, can you translate something for the kids? What does *'Idi ti na hui'* mean? One of them was complaining that A/C is not working, and this is what they were told at the front desk." (It meant "Go fuck yourself," possibly the most common expression in the Russian language. Five stars for crudeness. It is now most frequently featured on road signs in Ukraine, addressed to the Russian invaders.)

When I first landed at O'Hare airport as a child, *Rhapsody in Blue* had twinkled throughout the United terminal as my aunt and uncle hugged us, yelled, videotaped, and yelled and hugged some more. Hearing Jason, this gentle American musician, swear in Russian while the orchestra blasted the same music made me feel right at home then and there, in an unremarkable suburb of Tallinn.

The next morning, the sun shone as if it had never gone to bed—just like us. A rickety little bus jauntily bobbed up and down the hills, taking us to the Rakvere outdoor festival. At every bump in the road, we doubled over with nausea. The driver announced that we had a choice: to stop at a village souvenir shop or go straight to rehearsal. Before Jason had time to get to the front of the bus and respond, two freshly made-up and chipper orchestra moms clapped their hands. "Oh, we've got to buy those little weaved baskets! And weaved shoes, *lapti*?" After supplying the souvenir-shop babushkas with what was probably the equivalent of their yearly income in sales, the parents returned to the bus, sixty pounds of weaved goods heavier. Thank heavens for those women. The extra few minutes of sleep likely carried us through the concert. We may have traveled through other charming villages of wooden houses; along lovely streams; and past one-of-a-kind, not-to-be missed churches, but I saw none of it.

Finally, we reached Rakvere, an endless, idyllic green field in the middle of nowhere. Jason naïvely assumed that we would be greeted by festival organizers who would take us to set up onstage and do a sound check. Where did he think he was, Tanglewood? The only living creatures around to greet us were fluffy, adorable sheep. They bleated spectacularly, in unison, and I thought I heard a tune from Copland's *Appalachian Spring* also on the program. "Hey, Jason, they're in tune! Maybe you can hire them for the gig?"

Jason was looking more sallow by the minute. This was clearly not organized to his expectations. As everyone unloaded their instruments, we went looking for the stage. It was just a short walk away, surrounded by purple and blue wildflowers and more sheep, grazing lovingly. It looked perfectly set up to host an orchestra of our size. But it was missing the key element needed for the success of *Rhapsody in Blue*, the heart of the program: the piano.

We walked back to where the bus had dropped us off, unsure of what to do next. The concert started in an hour. Across the street was a two-story yellow building with French windows, and Jason and I decided to see if anyone was inside. The heavy doors were unlocked. We entered what appeared to be a large ballroom, with chairs set up as if for a concert. At the front was a gleaming, nine-foot Estonian grand piano. We would play *Rhapsody in Blue* after all!

With no concern whatsoever for propriety (What is this building? Who does it belong to? What if we are not supposed to be there? What if we are fined lots of money or killed by thugs after witnessing something bad?), we decided to have the concert there. We left a lonely harpist at the bus stop to direct any audience members across the street. We still had not given up on the idea that a concert needs people to hear it. The concert started about an hour late, and while an audience did show up, many were hungover (still not too bad, by solstice standards). When the clarinet began the intoxicating trill and scale at the start of the piece—a klezmer melisma leading into nonchalant blues, explosive jazz and a groundbreaking piano samba—I wanted to embrace him and every other musician onstage with me in celebration of this lucky happenstance.

* * *

The next performance was in St. Petersburg's Smolny Cathedral. We still had to get to Russia. This involved an overnight train trip across the border, which for some reason scared the wits out of our group. It was rightfully determined that, while my translation efforts were valiant, I could not keep up and needed help. A beautiful twenty-eight-year-old art docent and translator named Svetlana was hired to chaperone us on the Russian leg of our journey. She met us after the Rakvere concert and immediately captured the attention of our tuba player, Bud, a sub for a high school student who had cancelled at the last moment. He was twenty-five, and he and Svetlana began a very public and passionate make-out session right at the train station.

In the evening, we settled into our shared compartments. The train took off; lulled by its rhythm and exhausted after the sleepless night and emotional concert, I quickly fell asleep.

I woke up around two o'clock in the morning to Jason frantically knocking at the compartment door. The train was stopped. "Inna, I am so sorry to wake you. We need your help."

"What is going on?"

"We are crossing the border, and there seems to be a problem. We just don't understand what it is. We've been here for over an hour."

"What about Svetlana? Isn't this part of her job?"

"She locked herself in the compartment with Bud. We can't get her out of there, and they can't hear us." So, while Svetlana was shagging the tuba player, I was left to untangle a mess with the border guards. Just great. I wasn't destined to sleep on this tour.

A Russian border guard with a handsome crew cut, gun in tow, and vodka breath barked expletives at me. Russian cursing is so rich, it's almost like a separate language—one that I did not speak, while Svetlana likely did. The expletives were very difficult to decipher that early in the morning. My confused stuttering didn't help matters much. Finally, he shoved a picture in my face. It was of Madeline, our principal cellist, holding her cello in one hand and a white, long-haired kitten in the other. As any tour manager knows, traveling with a musical instrument requires a tedious amount of paperwork. Each student needed to have a folder with perfectly filled out, chronologically arranged, stamped documents accompanied by a photograph of the instrument. "Koshek nelzya! Zapreschayetsya!" the guard said. "No cats! Forbidden!" Why Madeline, usually so methodical, decided that it was okay to take a picture with her cat as an official document for her cello, I will never know. I pleaded with the officer.

"Please. These are students. Her cello is right here. The cat is back home in America."

For some reason, the mention of America only seemed to make matters worse. The guard shuffled his fingers together and put out his hand, palm facing up. He needed a bribe, and only then would the train move forward. This was turning out to be one expensive kitten.

When I explained this to Jason, he was shocked at the unseemly situation. "Is that allowed? It's not even legal, is it?" I reminded him that this was Russia, one of the most corrupt places on the planet. Even though both he and I knew that, it was strange to be confronted with extortion so plainly. We roamed up and down the corridor, knocking on the compartments and waking the young musicians and their parents, collecting a five here, a twenty there. One of the mothers cried, "Will they arrest us? Shoot us?" "Not this time," I explained to her. "Not if you have cash." I gave the officer a stack of oily American bills. The train emitted a triumphant screech, and everyone applauded. In two minutes, we were in Russia.

Our hotel in St. Petersburg was in Ligovka, a neighborhood formerly known as a place where *ugolovniki*—criminals—hung out, and its dreariness made me feel right at home. That's the old Soviet Union! The hotel's wrought-iron window guards—in the shape of a sun drawn by a child, with a slice of a circle in the corner and the rays coming out to the sides—gave me a nostalgic pang. All the first-floor windows of my childhood had guards like that, and I found them romantically beautiful, not rough and industrial. Here, they had a very practical purpose: to keep out the drunks and the thieves. Next to the hotel entrance, an old lady in a kerchief the color of asphalt sold fried pies filled with meat, sour cabbage, and potatoes, and their smell made me want to tug on my mom's sleeve and plead with her to have one.

The city center, though, looked nothing like the Soviet Union. It was as though an old, rumpled uncle suddenly was dressed in designer clothing. Nevsky Prospect—the main street, the one of Gogol's novella—was covered in Dior ads and Starbucks and the Gap and Russian potato chips and pastry shops. I remembered that first night in Vienna as a child. Russia had caught up to the materialist glamour of the West with impressive speed. But beneath all the surface glitter, the noble city stood on dark water, stern, proud. Bewitched, I forgot how I got there and why. I walked the streets in a waking daze, as lines of poems I couldn't quite remember collided in my head. "I still have the addresses where I'll hear voices of the dead." I strained to find the memories, to access the lost addresses of lines repeated over the years, like mantras. *"Na beregu pustinnih voln stoyal on, dum velikih poln."* There he was, the Iron Horseman, Peter the Great, on the Neva—the river dressed in granite, just like Pushkin said. There was Leningrad Prison, the site of Akhmatova's silent *Requiem* cry. Who's beast, and who's man? How long till execution?

Traveling back decades, I shadowed my parents in the Hermitage as they held hands and glided from room to gilded room. My mom became the symbolist Alexander Blok's "Beautiful Lady" and my dad turned curly haired and witty, young, audacious, like the Pushkin I used to imagine. Feeling stifled by the memories in the golden splendor of these rooms, I hurried outside onto the palace square, where I put a dollar into the hat of a man with a dancing bear. Now, if I could only find the ultimate childhood nirvana: an Eskimo pie, snowy heaven on a stick. A robust woman in a white cap sold them from a small cart. As I handed her the money, she asked me, "Where are you from?" Was it so obvious that I am not from here? I realized that I didn't know the answer to the question and blurted out, "London." Her eyes dreamy, she said, *"Solnishko"*—"little sun"—"Take me back with you." The ice cream tasted the same. Barely sweet coldness burned my tongue.

After a snack, I remembered that I was a Russian-speaking, Ukrainian-born, Jewish American pianist, here to play *Rhapsody in Blue*. I had never been to St. Petersburg, but I felt at home. Perhaps any place where a musician gets to make music—and where pixels of memories combine to form a three-dimensional likeness of your childhood—feels like home for a brief moment.

The concert in Smolny reminded me that the new Russia was a country of the very rich and the very poor. The cathedral space was full: More than a thousand people showed up to hear the Greater Baltimore Youth Orchestra perform Gershwin and Copland. The difficult repeated-notes section—the famous samba—at the end of the Gershwin must have drowned in the cavernous space, blending indistinctly instead of dancing playfully, but nonetheless, they loved it. From my days at the Tchaikovsky

On the stage of St. Petersburg's Smolny Cathedral with Jason Love and the Greater Baltimore Youth Orchestra, after our performance of "Rhapsody in Blue."

Competition, I could recall the rhythmic clapping: When Russians really like you, they start a march of applause in unison. In return, I played "La Campanella" for them. Children brought flowers to me on the stage, and afterward, I signed programs for a long line of audience members. The elderly women called me "Innochka," held my hands, and hugged me as if I was their long-lost granddaughter. One of them took the program I had just signed and squinted at it through a piece of a green broken bottle. I realized that she could not afford a pair of glasses, and yet, she had given me a bouquet of flowers.

A bit of family history: My father's grandmother Betya had two sisters and a brother. In 1941, Betya and her sister Manya were evacuated with their children, while their husbands volunteered to fight in the siege of Odessa. The younger brother, Izya; older sister, Genya; and the rest of the family stayed in the city as it fell to Romanians and Germans. Their fates differed. Twenty-year-old Izya was hanged in the street at the beginning of the occupation, but Genya and her daughter survived. After the war, they changed their names and moved to the suburbs of St. Petersburg. Genya became Irma and her daughter Meira became Klava. Klava now lived on the outskirts of Peterhoff, Peter the

Great's extravagant tongue-in-cheek homage to Versailles. I took the train to Peterhoff and met Klava right in front of the iconic fanciful fountains.

In America, we obviously were better off financially than the remnants of our family, strewn around republics that were no longer tied to each other by Socialist doctrine. None of these relatives managed to become Russian oligarchs, and they could not give me yachts, designer clothes, or apartments. But, as any Jewish grandmother would do, Klava brought me chicken cutlets wrapped in foil, perfectly spiced with dill, deliciously breaded, and lightly fried in butter. As I ate them on the bench, she laughed and wiped an occasional tear.

To celebrate the Smolny concert, we had booked a large table in a Russian restaurant and nightclub next to our hotel in Ligovka. It was convenient because the kids could be shepherded to their rooms after partying next door, and presumably, nobody would be late for the flight home the next morning. The table overflowed with the standard Russian starters: bowls of mayo speckled with crab and cheese and peas masquerading as salad; plates of burgundy tongue and rosy ham; earthy black bread; slabs of shiny feta with grilled peppers; smoked herring swimming through rings of onions in oil; fried pies with potatoes and mushrooms; and the prized dish, blini with sour cream and red caviar. Elegant crystal carafes of vodka punctuated the spread.

A Russian restaurant-cum-nightclub is an amazing thing. If you've never been, get yourself to New York City and take the B train to the last stop, Brighton Beach. The neighborhood is dubbed "Little Odessa"; everyone there speaks Russian, and the tchotchkes and food items at grocery stores bring a bit of *rodina*—"birthplace"—back to nostalgic ex-Soviet New Yorkers. As soon as it gets dark, the restaurants turn into wild, timeless dance parties where polka meets '80s Europop and the same kerchiefed grandmas who sold you cherry-filled fried pies earlier that day are suddenly decked out in gold miniskirts on a dance floor usually lit up by a disco ball. It's like mini-Eurovision.

This particular restaurant turned out to be even more exciting. There was a stage with a velvet curtain; presumably, we would be treated to some kind of Russian dance revue. We ate the appetizers and, warmed up by the vodka, hopped about ineptly to the Russian pop. (Why does it all, without exception, sound like polka? Even the ballads?) A neighboring table of Japanese businessmen gestured animatedly to the maître d', and one of them slipped him a fat envelope. I felt this merited no attention—until, a half-hour later, the velvet curtains parted, and women in doll, nurse, and pilot outfits strutted out in six-inch heels. We quickly returned to our seats. This must be the show! The disco ball then lit the stage in bedroom red, and to the delight of the young men of the Greater Baltimore Youth Orchestra and the dismay of their mothers, the women started taking off their clothes.

Jason was a wonderful, inspiring conductor and an endlessly kind, patient person. At this point, though, he lost it. "The goddamn idiots put us in the wrong room! We're done here! Out, everyone!" Our dinner ended in the hotel bar, where he downed tiny, free souvenir vodka bottles vehemently one after another. "Jason," I teased him, "you are learning the Russian way: loading up on free stuff!"

At the Sheremetyevo airport the next day, the customs officer claimed not to recognize the odd, shiny, snail-shaped object known as a saxophone. He insisted that it was not a musical instrument but possibly a weapon and wouldn't let us through. Our departure time loomed. By now an old hand at negotiating bribes, I was about to hand the wad of bills over, when the officer, nervous all of a sudden, changed his mind. His boss must have shown up because he pushed my hand away and waved us through. We made the flight with seconds to spare and broke into applause as the plane took off for home.

* * *

The Russia of oligarchs would reveal itself to me on my next tour, some seven years later. By then I had been living in New York, performing, and flying back and forth to Chicago to teach as a visiting artist at Northeastern Illinois University in Chicago. The tour was sponsored by Goskonzert, a concert-planning organization that had full control over the careers of

Soviet artists. It somehow had survived the fall of the Soviet Union, but of course, since the collapse, it had changed quite a bit. I had very little information about the upcoming concerts. Email exchanges were sparse and hard to understand. The last message had offered a fee that was ridiculously low, even for a young artist like myself; I said I would need a higher amount or would have to withdraw. I was in Chicago to teach and was staying with my parents. At five o'clock in the morning, we were awakened by a phone call. A frosty voice on the other end spoke in cutting syllables with a Moscow accent: "Inna. If you ever want to come to Russia again after this and have no problems, you will pack your bag, get on the flight tomorrow, and we will meet you in the airport."

"Or else?" I wanted to ask. But I didn't. The guy sounded scary. Instead, I mumbled something about needing to be paid my fee.

Incredibly, the voice said, "You will be paid what you asked. Such insolence. We haven't paid this much to any of our European visiting professors in years."

"I don't live in Europe," I retorted. "I live in the United States. It's farther away. Also, we usually do contracts." A signed contract arrived by email a half-hour later. I was going back.

This time I was playing a large solo program—Haydn; Brahms's F Minor Sonata; Ravel's *Gaspard de la Nuit*; Beethoven's *Fantasie* (a crazy piece that I had recorded on an all-Beethoven CD that year, along with the *Eroica Variations* and C Minor Sonata)—at cities on the train line that connects Moscow and St. Petersburg. My parents had just rewatched *Dr. Zhivago* and imagined me simultaneously getting crushed to death and robbed on the train. I would play in Tver; Torzhok; and Novgorod, a tenth-century wonder of Russian Orthodox architecture and the birthplace of Rachmaninoff.

Vladimir Ivanov, the Goskonzert manager I'd spoken to on the phone, picked me up at the airport. I was reading Gary Shteyngart's novel *Russian Immigrant's Handbook* on the flight, and Ivanov reminded me of the Groundhog character. He was enormous and had a tiny dachshund on a gold leash. He looked me up and down and grunted, "So you are the girl who asked for more?"

On our drive to Tver, he told me that I was a good-looking girl, but like all Jewish girls, I would get fat and old before I knew it. Such a shame. I was jet-lagged and tired and couldn't think of a comeback to this, so I just said, "No, I won't."

"Yes, you will." I wasn't going to win this argument, so I just napped.

On the way to Tver, we stopped by Tchaikovsky's little country house, where I wept, looking at his bedroom slippers, green and woven through with a silver thread, poised neatly near his little bed, as though he had stepped out briefly and was coming back soon. We drove through a landscape of flat fields, low-hanging gray clouds, and hundreds of birch trees—a cliché of the Russian landscape. I missed New York.

In Tver, I had tea with Ivanov and the venue director in the philharmonic management office. A gorgeous woman in high heels and a short skirt, her hair piled high, brought out the samovar, served us cherry jam, and poured the tea into tall glasses. The director slapped her loudly on her behind as she turned to take out the tray. "Masha is a great secretary," he said, winking at Ivanov. She giggled and clicked her heels. If there were samovar commercials in the '50s, I was living in one at that moment.

In *The Master and Margarita*, the devil visits Moscow in the 1930s and wreaks havoc on the day-to-day activities of the Socialist state. In one great scene, Satan sits on the stage of a full auditorium and considers the crowd before him. He wonders if the people of Russia are the same as they had been hundreds of years ago. "The main question," he says, "is whether these people changed on the inside." On my tour, the audience was the same as I remembered them from my previous experiences. They knew every note of Brahms and Beethoven that I'd prepared for them. They were fiercely, obsessively devoted to music, even if that meant spending a month's earnings on a concert ticket and flowers. They would make me feel at home anywhere, but I no longer knew the country where a fresh-squeezed orange juice in a restaurant cost thirty dollars. In my private train compartment,

I ate freshly cured salmon and watched Russian films on a flat-screen TV. Ivanov was eager to show me that Russia's splendor exceeded anything I'd experienced living in the West. After the tour, he organized a party for me in a fashionable Moscow restaurant, an extravagant fantasia of food and design with Asian themes, clearly inaccessible to anyone but the nouveau riche. "She plays very, very well," he told everyone, though I was sure he hadn't heard a single performance.

On my last night in Russia, my friend Zhenya from Odessa, who worked in international cultural relations, scored us tickets for a midnight tour of iconic *Master and Margarita* spots throughout Moscow. The tour began at the witching hour, in Bulgakov's apartment on Great Sadovaya Street, complete with a giant, black beast of a cat. After waiting for hours for the bus driver—who, like many passing characters in the novel, seemed to have gone missing—we traveled around Moscow in the middle of the night, from the "cursed apartment" where Satan and his entourage camp out to MASSOLIT, the literary club for respected Soviet writers; from the alley where the Master meets Margarita with her yellow flowers to the Patriarchi Lakes, where the editor Berlioz's head is chopped off by a tram. It was a surreal, mad rush around a city I didn't know well but felt intimate with, thanks to the many rereadings of the novel.

At five o'clock in the morning, we found ourselves at the Novodevichy Cemetery by a small porous gravestone with dark lettering. Even Bulgakov's gravestone has a strange and fateful story. One of his main literary influences was Gogol, the Ukrainian who later became one of the greatest Russian writers of all time. In one of his early stories, "Evenings on the Farm near Dikanka," Gogol revels in the colorful, magical, and mystical landscape of Ukrainian folklore, full of flying devils, corrupt deacons, anthropomorphic cherry dumplings, and heavy-lidded monsters. As I learned at the Odessa literary club at age ten, these stories formed a direct line to *The Master and Margarita*. This is especially evident in the magical chapter where Rimsky, the financial director of a theater, is attacked by the vampiric artistic administrator Varenukha, who has been turned supernatural through the shenanigans of Satan.

Gogol died in 1852, eighty-eight years before Bulgakov. During Stalin's purges in 1931, his remains were exhumed from his initial place of burial at the Danilov Monastery and moved to the Novodevichy Cemetery. The stone was discarded because of its symbolic connection to Russian orthodoxy, and in its stead, a statue was erected. Bulgakov's widow, Elena, recycled the stone for her husband's grave. Russia and Ukraine meet here, at this gravesite, inexorably tied for centuries through people, cultures, and blood.

Zhenya and I huddled together, drinking hot tea from a thermos. Dawn turned the sky blood red. I turned my head and saw the imposing, modern grave of Mstislav Rostropovich, the great Russian cellist. Between him and Bulgakov, clutching the hand of a childhood friend from Odessa, in a freezing cemetery at an ungodly hour, I finally felt at home.

8

THE MEDICIS LIVE ON

or How I Met Shpigelmacher Again

The Medici dynasty of Florence can be traced back to the late twelfth century. But while historians claim that the Medicis' immense power had dissipated by the eighteenth century, "Princess" Amalia di Medici, née Vargas, would tell you otherwise. A zaftig but elegant cross between Botticelli's it-girl Simonetta Vespucci and Ms. Piggie, she would kindly remind you that her family invented Western civilization and that for that dinner you must eat *magret du canard* or else remain hungry.

Amalia was a bossy amalgam of parody, myth, and self-invention and something of a patron saint to the young pianists of the Peabody Conservatory. Upon reaching drinking age, pianists auditioned for her and a panel of judges for the LaFesse Foundation Festival, sponsored entirely by her. If chosen, they would be taken to the French cities of Toulouse and Carcassonne to play solo and chamber music concerts; spend quality time with Amalia; and, in general, partake in daily European joie de vivre.

Some of these pianists would later be asked to play at Carnegie Hall's Weill Recital Hall as part of a three-day festival. The concerts never paid actual money, but few young pianists in the early stages of their careers would turn down an all-expenses-paid trip to France, a chance to perform outdoors in a place as sensuously lovely as Toulouse, or make it to Carnegie

Hall—even if this meant that we had to adopt a heavily right-wing mentality for two weeks, forgo thoughts of any romantic interludes, eat daily portions of the very fatty meat that Amalia would preorder for the entire table, and wistfully nod while she made such statements as "Salvador Dalí got all his ideas from my father" or "I am a princess, and don't you forget it!"

I had first met Amalia at a symphony concert in Peabody's ornate Friedberg Hall. She had floated gravely across the carpeted floor of the lobby, emerald chiffon skirt rustling behind her, with an entourage of bohemian-looking young men. She moved at a deliberate lento pace: She was very ill, very important, or both. Even before being introduced, I knew that I would have to weigh each word I uttered in her presence carefully. She was the subject of ridicule at many a Peabody party, but at the same time, we all wanted her to notice us and invite us to the festival. This immediately changed our demeanor from ironic to reverent when next to her. There was something profoundly sad about this vision of faux royalty combined with a deep love of art and music. She didn't have the studied elegance or snobbishness of actual royal patrons; the vehemence with which she perpetrated the myth of her title betrayed a murky, possibly unhappy past. The Peabody administration knew it had to keep her happy in order to continue sending its students and alumni to the festival, so it let the myth persist.

After I had already been coming to the festival with some regularity, she invited me to her house in Washington, DC. Hanging above the majestic staircase was a five-foot-tall banner of the Medicis' coat of arms. She descended the staircase, dressed head to toe in Versace, and pronounced that she would take me shopping for concert dresses. But first, she said, she wanted to play an LP for me. She took out the record from a white, unmarked envelope and started the turntable. First, we heard the warmly familiar hum of vinyl surface noise. Then, a tender A-flat major chord, a punctuated rhythmic bite, and the lilt of the appoggiatura that begins Beethoven's penultimate Sonata in A-flat Major. The slightly exaggerated yet inevitable lateness of the fast notes; the heartbeat of the left hand's sixteenths, brimming with life; the luminous, lean sound—this could only be one pianist. Unmistakably, it was Artur Schnabel, the teacher of Fleisher. It was a historic recording I had heard many times. Tears came to her eyes as she listened. She looked at me and, with utter conviction, said, "This was me, age fifteen, playing for Leon Fleisher."

We went to Bloomingdales, and she chose three gowns for me. One of them I still wear, a long, peach, gauzy thing. She loved me in her own way, believed in my artistry, and wanted to support me. Choosing those dresses for me to wear was a motherly gesture, and I had accepted it, which meant that I had accepted her.

Amalia preferred to invite male pianists to the festival. She relished the attention of young, talented men but was very hard on the women. Her summer fights with the female pianists of Peabody were legendary. After my first trip, lots had gotten cut off from the festival. I was expecting nothing less for myself when I first went to Toulouse with the LaFesse gang. Yet somehow, she and I got along. I admired her for making piano music and pianists the focal point of her existence. Whenever she would utter a particularly bullheaded statement, I would remind myself that she could have just bought herself a villa in Capri instead of bringing us to play in France every summer. "Oh, that Inna, she is totally crrrazy and wild," she would lovingly announce in her thick faux accent. The feeling was mutual, and as I was starting to perform more and more concerts, Toulouse had become a recurring summer stint, until I was done at Peabody.

To play far away from home carried with it a sense of reckless abandon and ease. I would descend on a town for a few days, get drunk on its quirks and characters, and walk the streets of a new miniature world that I discovered and would keep in the pocket of my memory until new experiences diluted it. I knew nobody. I would at times see my face staring down at me from a poster and get wonderfully, deliciously nervous at the prospect of adding a little bit to the cultural pulse of the place. And I would feel full to the brim, inspired and ready, juggling details of colors and images. I couldn't wait to make music in a way that only that environment conjured up within me at that

With Michael Sheppard in New York, long after our misadventures in Toulouse.

given moment. The cobblestone streets told me how to do this; the cracked rose walls of churches; the earthy, vine-covered bridge across the Garonne River; and the tiny chocolate mouse with almond ears I purchased near the Foundacion Bemberg, where I played amid gargoyles, next to a stone sarcophagus. And then I suddenly saw that my name, on a gargantuan poster, was "Inna Felik."

I wondered how this happened. I gently asked Amalia when I arrived at the Foundacion for my rehearsal on a smooth, buttery Fazioli piano. "Well, darrrrling, your name just had to go. This is an elegant society. It was just too phallic." So it wasn't an accident. I had never thought of my last name in this way. And why had she only thought of this now? It wasn't my first time there. I was tickled and could not wait to share this absurdity with my roommate and friend Michael Sheppard. He had a wicked, outlandish sense of humor similar to George Carlin's and could have easily made a career in comedy, had he wanted.

There were a few other projects to discuss with Michael before the evening's concert. I had a rendezvous the following morning, and it had to take place quietly, without Amalia's knowledge, lest there be judgments or misgivings. It had to end before we moved on to Carcassonne. And I had to figure out what to wear. It had to be something flattering but not too flirtatious, something that said, "See what you missed when you stopped writing me fifteen years ago?"

* * *

A month before I had left for that Toulouse trip, I was practicing in my parents' Chicago townhouse, taking too many email breaks in the cool basement, and hiding from the scorching afternoon heat. One email from an account labeled "Leopold the Cat" made me jump—the subject line said "Misha Shpigelmacher." For years I'd thought about my best childhood friend. Misha's family had immigrated to Holon, Israel, around the same time as ours went to the States. At first, we wrote each other long, elaborate letters. His were illustrated with caricatures of Saddam Hussein, civilians in gas masks, strange buildings on stilts, the many different Orthodox Jewish hats, the walls of Old Jerusalem, and a never-ending parade of new characters. I tried to hold my own, unsuccessfully, by providing him with drawings of the obscenely made-up twelve-year-olds with bangs like shelves and plastic eyelashes who made my junior high school life a misery. What else was I to draw? Mozart? Schubert? Mr. D?

Just six months after he; his sister, Rimma; and their parents got to Israel, Misha's father, Nolik, was killed by a truck in a bicycle accident. Soon after, his letters to me slowed to a trickle and then just stopped. Nonetheless, the memory of his particular brand of Odessa humor, combined with an intelligence and spark that I had since failed to find in men of twelve or older, had kept him in my consciousness through years of relationships and dating. I had eventually decided that he probably didn't like music or art, spent eighteen hours a day in front of the computer, and did not venture outside an office for years. I also hoped he had become completely unattractive in every other way, as well, and totally uninteresting to me as a friend or anything else. So I tried not to get too excited when I opened the email. It read, "What's up Inka?"

My response to him was "Holy shit."

My marriage to Max had fallen apart four years before. I was done with Peabody and was trying to figure out the next steps in my career—whether to launch into a doctoral program with another teacher or focus on traveling and playing concerts while trying to find a position. I wanted, or expected, nothing from the sudden reemergence of my childhood friend, only to spend a little time on a giddy memory trip. It turned out that he had thought of me because he had been up one night, rereading *The Master and Margarita*, and got to the part where Margarita carries ugly yellow flowers just like the ones he had once given me. We had first read the book together in Odessa. Again, that fateful book!

We emailed each other nonstop for a few weeks, and suddenly, he announced that he had bought a plane ticket from Tel Aviv to Toulouse. We agreed to meet in Toulouse near the former apartment of Antoine de Saint-Exupéry, author of *Le Petite Prince*. No photographs were to be exchanged until then, and our code phrase would be, "Would you please draw me a sheep?" Always a sucker for clandestine adventures of this sort, of reunions, codes, and literary references, I agreed.

My mother worried. "What if he is a liar, a loser, or a pervert? Do you really need this now? You know, he is probably fat and bald. Will he distract you from practicing? What will you wear?"

When I arrived in France, it was the very morning of my concert. Amalia was convinced that I would have to cancel, so she had prepared at least two backup artists. Contrary to her expectations, I felt buzzed with a manic, jet-lagged energy and was eager to play. Dropping my suitcase backstage, I catapulted onto the stage of the ancient Foundacion Bemberg and sank my hands deep into a Brahms sonata.

An artist might never play as freshly and directly as during childhood. That's when the music flows like words, without premeditation or the pressures of consequences but with the utmost sincerity. That summer, I was trying to reconcile the strength of my own musical personality with my studies with Leon Fleisher. I had just finished my work with him at Peabody, but his ideas about music still felt uncomfortable, making my sound at times brittle and cold.

Playing the piano this way could be like looking in the mirror and seeing a different person. I was still the only one who could hear and feel this discomfort. In the process of assimilating these ideas that differed so dramatically from what I had been used to, I was overthinking everything. Others had told me that I was growing as a performer, that my sense of musical structure was more mature, that my control of the piano was becoming more masterly. But I wanted the music and my voice to come naturally, with the same freedom and imagination as before. Until that began to happen, I could not find peace. It takes years to reconcile the intellect with intuition and emotion so they work together seamlessly; this process was agonizing for me.

That evening, though, thoughts of childhood, combined with the delight of being in Toulouse, filled me with a brightness and ease. It was as if I had slipped back into my own skin, and my mind relaxed as I played. Even as I performed, I couldn't wait to get to my hotel room to prepare for the reunion.

* * *

"Honey, wear something low-cut, just in case," Michael said. "Show the girls off. And anyway, what does he look like? Should I leave tomorrow night, just in case you two need to, you know, relive your elementary school days, play doctor, or whatever?"

The thought of something physical, the merest hint of an adult kind of relationship, felt sordid to me. I instead hoped to slide down the rabbit hole, into the diorama that was my childhood in Odessa. I wanted to find Misha the same now as he had been then. So no, I would not need the room. The next morning, wearing a simple, long summer skirt and blouse, I waited in a café next to the Hotel Saint-Exupéry. Shpilka was already fifteen minutes late, and I began to carefully look around to see if he might also be waiting for me at the café. In my mind, I tried to take his childhood features—longish nose; prominent ears; dark, straight hair and floppy bangs; a big forehead; and a lopsided grin—and stretch them out in the manner of a Giacometti sculpture. When a barely proportional result had materialized in my brain, I began to look for a match in the surrounding customers.

One brown-haired guy at the bar with a backpack seemed to have the necessary traits, though he looked a bit wrinkled and rough around the edges. It was odd that he was drinking a vermouth so early in the morning, but who knows? Shpigelmacher could certainly look older, a rugged woodsman type, thanks to the rigorous army training and the notorious closeness the

Israelis feel to the soil. For that matter, he could also have picked up a drinking habit. I had to keep reminding myself that I really knew nothing about him—other than what a few very long, intense, bright, and open emails had told me.

Tragically, Nolik, his father, had died in a car accident almost as soon as the family had arrived in Israel. Shpilka was only ten. Despite this, he had remained as funny as before the tragedy. He still drew caricatures and wrote plays and stories. He had majored in physics, math, and computer science and dedicated seven years of his life to the Israeli army. He now worked for the Israeli government in a technological capacity, doing something he could not—and still won't—go into. (I claim that he was actually manufacturing shoelaces on the Lower East Side all along.) He also was researching a dissertation through the Weizmann Institute of Science in Israel. He had taken many dance classes, especially salsa. He read the same books as me and saw the same films. He had traveled for three months in South America recently; was fluent in Spanish, Hebrew, Russian, and English; and knew some Arabic. He had hiked Israel through and through, played basketball, and gone on diving trips. It seemed that he was a serial monogamist and a very cheerful, open person. I didn't know why he wanted to come and see me—probably for the same reasons I wanted to see him.

After a few moments, the stranger at the bar noticed me examining him and began to wink at me suggestively while tossing his long bangs as though he had a fleet of small creatures to evict from them. His eye contact did not waver for a second, and I began to realize my mistake as he stood up and made his way toward me. Seething because Shpilka was late, I thought of ways to lose this guy, and then I heard, from another direction, "Inna?"

A thin and athletic guy with clever and kind eyes; slender, elongated features; a giant backpack; a T-shirt with Hebrew words; and very serious sideburns was hugging me, and I spoke the requisite phrase: "Can you please draw me a sheep?" To this, he took out a folded paper with a pen drawing of a sheep, munching grass on a small planet, à la *Le Petite Prince*. "I drew this on the train," he told me.

This is the drawing Misha took out of his pocket when I said the code phrase "Can you please draw me a sheep?"

The day flew by. I missed not only Michael's afternoon recital (he would understand) but also the train trip to our next performances in the medieval walled city of Carcassonne, about an hour away, where we would stay for a few days. I asked Misha to cancel his hotel reservation and come with me. I was sure we would find him a place to stay there, and it seemed that we had only skimmed the surface of the past fifteen years. We talked nonstop, switching between Russian and English, his language peppered with Israeli expressions and gestures unfamiliar to me.

On the train to Carcassonne, I looked into his face carefully and saw ages reflected in it: a hint of my great-grandmother's eagle nose; of black-and-white photographs of class B from School 119; and the brown, square backpacks we wore in fourth grade. But these were fragments; I could not place the boy within the man or vice versa, and this collision of images—then with now—was making it hard to breathe. More than anything, I suddenly wanted to be by the piano, to play like I was in a forest, walking by an ancient clear river, following it blindly, listening to it, and letting it lead me away, away, to the one thing that was constant and unchanged within itself—the music. I was suddenly angry at Shpilka and faulted him, silently, for my having spent the day away from the piano. Pianists are either practicing or wishing they were practicing and usually hold others responsible for any circumstances surrounding the latter.

In Carcassonne, the musicians had rooms in an inn at their disposal, all paid for by Amalia for the duration of the festival. I knew that one of the rooms would become vacant that evening because a singer was leaving to go back to the United States. I suggested to Misha that he ought to stay there and that I would check with Amalia but was positive it would be no problem. He hadn't planned on the Carcassonne trip and had not made any reservations in the town, so I felt it was my duty to help out. However, because we arrived separately from the group, I had no idea where to go. I had a phone number but no hint of the name of the place, the owner, or the street address. When we arrived in the city, I went to a phone booth, dialed the number, and in my best and most proper emergency French asked whether Amalia's party had arrived yet and whether I could drop my bags off. The voice on the other end barked at me, "You call so late! Unbelievable!" *Click.* It was nine at night. I had no idea where to go or what to tell Misha. No problem, I thought. It's a small town, with lots of charming, winding alleys; cafés; and little squares. We would wander around, have dinner somewhere, and think of something.

We walked for a few blocks from the station, passed a small church or two, and entered the labyrinth of streets approaching the old walled center. Carcassonne is a medieval city on a hill, overlooking green valleys, and the Ville Basse is its more expansive lower part. This is where our inn was supposed to be located—just steps from the moat, the bridges, and the castle. Our conversation, like a game of Ping-Pong, was swift and light and always moving and changing direction. It now felt utterly comfortable, with the turns and the jokes that only two Odessites could exchange and understand.

As luck would have it, every café seemed to be closing in front of us. The first open restaurant we saw was called Les Trois Rapiers; as we came in, I heard the familiar roar of Amalia's untraceable Euro accent: *"Quel Horrrrrreur,* it was a rrrrotten, terrrrible performance. I wanted to press a button and make him go away." In the small dining room, Amalia was presiding over a long table. We were saved from a night of wandering around, although in a beautiful French medieval town, how bad could that have been? We tiptoed in quietly.

Everybody seemed to be eating a mystery meat. There were two empty chairs—I sat down with Misha next to me and quickly ordered *moules marinières* for both of us before Amalia had a chance to notice. Thankfully, her spirits turned high when she saw me.

"Inna, my darrling! I was so worried. I am glad you made it. And this is your friend?" She did not seem to mind at all that I had arrived separately and with a stranger. I'd managed to catch her in a benevolent mood.

"Who him? Oh, yeah. Imagine, we ran into each other after all these years!" The last thing I wanted Amalia to know was that I had a date with a guy, even if it was just a childhood friend.

A plate of mussels arrived in front of us, and I blissfully inhaled the garlicky aroma. No duck fat for us tonight. The conversation moved lightly from the unfortunate concert from a few days ago, when a buxom pianist broke the piano bench, to this afternoon's concert of piano transcriptions and virtuoso showpieces that Michael had played brilliantly. And from there Amalia urgently slid into that very slipperiest of topics, the Israeli-Palestinian conflict. Learning that Shpilka had spent a great deal of time in the Israeli army, she produced some uninhibited commentary that clearly made him uncomfortable.

Shpilka, swallowing his tongue for a few seconds, replied carefully, "This is a complex subject that I cannot elaborate on in just a few sentences, and it is hardly a topic for such a lovely meal."

Disaster seemed averted, but Amalia's eyes now had that certain look I had learned to decipher, the look that said, "You disagreed with me. You are toast." She did not like him. After plates were cleared, she pulled me aside and said, "Don't you get mixed up with those liberals, you hear? They are a nightmare. They will destroy our country and theirs, too. They will use you every chance they get and leave you dry."

There was no point in arguing. I just listened. It did not seem like a good move to ask her whether it would it be okay to bring the liberal back to the inn and give him a spare room. Instead, I casually asked if Oona the singer had really gone home and learned that, yes, she had, and her empty room was next to mine, that we shared a bathroom, and that I now could have her key. So I had a suite at my disposal. This sounded almost like some romantic setup, one I hadn't looked for and didn't particularly want at that point.

I told Shpilka that if we stayed around a bit after everybody left, I could sneak him into his own room, next to mine, and that we would share a bathroom. An agreeable and easygoing chap, he went along with it. The group had left the restaurant, and we lingered a little while longer, when I finally asked the question that had been troubling me for so long: "Why did you stop writing me?"

He looked away and then back at me. His eyes darkened with concentration, which changed his entire bearing from easygoing and fun loving to fiery and extremely focused. He spoke slowly.

"I wanted so much to write you, to connect with you, and to understand you. But the Inna I knew, the one from the stamp shops, from the dumpy building site, the one with the big bow, did not exist anymore. There was a young concert pianist in a very different country from mine, but I knew nothing about music and could contribute nothing to your life in the way it was developing and I . . . well, after my father died, when we just got to Israel, I had so much to do. I felt it was best to let each other be."

We walked to the inn quietly. It was called Tete de Lard, or the Pig's Head—I now had the address, which was only a block away from the restaurant. I saw Michael leaning out of the window, trying to hide behind the window shutters and catch a glimpse of the guy I was with. He winked at me and pantomimed fellatio. I couldn't stand him breaking the mood. "Get lost," I mouthed, and he got it and disappeared behind the curtains.

As I closed the door to my room that night, I decided I would not think about my upcoming performance. I had to focus on Brahms and the Schumann lieder I was to rehearse the next day and when I would find time to practice, but I could not help but take a peek at Shpilka in the other room, getting ready for bed, by now shirtless and, as it turned out, perfectly toned. It occurred to me that I had to call my mom and tell her that he was most certainly not fat or bald but, in fact, kind of hot.

In the morning, we waited until all others in the LaFesse group had left the building so that we would not be seen leaving together through the same door. As soon as the two of us stepped outside, we were greeted by a large man with beady eyes, somehow made smaller by his very small glasses, with a cartoon pig on his T-shirt and a bare, well-oiled head. With deep disdain he screeched, "Welcome to my eeenn. I trhust you 'ad a gewd night?" and then, unexpectedly, under his breath, "Argh, your kind is all the same."

What did this mean? What was he talking about? Israelis? Jews? Soviets? Expatriate Soviet Jews? Musicians? Long-lost childhood friends who had found each other again?

Somebody had seen us last night, somebody besides Michael, who would never say anything. They clearly had given the innkeeper the impression that I was sleeping with strange men in his hotel. In all honesty, it could have looked bad. There was a man from outside the group, and he did walk in at night and left with me in the morning. I hadn't considered this. I had thought that because Shpilka was giving up his hotel reservation in Toulouse, it was nice of me to help him find free accommodations. After all, he had come all this way to see me.

And then that other voice in my head woke up, the one that had already gotten annoyed with Shpilka on the way to Carcassonne. *You are here to rehearse and play a concert, on a professional engagement. Childhood friend or not, the audience must be pleased; the presenter, happy and ready to invite you back. What are you doing? Tell him that it was nice seeing him, but you have work to do.*

* * *

And yet I didn't do that. I had nowhere to practice in the morning, so we spent it exploring the medieval city behind the walls. Shpilka bought a bag of sour cherries, and we sat on the wall, spitting the pits into the moat. He took out a notepad and quickly sketched a new character—a piglet's head and a tight T-shirt with the words "I Love Ukrainians." It was as if we were continuing our collection of made-up cartoon characters from fifteen years ago in Odessa.

Was our repartee the comfortable interaction of childhood friends or two adults getting to know each other in a different way? Eventually, I begrudgingly had to leave the castle walls and make my way over to the church to rehearse the Schumann lieder with Artemisia, the soprano.

Schumann composed his *Frauen-Liebe und Leben* (*A Woman's Love and Life*) during his "Year of Song," 1840. In that same year, he wrote his *Dictherliebe* and *Liederkreis* song cycles and finally married his beloved Clara Wieck after a long legal battle with her father. *Frauen-Liebe und Leben* follows a female protagonist through her first meeting with her love, through their marriage, and on to his death. The piano writing not only supports the voice but also fully and independently creates the mood and emotional content of each poem, as if setting the stage for the singer with the utmost detail. This was my first Schumann song cycle. It was eerie and tender to dive into it in the darkness of the empty five-hundred-seat auditorium with a few flickering candles, in view of the pale, painted saints, behind shuttered windows that kept out the warm daylight. When the melody from the opening came back in the eighth and final movement of the cycle, my breath caught in my throat, and the hairs on my arms stood on end. A light breeze fluttered through a crack in the doors and ruffled my score.

Once we had finished the rehearsal, I still had a bit of time left with the piano onstage to work on Brahms's Sonata in F Minor, which he had composed when he was only twenty. I started by playing through two of the more lyrical movements. The andante espressivo begins with a quotation by Otto Inkermann:

> Through evening's shade, the pale moon gleams
> While rapt in love's ecstatic dreams
> Two hearts are fondly beating.

The music begins simply, with Brahms's special fingerprint: thirds descending in the right hand, and thirds in the left murmuring gently. The feeling of multiple voices or instruments involved in an equal exchange, not a typical melody-accompaniment situation, persists throughout the movement, whether the textures are thick and sonorous or shimmering in a higher register. The final few pages of the movement—the coda—are some of the most mystical writing of the entire work. Here, an entirely new melody is born in the right hand, with the left rumbling low, like a primordial river. The melody swells and grows, and it is as if the entire planet's large heart is expanding, filling to the brim, finally calming and ending with celestial harp breaths. "Rückblick" ("Looking Back" or "Remembrance"), the fourth movement of the piece, brings back some of these melodic elements but as a stark funeral march with implied trumpet calls and timpani rolls. A brief foray into the searching, meandering harmonies from the second movement is just a wistful reminiscence, and then the darkness takes over.

I am not sure whether it was the mystery of the empty church or the new presence in my life of a person who could connect me to the world I came from, a world that did not exist anymore, but I'd never before given as much of myself to these movements as I did then. It was like discovering the music anew. When I was done, I wished that there was an audience to hear it. Who knew if I could do it again just as well tomorrow? I looked toward the slice of light in the door and saw that Shpilka was standing there, listening.

The next day, as Artemisia and I helped each other with the zippers for our dresses before the evening recital, she let it slip that Amalia was very angry with me. I wanted to hear details.

"Well, I think she is jealous. He is cute! And anyway, who cares. It's your business."

"What in the world are you talking about?"

"Well, I ran into Amalia at the grocery shop. She was getting chocolate for the reception, and she went into a tirade how you are too wild and oversexed and how you had thrown an orgy with some ultraliberal Israeli guy you picked up. I think she might have said that more people were involved."

"What? That's crazy! Nothing happened!"

"I told her that it wasn't some guy but your best friend from childhood who came to see you and to hear you play and that I was next door to you and that things were completely innocent and really nice. But she didn't believe me. She is just hungry for scandal, you know? She loooves gossip. I wouldn't take it personally. Our Schumann will be great; your Brahms, too. She'll forget all about it."

This was completely perverse! It was very clear that Mr. Ted the Lard from the hotel had told Amalia some ridiculous fable, and she was only too happy to spread it around. I didn't know whether to laugh or get very, very angry and throw things. Again, I felt that nasty little feeling of annoyance with Shpilka. Why did he have to come here and meddle in my relationship with Amalia and the festival? After all, I was thankful for her. She was definitely a character, but she had brought me to Europe many times, and she had given me numerous opportunities to play at Carnegie Hall. I should tell her that he is a very respectful guy and that the whole thing was not only innocent but also very moving. I should be calm and polite—I had a part in all of this and needed to tread carefully. My greatest responsibility, however, was to play as well as possible. I knew that if I played a great concert, then all would be fine.

Shpilka waited for me outside, dressed in a dark, linen dress shirt, and escorted me to the concert in silence, clearly not wanting to break my concentration or interfere with any of my thoughts. I said, "Misha, after the concert there is a reception and dinner, but I am not sure it is a good idea for me to bring you. I can explain later—it is nothing that you did. The hostess of the festival is a little extreme in her opinions, and I have to smooth things over."

It was the first time I had spoken his actual name in twenty years. He seemed nonplussed but calm as always. "Of course," he said. "I understand."

The church was packed, and the audience gave a warm ovation once the concert was finished. One of the Peabody deans was in attendance, and she came up to me and took my hand, saying in my ear, "Dear, you played so beautifully. I am sorry Amalia is behaving in such a way, I am sorry that it's you this time. It seems that every year, there is some female artist who is the scapegoat."

Finally, I saw Amalia circumvent the people lined up to congratulate me. She briskly came up and exclaimed, "You are an amaaaazing pianist. I am so sorry there was such a horrible story with this man. *Quel horreur*." Her voice reverberated through the space, over the heads of well wishers, to the entrance of the church.

"Amalia, you know this is untrue. I really apologize for the way it may have looked, but I only wanted to help my friend who would have nowhere to stay that night, as he didn't know we would be in Carcassonne and did not make reservations. You know me better than to believe some story."

But she would have none of it. And suddenly, something snapped inside me.

This is a situation that may replay itself over and over in a young musician's career. Classical music has always depended on the kindness and generosity of patrons. Often, a young artist's relationship with a patron can advance their career more steadfastly than the quality of their actual playing. One can ingratiate themselves endlessly. Or one can tell an insensitive patron to buzz off, like Mozart did to Archbishop Colloredo. (To Mozart's relief, Colloredo then proceeded to literally kick him in the pants and out of Salzburg.) Or one can aim to strike a careful balance, which is what I had been trying to do, until that moment. My relationship with Amalia was fraught with difficulty. Patrons have power over the artist, the festival, the concert series, but the artist has the talent and the pride. For a very young performer, it can be terrifying to stand one's ground: "What if I am never invited back?"

I remembered how I visited Amalia in her home in Washington, DC, how she passed off Schnabel's recording as her own. I had just performed a moving concert with an immensely difficult program, but she still had to humiliate me for supposedly canoodling with Misha. She wanted to control me, to know that she could orchestrate the situation, like a puppeteer. On a deeper level, she wanted to be able to play music. Something about this dichotomy was sickeningly fake, like that Medici banner. I would not partake in the juicy drama she so clearly wanted to play out, even if it meant I would never be invited back. I realized that I no longer needed this engagement. There would be many, many more.

Backstage, as I changed out of my black high-heeled concert shoes, I told Artemisia, "You know, I am not going to go to this dinner. I can't take it. It was such a good concert, and you know, I am so rarely happy with how a concert goes. I just want this night to remain positive in my memory. And I don't want to defend myself against some stupid gossip."

I went to the inn. Misha was waiting for me in his room, reading. I asked, "What would you like to do, if we could do anything now?"

"Inka, I'd like to go to Paris with you. I've never been."

We packed quickly, walked to the train station, and waited for the next train to Paris over Coronas and pizza. We got a small, cheap room in Quartier Latin, overlooking Notre Dame. With no festival patrons or nosy hotel owners around, we were free to do exactly what felt right and natural—be together.

Three days later, I phoned my mother from the Toulouse airport. My tickets to the United States were from Toulouse, so I had to return there by train in order to fly back. Misha, of course, came with me, though his plane tickets to Tel Aviv were from Paris. "I'll figure it out," he told me. "I need these extra hours with you. You know?" On the train back, we drank wine from the same bottle, ate sandwiches while he drew silly pictures for me, and kissed a lot. I told all this to my mom.

"Just what people should do on a train from Paris!" she noted. I was crying big, awkward, uncontrollable tears and look-ing at sheets of paper stained from ham and cheese sandwiches and tomatoes, filled with little cartoons, some of Amalia and Ted the Lard; some illustrating complicated poses from the Kama Sutra (man, wife, and peacock); some making fun of my previ-ous boyfriends.

"Mo-o-om, what am I going to do?"

She tried to console me. "Just wait and see." I was so glad that Mom listened and could be calm and reassuring when I needed her to be. I could talk to my dad about anything, but I never liked burdening him too much with stories about my rela-tionships, and I think he was more than happy about this. He just wanted me to be fine. Mom was the one to listen to details, and she heard them patiently, over and over again in this case.

We would weather the long months apart, living for our phone calls and emails. He would come to visit me in Baltimore and Chicago, and I would go to Israel, where I began to under-stand him not just as my childhood friend but as a brilliant sci-entist, an inventor of uncanny tenacity and sharpness, a man of unwavering ethics and a profound sense of loyalty to people he cared for—somebody I knew would change the world in some way. His stories from his years of army service and in the Talpiot (an exclusive science program for the brightest Israelis) finally came to life for me.

I fell in love with him all over again when I visited him there, a few months after our trip to France. Going through security on the way back to the States felt like having my guts ripped out. For the first time in my life, this felt real—not an idea, not being in love with love, not a drama that might help enrich my art. And it felt horrible. Even the tough El Al security guard gave me a kind smile and a pat on the back as I wept my way through the line. But Misha and I knew that what we had was worth fighting—and waiting—for.

By 2005, I was living on Long Island, where I was pursuing a DMA degree at Stony Brook University. The cell service was terrible; not talking to Misha every day was torturous. I made use of the quiet hours and practiced for my concerts, but the pull of nearby Manhattan was strong. Meanwhile, Misha was applying to MBA programs. He was accepted at Harvard, Columbia, MIT, and Wharton, but he picked Columbia to be with me in New York, eighteen months and countless airfare miles after our meeting in Toulouse. We found a walk-up on 103rd Street and Central Park West. By then, I was a Yamaha artist, and Yamaha had generously provided me with a cabinet upright piano. We would have it all—the park nearby, a subway stop for the B and C lines (we could feel the vibrations of every train underground!), the fire escape, the bed-sized bedroom, and whole-wheat chocolate-chip scones from the Silver Moon bakery two blocks away.

As soon as the apartment was ours, I stuffed a taxicab with helium balloons from a party store and crouched on the floor of a cab as it took me uptown. No more excruciating goodbyes in the Airport Ben Gurion or O'Hare or Kennedy or Milan Malpensa or LAX. No more bed-and-breakfasts in Zichron Yakov and Rosh Pina and Jerusalem—at least, not as Misha's guest from the United States. No more staying in the basement of my parents' house in Skokie without a place of our own. He was coming here, to stay, and I was about to fill our new home with balloons.

Interlude

WHAT'S SO GREAT ABOUT BEETHOVEN ANYWAY? LUDWIG VAN BEETHOVEN, *EROICA VARIATIONS*

I raise my shoulders high, then drop them and bend to the ground, blood rushing to my hands, filling each finger with heaviness and warm calm. I peek onto the stage. Hey there, handsome. Though this one is kind of short. Maybe five feet, at most. A little dusty, perhaps a bit raspy and out of tune. But who cares? Is there anything more poetic, proud, elegantly debonair than the wing of an opened piano, poised for flight?

A week from now, I will be on the stage of Carnegie Hall for my debut solo recital—and now, I am about to play the same program for the elementary schoolers of Grant Avenue Elementary School in the Bronx. They have been told to sit still. Why? Why on earth should they fold their hands in their laps, looking frightened and small? They are about to hear some of the wildest music ever written: Beethoven's *Eroica Variations*.

This piece has been something of a charm for me over the years.

Three years earlier, I am practicing in a piano bar in Verbier because there are no practice rooms available. Tomorrow I'm supposed to play for Petrushansky, and judging by today's master classes, he is tough. I am hoping to study with him long term and want to make a solid impression. At first, I barely notice the curly-haired guy in glasses bopping to Beethoven at the bar. I am trying to choose what to perform for Petrushansky. Should it be this? Or maybe Schubert's *Wanderer Fantasy*?

The guy waves to me. "What is this piece? It's hilarious." He offers me two tickets to his concert tomorrow at the main Verbier Pavilion. "My concert is tonight. These seats are in the front. You'll sit next to some pretty uptight people, but the sound is great!" I look at the name on the tickets and then look up to see Chick Corea turn around and leave abruptly, probably late for a rehearsal. I am left standing next to the white piano with my mouth open.

Two tickets to his big tent concert! So he was the weirdo listening to me practice Beethoven for the past hour on this out-of-tune piano? The next day, I'm dancing in the front row of the Verbier tent and obviously disturbing my neighbors in pearls and Chanel. Chick could not possibly have known that he picked out my good-luck Beethoven piece—the one that will get me into Petrushansky's studio, that helped me understand Fleisher's musical philosophy.

One of Beethoven's most merry tunes, the theme of these variations made it into his Third Symphony, *Eroica*. While he was composing that work, Beethoven was also writing to his brothers about his impending deafness and his wish to end his life. Amid unfathomable suffering, he composed some of his most joyful music. This paradox allows us a peek into the core of his creativity. Beethoven's music is not always meant to be beautiful or pleasing. It can be brutal, disturbing, purposefully excessive, rude and simultaneously transcendent, sublime, bubbling with life, and impossible to categorize. Also, it's often really funny.

Twenty-five minutes of nonstop rambunctious hilarity, the *Variations* open with a crashing E-flat major chord—and then, Beethoven gives you one note: E-flat, the root of the home key. A rest. And then another note: B-flat, a fifth above the E-flat. Then another B-flat. Each note is interrupted by a hiccupping rest. Another E-flat. Is this a joke? Then, a warm line in the left hand that sounds like a bassoon and circumvents the poles of E-flat and B-flat, hinting that something lovely and tender may come from all this nonsense. The next variation hops to life, and finally, the famous *Eroica* motive lands in the listeners' ears, bringing much relief after the goofy introduction. After we hear the theme, we go on a journey, where each short segment tries to outdo the previous one with its audacity and humor. Here is a virtuosic rush of notes in the right hand, tossed off with nonchalance and ease, accompanied by a studious, careful left hand. Here is a mad whirlwind in the left hand, accompanied by a tight-lipped and proper right hand. Here are crashing, repeated chords alternating with timid, ascending notes. Could this be deaf Beethoven's downstairs neighbor, knocking on their ceiling with a broom, then walking upstairs to nosily listen at the door? Here is a pompous, tongue-in-cheek waltz. A silly, high-pitched canon. And then, the lyrical, operatic marvel of Variation 15, which seems to have wandered into the piece by mistake. These adventures are capped off by an energetic fugue that turns into the theme's much-awaited return, a finale so satisfying it feels like a Hollywood ending.

At the elementary school, I walk to the piano and pat it on the side. "Who is ready for some Beethoven?" The students' sudden cheers are contagious, and I abruptly sit down and break into the daring opening. They become silent and engaged, listening to this long, complicated work with obvious wonder. I see a reflection of a pigtailed girl in the piano's lid during the goofy opening variations; she is giggling already. We haven't even gotten to the stomping-feet part!

What's so great about Beethoven? He makes children laugh.

9

A RETURN TO ITALY

I lovingly inhaled the freshness of my sandwich—tomato, basil, and cheese. Around me, passengers were unloading their bags off the trains onto the platforms of Milano Centrale. They argued, laughed, swore, and protested in Italian, and hearing the language was like stepping back to 1989 during my family's immigration journey. The memory was pungent, almost painful. I looked around, half-hoping to see my parents, in their thirties, with the two monstrous suitcases. Back then I would not have been allowed to buy a sandwich at a train station for fear of con- tamination and bad hygiene. Nor could we afford the extrava- gance. Who knew that a fresh panini bought at a little stand in a Milanese train station would taste better than anywhere else outside of Italy? I swallowed the last morsel of fragrant tomato and went to find my next train, to Bologna Centrale.

Two days ago, I had no plans to be in Italy. I had been enjoy- ing a peaceful and stunningly scenic journey up to the Verbier Festival, held at a pristine ski resort in the Swiss Alps. To get there from the Zurich airport, I switched trains three times, and the higher the altitude was, the tinier the train. The one that brought me to the Verbier village looked like a Christmas toy.

I was greeted by Florence, a sharp, redheaded, British psy- chiatrist who was going to be my host. She took me to her house on top of a hill overlooking the entire village. I had landed in

The Sound of Music. Around me, rolling meadows bloomed in the purples and yellows of July, and snowy peaks glistened and resonated with the hypnotic music of cowbells. The cows peeked in and out of the fog, chiming away distantly during the day. In the mornings, they came down closer to the house, greeting me gently as I went for misty morning uphill jogs.

The house, a typical Swiss-style chalet, smelled of pine and banoffee pie, Florence's specialty. Long wooden beams supported the gently sloping roof, and on the little hooks in the beams hung long strings of rosemary, thyme, and garlic. Two proud Persian blues roamed the chalet, ignoring me and my roommate Fei Jin, a pianist from China. As I settled in, I entirely forgot that I was there to play the piano and learn. Everything felt luxurious and unreal.

The Verbier Festival is one of the music world's most exclusive summer events. Only top-selling names come to perform in its giant white tent, set up amid mountains, chalets, luxury restaurants, and ski shops. Every village store becomes an emblem of classical music. I got a kick out of the large posters of Evgeny Kissin and Gidon Kremer smiling geekily in the windows of extravagant lingerie boutiques. There is an orchestra of young musicians, handpicked from around the world by the festival's administration, and also a very small academy for young soloists who come for performances and master classes with world-renowned older artists. The academy accepts just a few people per instrument. It is nearly impossible to get in, as thousands around the world apply. This is where a high-powered recommendation letter can speak stronger than the most exquisite audition tape. I tried for a few years and, with a letter from Fleisher, was finally invited to come. When I received the acceptance call and reported it to him, he raised his monumental eyebrows and mumbled skeptically, "So, you got in." He was never one for much encouragement. But his letter had done the job.

As I felt consistently more unsettled with Fleisher, I looked for solutions and, through friends and fellow musicians abroad, learned about Boris Petrushansky, who taught at the Accademia Pianistica Internazionale in Imola, Italy. This man was reputed to be an imaginative, exuberant teacher in the tradition of

Neuhaus and the old Moscow school. The "Russian school" of piano playing, to which it belonged, has so many connotations at this point that it is nearly impossible to define—just as with any other "national" piano school. In my early musical experience, it meant a relaxed physical approach that came from the shoulder, so that the arm weight was carried into the fingertips, and a detailed, refined approach to sound—making the piano sing, coaxing luminosity and liquid legato out of the instrument Stravinsky referred to as just another kind of percussion. But some now associate the term with the kind of bombastic playing that does well in international competitions thanks to its athletic infallibility, while others link it to sentimental and indulgent performances. (Fleisher often alluded to the latter two definitions.) As with any artistic terminology, all these ideas certainly stem from reality to some degree, but they are limiting nonetheless. If a great teacher imparts musical lessons to a student, and that pianist then passes them on to their own student without internalizing, shaping, and changing the ideas in relevant ways, simply mimicking them, then the original insights can become mannerisms that make the music sound insincere, even tasteless.

Petrushansky had studied in Moscow with Heinrich Neuhaus, teacher to the great Odessa-born pianists Sviatoslav Richter and Emil Gilels, and with Lev Naumov, who was known for flights of the imagination that drew from poetry, theater, paintings, and anything and everything around else him, leading to very dramatic, colorful, and unusual interpretations. Naumov had many prize-winning students, but what drew me to Petrushansky was the poetry and lyricism with which he treated sound. I felt that my training with Fleisher had affected my own natural sound and I had become far more analytical than before. While this was not a bad thing in and of itself, it prevented me from playing in a way that felt like my own. I thought I needed somebody like Petrushansky not only to help me feel comfortable with my own sound but also to broaden my palette and really make the piano speak. Neuhaus's motto had been "Playing the piano is easy," and I wanted to feel that ease, that complete physical relaxation and oneness with the instrument. Petrushansky and I wrote back and forth for a while, and while he liked my recordings and was interested in meeting me, there seemed no feasible way for us to get together. He had no plans to be in the United States, and I had none to be in Italy. I had put the idea on the back burner and focused on completing my studies with Fleisher while persisting on finding my own way. I figured that eventually, somehow we would meet.

On the first morning of the Verbier master classes, I took the downward path from Florence's house to a small hall about a mile away. For that morning, I had prepared Beethoven's *Eroica Variations*, a piece I learned at eighteen and resuscitated that spring, when I was twenty-four. This piece tests the virtuosic limits of the pianist while challenging them to sound like an orchestra; it shares the theme with the finale of Beethoven's Third Symphony. It was this piece that had so pleased Fleisher when I played it for him at Peabody.

I expected the pianist Stephen Kovacevich to be that morning's artist-teacher. At ten o'clock, the festival manager brought out a man in a linen summer suit and a matching tie and handkerchief. He had a graying mane of hair and fiery, green eyes beneath wire-rim glasses, and he projected an air both intellectual and ardent. The manager announced that, due to illness, Mr. Kovacevich had to cancel his Verbier duties. But instead of him, the festival was proud to welcome one of Europe's foremost pedagogues and pianists, Boris Petrushansky.

Unable to contain my excitement, I raised my hand and introduced myself, and with characteristic Russian Jewish sarcasm and warmth, he exclaimed in Russian, "If Mohammed does not come to the mountain, the mountain comes to Mohammed!" Obviously, he was the mountain.

I did not get to play until the next morning, but the first day of lessons was enough for me to realize that this man was someone truly special. There were five pianists in the group—two from the States, including myself; one from China; one from Germany; and one from Bulgaria. A sizeable audience had filled the little hall to hear the master class. One of the musicians played Scriabin's Sonata no. 5, a maddening, wild work of sensuous abandon. He executed the piece with obvious, painstaking attention to the details of the score and with a bright crispness: It sounded as if silver coins were thrown on the floor, hard, from the elbow. Petrushansky spoke some German, immediately translated by a translator into English. He praised the student's respect for the intricacies of the score and his quick fingers but urged him to go deeper.

Getting more and more inspired by the moment, he used seemingly far-fetched images, earthy ones, of smoke and steam rising from cauldrons in the earth; of pedaling in a way that sounds like a whirling mass of water rising and then cascading down with enormous horsepower; of the wide-eyed, fragile innocence of the melody that takes over after the opening—perhaps a leaf that is shaking back and forth, about to break off, and then falling slowly. He spoke like an actor or poet, mesmerized and spontaneous, and it was impossible not to hang onto every syllable. He quoted whole stanzas of Boris Pasternak from memory, gently moved the student aside, and sat down to demonstrate, and I realized that the sound he made at the piano was different from any sound I had heard previously. It was as if the piano suddenly opened up and spoke in a liquid, throaty, heated voice. There were not separate notes or phrases but sound worlds—exactly the ones he described, coming to life. What he did with pedal was nothing short of amazing. There were dozens of gradations in how he used it, creating echoes, connecting sounds that I never thought could be connected until they made new ones, then fluttering the pedal until they evaporated like a flock of small birds, disappearing in the distance.

I always thought I could make the piano talk colorfully, passionately, and convincingly, but this was something new, a way of playing and treating musical material that was creative and alive but clearly stemmed from a deep technical knowledge of the instrument and from total physical freedom. I had never been a tense performer and always felt free and relaxed with music and the piano—that is, until my Fleisher years. But this was another level of freedom, a fluid way of using the entire hand, arm, body in the most relaxed way possible to make sound. It was also another way of hearing, of imagining the most vivid and lively possibilities for the notes before they sounded.

For the next day's lesson, Petrushansky called me to the stage and asked me to translate for the American pianist, who played some Chopin. He clearly didn't like her playing and spoke ruthless Russian. I had to politely translate for the pianist and the Swiss audience. The exchange went something like this:

HE: (to the student) Do you understand? (to himself) God-dammit, she doesn't understand anything. This is ridiculous. Terrible! (to the student) Look at your fingers. It's as if you are picking up something disgusting. Caress the piano! *No! No! No!* This is not the way. There is no accent here. The phrase *has* to go down! Don't you hear it? Play it again.

ME: (to the student and the audience, sheepishly) The maestro wants you to try it again, this time with a diminuendo.

His hot temper didn't do anything for my nerves, and I knew I had to play the next day because we had run out of time. I chatted with him after the class, and he seemed pleased that I happened to be there and well-disposed toward hearing me play. I had never felt like a student when I performed, but here, I suddenly felt like a little pupil, wanting to impress this Russian master. I just knew I had to play well.

The next morning, bright and early, I arrived at the small hall to warm up. Once the class began, I expected to get through about two minutes of the twenty-five-minute *Eroica Variations*. In a master class, the performer usually plays through a piece, and the teaching artist withholds comments until after the performance. During the previous day's class, each student had been stopped after about five minutes. Petrushansky's eloquence and wealth of advice could not remain bundled up inside of him for the duration of an entire piece. He heard so many things that needed fine-tuning, improvement, or elaboration that he had to stop a student early on, if not straight at the beginning. I would learn this in due time. But this time, I was amazed to get past the five-minute mark with my Beethoven and, after each variation, expected to hear a "Thank you" that would signal me to stop. But it never came, and I played through the variations, to the last "Cantabile" variation on to the winding fugue and joyful,

With Petrushansky outside Accademia Pianistica Internazionale in Imola.

hilarious finale. I now wish I cherished that moment more because I would never again get to play a complete piece in one go in a lesson with him.

He looked familial, almost paternal, as he came up to me and said, *"Molodets"*—"Well done." He went on to say that he wanted to introduce me to Franco Scala, the director of the Accademia in Imola. I was surprised, as I didn't feel all that sure that I had played my best, but his reaction meant that he heard the real me, my own voice.

* * *

Accademia Pianistica Internazionale was a small but very prestigious and exclusive piano academy in the tiny town of Imola, in Italy's Emilia Romagna region. It seemed appropriate that Imola was also famous for its Formula One racetrack: The Accademia produced an equally large number of competition winners in the piano world. I didn't care, though, if it was an airport hangar or a farm I had to go to and whether I was the only pianist there or I had to compete against a battalion of other players. If I had to go and audition at the North Pole in order to study with this man, I was happy to do it. Two days after my lesson with Petrushansky, I boarded a train in Zurich to take me to Milan, then on to Bologna, and finally Imola.

To get to Imola from Bologna, you had to take another twenty-five-minute train ride through Emilia Romagna. Later, each subsequent arrival at the Bologna train station would like a visit to an old, familiar apartment. There were the four ticket windows, with the people attempting and always failing to line up; a large smoking room; and a waiting area with the energy of a gambling parlor. A bell sounded every minute or so, and a singsong voice called out, "Partenza!" or "Arrivo!" followed by seductive-sounding destinations like Venezia Santa Lucia, Roma Termini, or Firenze Maria Novella. Before my departure, I always made sure to pop into a small shop for some colorful, unexpectedly high-quality makeup. One late night, when every train service worker seemed to be on a prolonged strike, I waited for a train to Florence and had dinner at the only open restaurant, a McDonald's. I ate the freshest, tastiest chicken salad in my recent memory, with thin slivers of parmigiano; fresh vine grape tomatoes; and happy, crunchy seasonal greens.

The *binarios*—underground passageways that connected the departure gates—smelled of urine, cigarettes, and espresso. For fifty cents, the coffee machines at every staircase produced tiny plastic cups half-filled with thick, dark deliciousness. Over the years, across my many subsequent trips, the station got a slick makeover—every *binario* had a flat-screen TV, fancier candy machines, and newly painted benches, and they started smelling fresher. It was as if the old apartment got a face-lift. But the energy was unchanged: The passengers gulped down their little cups of fuel, smoked incessantly, littered, lingered, rushed, and argued.

Emilia Romagna is a relatively flat region, not as voluptuously scenic as Tuscany but, in the springs and summers, lush with fruits and sunflowers. Imola greets you with a dilapidated, pink, little station. A long, maple-lined boulevard quickly takes you into the town, passing tiny bakeries and bars, and on to medieval city gates almost entirely covered by wisteria. (My suitcase would hobble after me on the cobblestones like a faithful puppy, awkward but not heavy enough to prevent me from popping into a bakery for an espresso and a morsel of something filled with weightless hazelnut mousse.) The clock tower in the middle of the square serves as a meeting place for the Imolese. The shops here are smaller and more expensive; the bars, larger, wider, intricately decorated, and stuffed with vases of chocolates and biscotti. Ubiquitous old gentlemen in suits and hats arrive on their crusty bicycles to sit outside the bars at small tables with their beers, looking you up and down. Take a right at Via Emilia, turn left at the coral-colored church, right at the lingerie shop, and keep walking until you suddenly see a medieval cake-like thing. This is La Rocca Sforzesca, a castle reputedly designed by Leonardo de Vinci. Today, it houses Accademia Pianistica Internazionale "Incontri col Maestro."

The Accademia consisted of a hall downstairs and four large studios upstairs, plus a little office and a large, circular veranda overlooking the castle grounds, the moat, and the surrounding town. In the brutal summers, the old stones preserved a pleasant chill. In the bone-chilling Italian winters, one had to climb a ladder in the building's only bathroom and find the correct switch to activate the heat in the studios. A lot of the time, you could still see your own breath as you played.

When I finally arrived at Imola, I was greeted by Maestro Franco Scala, and thrown off by his appearance, I mumbled something unintelligible instead of my planned *"Piacere."* The academy's director must have looked like a screen legend in his youth. I played the *Eroica Variations* for him and Petrushansky, and they chatted for a while afterward, making me feel completely invisible. Finally, Petrushansky told me that Franco wanted me in the academy but that I would have to play an official audition in a few months. Earning an artist diploma at the academy simply required a certain number of lessons over several years and a successful "final exam" performance. Could I come back to Italy to do this?

I hadn't yet figured out how I would study in this artist diploma program. Would I move to Imola, get a bike, learn Italian, and pass my winters in this sleepy Felliniesque town, or would I just travel there every month for two-hour lessons? How would I pay for all the flights? I didn't like the idea of exams, auditions, or being treated like a student. I simply didn't feel like one anymore. I had my own concerts to play and career to develop. If I wanted to make this work, I would have to combine it with finishing my doctorate at Stony Brook. I wanted this opportunity to work with Petrusha, as I would call him, and, in a way, get back to my pianistic roots, so I had to make it work. I could travel to Imola when it was possible, have many lessons over a few days, and then go back to the States. Before going back to Verbier, I agreed to return for the formal audition in August.

Petrusha told me that he would be judging a piano competition outside of Piacenza at that time. "Even without me, I think you could win," he said, "but with me there, it will help." It was like he was saying, "If you come, there will be a ribbon waiting with your name on it." This didn't sound very convincing from an ethical perspective, but I'd been told so many times, this was how competitions worked. So I figured, what the hell? Nothing wrong with having a jury member who actually likes me and who will be my teacher! Everybody else did this, so why couldn't I? My plan was to come to Imola, play for him, and take the train to Piacenza. Hopefully, once there, I would find a place to stay, figure out the details of practicing, and spend a few days amid the joys of Tuscany. Then back to Imola, my audition at the Accademia, a day in Florence, and finally to the States.

So two months after meeting Franco Scala, I came to Italy again—with the support of Hilda Goodwin, the woman who had called me "Ms. Chutzpah" in my early days at Peabody. I arrived at the Santa Maria-Teresia convent in Imola and pressed the button marked "*Offizio*." I was buzzed in once just enough time passed to make me wonder if I was in the right place. I found myself inside a four-story stone complex, in a darkish overgrown garden with a small statue of the Virgin. A stubby, short-haired grandma stomped down the staircase. She wore a squarish wool skirt that brought to mind the Soviet Union. She grabbed my suitcase, jabbering at me in unstoppable Italian. "*Mi chiamo Mamma Maria*" was the part I understood. At that point, my Italian could really be boiled down to two important phrases—"What is the price of this ice cream cone?" and "Where is the bathroom?"—but Mamma Maria paid no heed to my sad attempts to tell her that I spoke almost *niente*. Starting at that moment, she settled into the first of many long-winded, loud, and totally one-sided conversations in Italian with me.

The convent operated like a black-market hotel. Arrangements between nuns and students of the Accademia Pianistica were made the day of arrival, usually by the students' professors. For twenty-five Euros a day, I had three meals, a hard bed with a giant crucifix watching over me, and a 9 p.m. curfew. The curfew meant that if by 8:59 I was not inside the wrought-iron gates, then I would be left to my own devices. On summer evenings, with the locals out for their *passagiata*, this curfew felt like punishment for being too poor to afford a real hotel.

Passagiata is an activity Italians love, and it is best performed with someone on your arm. (No shame in doing it solo, though.) Picture proud peacocks, strutting down the street—whether it's pedestrian friendly or not. Ignore the cars; they honk for a while and go the other way. Fellows on scooters pass by close enough to rub cheeks. Or they might make an obscene gesture involving the elbow. Blow them a kiss; they are charming. Armed with an enormous cup of gelato and maybe a cigarette that you really don't have to smoke as long as it looks cool, walk back and forth slowly, checking out other people's outfits. It is a wondrously relaxing and engrossing activity, and it can be performed anywhere. When really at one with the *passagiata*, lulled by the slow rhythm of the walk, you can consider the earth's rotation and your small role within the human race: to walk slowly and consume great quantities of ice cream.

No *passagiata* for me on those first few nights in Imola. Under the watchful eye of Mamma Maria, I chewed dutifully. *"Mangia, mangia! Poverina stanca, mangia!"* This was Italian food for people with dentures: burrata mozzarella, some kind of cooked vegetable, soft pasta, and fish steamed with a simple sauce. It was bland and strangely calming, but I wanted to be outside, inhaling bresaola or prosciutto accompanied by fizzy, blood-red lambrusco and watching armies of Italians parade by me in their skin-tight garb. Lying in the small bed with a tiny light, protected from the joys of the outside world by heavy shutters, a wooden Jesus, chamomile tea, and a fat Russian novel, I wondered if every night in Imola from now on would have to end at 9:00.

The next morning, bright and early, Petrusha picked me up and took me to his house on a hill outside Imola. We had a three-hour lesson on the Brahms F Minor Sonata on his beat-up Steinway. I'd played this piece so much that it was crusty around the edges. His demonstrations of how to make a theme bend and flow in just the right way were forcing me to listen differently—not just with character and form in mind but also with a very particular focus on how to make each note alive, as if breathed or spoken. This had to do with both hearing the sound in great detail and being able to predict how it would connect with the other sounds to become like natural speech. I began to feel that at any given moment, the music could be a living creature. If I did not give it life, though, it would die before having a chance. This experience was entirely new, one that I would conjure up many times in the future when practicing or performing. It was a practice that helped me prevent music making from becoming a routine, even though it was one. As with anything new, it would take time for me to really absorb it. But as I did over months and years, it took my playing to another level.

That evening, I wandered along Imola's small streets and by its shops. By eight o'clock, I had somehow found myself at a trattoria in the company of a curly-haired, dewy-eyed Sicilian pianist named Alfredo who had also come to audition. I didn't understand a word Alfredo said to me, but he was needy. I enjoyed my solitude, and his banter and predictably handsome features got in the way. To be polite, I decided to try and lie to him in Italian: *"Io sono sposato, mio marito habite a America"*—"I married, my husband living on America."

But this made no difference to Alfredo, who was ordering lots of wine and pasta with *lardo*, an Amalia specialty. Mistaking *lardo* for *lardon*—French for *egg*—I was disappointed to find out that I was having jellyfish-like slices of pork fat for dinner. I ate no food and drank twice the wine. At 8:50, I decided to turn into a pumpkin and told Alfredo, "Sleep I must in convent." Before he had a chance to protest, I put some Euros on the table; made a hazy goodbye gesture; and dragged my feet, jellyfish-like, for my nightly date with Mamma Maria. After the *lardo*, I looked forward to her healthy food.

I don't know whether Alfredo was accepted into the Accademia. I never saw him again. Perhaps I got it all wrong, and he was not a pianist at all and had nothing to do with the auditions but was just some random Italian guy. The next morning at breakfast, Mamma Maria seemed either furious, excited, or both: *"Un uomo ha venuto sta mattina, ha lasciato quel cosa per lei."* She was telling me that a man had come in the morning and left something for me. This could be a little scandalous, for men were not allowed into the convent, and the nuns would definitely be wondering how I found the time to pick one up. She presented me with a paper package, holding it carefully with two fingers, like it had been dipped in poison. I unfolded it, and a black gauze scarf with beaded flowers fell out, fluttery and nocturnally glamorous. I would go on to wear it for concerts, covering my shoulders with it before and after the performance. The first few times I put it on, I wondered what had happened to Alfredo, until the memory of him faded and the scarf was just a strange, beautiful gift from Italy.

* * *

The competition, held in Val Tidone, a town snugly situated among the luscious hills of Tuscany, began with a meeting in the town hall. The meeting was held strictly in Italian, with no hope for translation of any kind. This peeved the more than ninety entrants, who had come from all over the world. The number of pianists was unusually large, but this was not surprising, seeing as the Queen Elizabeth of Belgium competition had just come to a close, and the pianists had simply migrated south to try their luck again. In some ways, jurors and competitors are nomads who survive by traveling from one contest to the next. The only difference between them is that the competitors mostly lose money, and the jurors keep the cash.

During the meeting, we were told by an angry young competition coordinator named Benvolio that we would get thirty minutes of practice a day. We then drew lots, and I found out I would have to play the following morning. Most competitions offer musicians ample practice time, at least a few hours. A half-hour was ridiculous, but it also made me feel like this was a Tuscan vacation. What else was there to do, other than meet people, sit in a café, enjoy life, and hope for the best?

This competition wasn't offering a giant prize or concert opportunities, just some money and a few televised performances for the three laureates immediately afterward—a nice bonus. Usually, large and important competitions have prerecorded auditions and then accept about thirty people on average. Then comes grueling rounds for which each competitor must prepare hours and hours of music. Luckily, this little competition was practically stress free, as the repertoire was not huge, and the haphazardness of the practice situation put everybody in the same boat, relaxed and generally carefree. This one wouldn't make or break anybody's career.

The practice room assigned to me for that day was only a few blocks from the town hall. When I entered the required room in the small building, I found myself staring at the beards of Vladimir Ilych Lenin and his sidekicks, Marx and Engels. "How perfect," I thought. It turned out to be the headquarters of the town's Communist Party. The room was painted red, and the Communist fathers' portraits sternly looked down at my hands as I quickly warmed up on the upright piano. They were not very good portraits; if Lenin, Marx, and Engels had a cartoon show on Nickelodeon, this is what they would look like. I had to stop myself from playing the Soviet anthem. After some scales, Brahms touch-ups, and a few moments on "La Campanella," I was kicked out by a studious-looking Russian guy with long, greasy hair; glasses; and a giant stack of Chopin's music. "Good luck getting through that in thirty minutes," I thought, leaving the little room. As I shut the door, he began the fastest and cleanest Chopin Etude, op. 10, no. 1, I'd ever heard.

There turned out to be absolutely nothing to do in Val Tidone but enact imaginary jokes: "A Turkish Baha'i pianist, an Estonian pianist, a Ukrainian American pianist, a Roman pianist, and a Florentine pianist all walk into a bar . . ." It was a fun-loving bunch, and I immediately bonded with a slightly older pianist from Florence, Alessandra Ammara, a down-to-earth firecracker simultaneously spirited and calm. She had come from the Queen Elizabeth competition in Belgium, and we bonded while gossiping about jurors and competition politics; laughing them off between glasses of wine; and then moving on to much more serious musical topics, like Messiaen's chamber music and the late Beethoven string quartets. We finished off the evening in the apartment Alessandra shared with a group of Italians, cooking a large pot of pasta with eggplant sauce and delving deeper into musical discussions. It turned out that we both had worked with Fleisher at some point, and we talked about Schnabel, Schubert, and Fleisher's amazing recordings with the Cleveland Orchestra. I knew I had found a kindred spirit for life. We made plans for me to visit her in Florence after my Imola audition, and I went back to my hostel.

The next morning, I was waiting backstage, downstairs in the tower. The ease and lightness of the previous night had evaporated, and I would have sold my soul for a place to warm up before the performance. I clearly wanted too much. I was about to go out onstage and delve into "La Campanella" cold. Each entrant had to start with a swashbuckling etude. This was probably to test how all of us would play technically difficult stuff without having practiced or warmed up. It was stupid but quite typical of a competition—the art of music-making separated from the pursuit of technical virtuosity.

I had no cell phone and had been unable to get in touch with Petrusha the previous day, but one look at him, sitting among the very prominent and very mafioso-like jurors, told me that he expected to be elevated to Olympus by my performance. After I finished my program of Liszt and Chopin, I figured there was no reason to return to the Communist headquarters at all because there was no chance of me being in the finals. They had to pick eight people from ninety, and I just hadn't played well enough.

When I illicitly called Petrusha from a pay phone during lunch, however, he told me I had played great and would definitely be in the finals. This sounded fishy, but I didn't ask questions. I ran over to the room with the Three Soviet Stooges and, I am embarrassed to admit, kicked out an eleven-year-old pianist, claiming seniority. When the Brahms F Minor needs to be performed and you have thirty minutes, you do what you must. By the next night, I had received formal confirmation that I made it to the finals.

The morning of my final round, I woke up early. The other girls I was sharing a room with were still in their beds when I left. I spent a little longer at the corner espresso bar than I intended, but I was in no particular hurry, as there was, again, no place to warm up. When I saw that it was soon time to play, I went upstairs to change into concert clothes.

Inserting my key into the door, I became aware of a sound I could not identify. It was nasal, definitely tonal, seeming to come from multiple corners of the room. The door opened, and I faced eight male accordionists, immersed in rehearsal. They were situated on the girls' unmade beds; none of the beds' actual occupants were in the room. The most surreal part was their choice of repertoire. They were playing an accordion arrangement of Beethoven's late String Quartet no. 15. This music had been in my head for two days, ever since Alessandra and I talked about it. Its intimate character worked well on accordion, and it sounded like a Central European folk dance. All this was fascinating, but how was I going to get over to my bed and retrieve my clothes when a two-hundred-pound man with an accordion was sitting on top of them, immersed in the second theme of this beautiful work?

Eventually, I politely squeezed through, to their great annoyance, and pulled out my black, frilly clothes from underneath the accordionist. They grumbled at me in what I guessed to be Czech because I was teetering on the edge of understanding the words without actually grasping onto their meaning. I never found why they were there.

I ended up getting second place in the competition, which I was quite happy with. The winners' concert was to be televised, but for some reason, it had to start at eleven at night in a dungeon of a wine cellar amid lavishly priced wine bottles and even more lavishly dressed night owls. After the concert, at around 1 a.m., the multicourse celebratory dinner began. Most of the male judges became hopelessly drunk, and the more they imbibed, the more they hit on the women. Luckily, the group did not include my teacher-to-be; he had already gone back to Imola. I would never see him behave in any way other than absolutely gallantly.

* * *

I was accepted into the Accademia, and for the next three years, I traveled to Italy every few months. Sometimes, I came for just a few days, with daily five-hour lessons. Sometimes, they were more spread out, and I allowed myself short trips to Florence, Verona, Venice, Rome, Siena, and Ravenna.

On one such jaunt to Florence, Alessandra met me near the cathedral of Santa Maria dei Fiori, our usual meeting place, and said that we were going to take a short trip back toward Bologna. There was somebody she wanted me to meet. The lonely station where we got off looked and smelled like a large public restroom. The town's name was Crevalcore, and I thought it should bear the distinction of being the ugliest town in Italy. Before I had the time to wonder why she had brought me there, two guys with giant bouquets of field flowers were hugging and kissing us. "Inna, meet Clark!" One of the guys, tall, green-eyed, and tan, bent down to kiss my hand elegantly. We stuffed ourselves into a jeep and bopped up and down a long road between corn and sunflower fields and pear gardens, through a few ramshackle neighborhoods, and past a lonely church and cemetery, before we violently veered left. I saw giant iron gates and then a rugged, weedy, murky castle with two towers and a big garden; a table set outside; candles hanging from trees; and a large group of noisy people chomping on breadsticks, cheese, and fresh tomatoes. This was how I met Peter Pan.

Clark Lawrence was an arts history major who had moved to Europe after college in Maine and never looked back. He rented a part of the fifteenth-century Castello di Galeazza to use as a bed and breakfast, recital and exhibition space, ever-growing garden, and meeting place for a zany international community. As a local paper wrote, to the immense displeasure of the castle's stodgy aristocratic owners, it was "something resembling a hippie commune." To me, it was a bohemian paradise in the middle of nowhere.

Clark started the Reading Retreats in Rural Italy in December 1996. He had wanted to welcome small groups of people to a quiet, nontouristy place in the country where everyone could bond by reading the same books and discussing them over dinner. Soon it became clear that people just wanted to pick out books from the giant library and read whatever they wanted, so the traditional book club fell through. Clark made his living taking care of the castle for an aristocratic owner, and he hosted concerts, art exhibits, and other events there. People would come from other European countries at first and then from as far as Australia and the United States. Sometimes these were groups that wanted a place to study Italian or get together for a class about opera or just live in the countryside and visit nearby Ferrara and Modena. In the evening, everyone got together for late dinners that they prepared together, forming a cheerful, colorful, improvised family.

Clark employed "interns" who usually came from American, Australian, or English colleges, thinking that they would take part in some academic research or curate an exhibit or teach something to somebody. They ended up washing dishes; weeding the garden; helping to cook; biking to town for groceries; and relaxing into the slow-paced, lulling lifestyle of the castle that had become an escape, a place for contemplation, and an opportunity for rustic down time for so many. Everybody who stayed pitched in a little bit to help, as an old castle is not easy to take care of. For forty Euros, one got a bed, three communal meals served in the garden in the summers and in the heated kitchen in the winters, and all the wine one could want to drink. Sometimes, Clark hosted exhibits of unknown and brilliant painters, like Yuri Zurkan, who came from Odessa and who looked as if he had stepped out of Tarkovsky's *Andrei Rublev*. Yuri painted haunting fantasy portraits in the style of Fra Angelica and reportedly was offered a commission by the Russian oligarch Roman Abramovich to paint the Virgin Mary holding a soccer ball, to honor Abramovich's purchase of a British soccer team. (Yuri declined.)

That first evening at the castle, Alessandra and I gave a miniature impromptu concert in the library on an old upright with yellowed keys. Over the piano hung a painting that could have been a dark Miró, and candles lit up the room. Zurkan's painting of a knight stared down from the wall, all nose and feathers, and the rest of the space was taken up by books, books, books. People and their wineglasses looked permanently sunk into the two ottomans and the couch, loving everything that came out of the little piano. The omnisexual Clark poured more wine, and nobody's behind went unpinched as he handed out small sandwiches on plates. A fluffy tiramisu appeared, brought out by Stacy the Australian intern. For many hours, we stayed and talked in a variety of languages, getting noisier and rowdier as the night progressed.

There were six rooms for sleeping, some large, some small; one kitchen and two modernized bathrooms; many staircases; and a tower that was officially off-limits but could be climbed anyway if the owners were not around. Because they were never really around, exploring was not a problem. That first night in the castle, I slept in the little, rhombic room next to the library, with old frescoes of fawns and hunting scenes and coats of armor. Eight-foot-tall shutters opened onto the garden, where the invisible, brutal Italian mosquitoes ruled the night. I had to pinch myself to believe this place. From then on, I had an invitation to stay at the castle whenever I came to Italy for lessons. This involved a few more train rides to and from Imola but was just about the opposite of staying in a convent.

I never understood and still do not understand how the dwellers of the castle survived from day to day—but they did and were some of the happiest people I have ever met, with Clark as their captain. His gentle manner, unfiltered humor, openness, and talent for making reality out of pure fantasy made him a dream host and something of a Peter Pan. He still hosts some of the most magical parties in Europe. One stormy evening in late fall, I arrived at the castle soaked to the brim, exhausted after having taken the wrong train, which had brought me to a ghetto on the outskirts of Bologna. Julia, a British translator from Bologna and a friend of the castle, picked me up at Crevalcore. My arms were sore from an especially grueling session with Petrushansky, and I could barely lift my bag. I was generally annoyed at everything and everyone. I climbed the grand main staircase, which was lined with perversely big pumpkins, and made my way into the library, past the old chest near the entrance. The next moment I was screaming, my arms whirling like a windmill as I wrestled with a giant ghost of satin sheets. The ghost grabbed and groped and pinched me everywhere, making obscene sounds before breaking into a guffaw. Clark emerged from the cut-up sheets. "Just practicing for the Halloween party!" he announced.

And some party that was. The castle had been transformed from the summer resort I remembered into a ghoulish, web-encrusted haunted house. Clark singlehandedly turned the nearby forest preserves into a horror trail, with hand-made monsters waiting at every turn, riding down pulleys, using every branch and crevice in the earth to give you a heart attack. At the end of the trail, he, dressed in a clown suit, waited with a chain-saw. As screaming guests appeared, he turned on the chainsaw and chased them back into the castle, where a dinner of pumpkin soup, pumpkin tortelli, and quail awaited them.

Clark loved music. He listened to recordings passionately, always curious, deliberate in his questions, and definite in his tastes. Playing concerts at the castle, whether on the little upright in the library or a rented grand in the stables or the garden, I opened up completely to him and a small audience, taking what I learned from Petrushansky, trying to implement it my own way, channeling the magic of this place. Everyone has that place they travel to in their mind when they want to get away. For me that place is the Castello di Galeazza. When I want a boost of inspiration, I mentally transport myself to the castle from wherever I am.

* * *

Each time my train would roll into the little, pink, dilapidated station at Imola, I had the uncanny sensation of arriving home. This really didn't have much to do with where I currently lived or where I was from. The truth was that I had found a musical home and a teacher from whom I learned—not in subtle ways but in hungry bites. Filling the time between excruciatingly intense, exhilarating lessons and practicing, I made a point of stopping at a few favorite little spots: Pasticceria Rocca, with its tiny cream puffs of coffee and chestnut filling; Calzedonia, the cartoonishly colorful stocking shop; and a few others, marked on the map of my mind like colored chips on a board game. I savored each stop, filled to the brim with my latest lesson. Looking at clothing prices and savoring pastries, while in my head mulling over every sound Petrusha had shown me, thinking about pedaling, questioning the truth behind certain musical gestures—this felt like the complete package, the pleasantly mundane and the once-in-a-lifetime exalted meeting in one place. During winter visits, the Emilia Romagna cold seeped through to the bones, to be warded off with hot, milky coffee and a novel at the convent. More than anything, I knew that I was undergoing a personal renaissance. Making music became lush and rich, a delicious challenge, a communion with the piano so powerful and physically satisfying that it made all my previous tribulations worthwhile.

Exams at Imola were more demanding than any American conservatory or university. The day before, you had to give the faculty a choice of two two-hour solo recital programs and two concerti, and during the exam, the faculty acted like a competition jury. Winning competitions was a very important goal at Imola (too important, perhaps), so the exams were designed to emulate them.

One of Petrushansky's neighbors—and one of the people who would eventually serve on my exam committee—was a legendary Russian pianist. He was known for his recordings of Liszt, and I'd been hearing his name for as long as I could remember. One of the most problematic things in my profession is the idea of "untouchable greatness." This is especially prevalent in, though of course not at all limited to, the old Russian school. The Russians simply knew better how to play the piano, supposedly, and nobody in the world could measure up. There was their way of doing things, and there was the wrong way. This attitude lives on in many piano lessons around the world, still—the ones that tell the young pianist exactly what to do while squashing their desire to explore and ask questions and doubt and try again. What if I simply didn't like something that a "great one" did? What if I didn't think it was that great? Why did there necessarily have to be a right way and a wrong way when we were dealing with something as fragile as human emotions transcribed on paper in little dots and lines?

In my second year of the Artist Diploma program, I was playing an exam with Brahms's F Minor Sonata #3, which I had also played at the Val Tidone competition. I had learned it with Ann Schein and carried it with me through life like a suit of armor. As long as I had my Brahms in my hands, I felt invincible. Petrushansky had given me a fresh outlook on the piece, and I felt great about it.

During the second movement, I heard a boisterous snore. As I did my best to bring to life the epigraph at the start of this mesmerizing music, which slowly unfolds from shy, soft, falling thirds to a passionate, valedictory hymn—"two hearts beating as one"—the legendary pianist, his head nestled in the crest of the Henle score, was having a nap. Later that afternoon, I pointedly asked Petrushansky what the napping adjudicator thought of my playing. "You don't want to know," he said. When I pressed him, he told me, "He said you should go back to your husband or boyfriend or lover and make fried schnitzel for him in the kitchen because playing the Brahms F Minor is not for small girls." Had Petrushansky's neighbor somehow gotten wind that Fleisher had once called me a really good German milkmaid?

"*Bezobraziye*," added Petrushansky—"disgrace." "Just ignore it." Petrushansky had always been different from many of his older colleagues. And of course, I'd ignore it, as I always had. Women who play the piano (feel free to substitute the name of any other instrument—or just put *conductor* or *composer*) have been letting this crap roll off their backs for centuries. What choice did I have?

What was so unique about Petrushansky's teaching? I would be able to identify it after I went back to see him a year after I received my artist diploma from the Accademia. I went to Verona and switched trains to Pine, a village in the mountains near Trento and Bolzano, close enough to the German border that apple strudel popped up on the menu of every establishment. Petrushansky taught summer courses there and invited me to come and play for him. I checked into a small hotel where the average age of the guest was eighty, a calm and genteel place that you might visit to enjoy mountain air and bath treatments. As I walked that evening to greet him, I was swallowed up by the memories of Verbier and meeting him for the first time. Pine also had an Alpine feel, with pristine wooden houses, clouds you could almost touch, and many hilly walks. Unlike Verbier, thankfully, it lacked an A-list crowd, which it made up for with twelfth-century churches, matronly old ladies with *sacchetinos*, and elementary school children singing and playing in squares.

At the music hall, I listened to him give a lesson on Beethoven's Sonata opus 53, "Waldstein" to a sixteen-year-old boy from Kyiv. I realized with a jolt just how much I had learned from Petrushansky and how so many things had already become a natural, integral part of my own playing, giving it a quality of sound, pedaling, richness, and detail it didn't have before. I thought of how he phrased and shaped sixteenth notes to make them sound like a constantly moving stream, the way his playing spoke vividly, sensuously, but always relevant to the music and the composer. The way his imagination boiled wildly, how he oversaw musical intentions from a bird's-eye view while conjuring up something spontaneous and magical. I remembered how his imagery had struck me at first and how I could not always relate to it and how I then gradually began to see it not just as a bunch of pictures but also as a way for an artist to connect to the music and audience, a way to deeply process all experiences, musical or not, and smoothly mold them into sound.

The boy finished playing the last movement of the sonata, nicknamed "Aurora" by its editors. The movement does bring to mind an opening-up, an exuberant awakening, and Petrushansky was at his metaphorical best here—invoking Apollo's chariot, nymphs, rivers, and the light of Ovid's *Metamorphosis*. That seems a bit over the top, and it only worked because he demonstrated exactly what he meant. He showed the boy how this music, often played in a mechanical, nagging way that makes one's ears itch, was in fact melodic to the core in every small, fast note. Hearing the transformation in the boy's playing was like seeing an airplane leave contrails in the sky at sunset, swirling fast lines of intense pink color. In Petrusha's teaching, the imagery and metaphors were rich but related precisely to the context of the music, revealing ways for it to come alive. His imagination is what set him apart: It was wildly uninhibited and completely inspiring.

It's easier to sculpt sound on Yamaha and Hamburg Steinways; you never have to fight the action because it is light and responsive, and the sound catches reflections like a diamond, reverberating with dazzling colors. I told Petrusha that when he played, he reminded me of a giant seabird, with great open wings, as if it were practicing tai chi. He liked that. He was dressed in a summer blue-green kimono that made him look like a cross between a fighting master and Poseidon, with his beard and white hair untamed.

I played two fantasies for him: the rarely heard, whimsical Beethoven op. 77 Fantasie and the great Schumann Fantasie in C Major, op. 17. Upon submitting the latter in 1839, Robert Schumann wrote, "My Fantasie, won't you be so good as to publish it?" At some point, this masterpiece had been nothing more than somebody's child, barely born, and that somebody was Schumann. And he was begging some guy to take notice. This fact, and the two words together—*My Fantasie*—bring tears to my eyes. Its three movements are, in turn, daunting, intimate, ebullient, passionate. At first planned as a tribute to Beethoven, who died in 1827, it became an expression of love for Clara Wieck-Schuman, like much of his music. "Ruins," "Triumphal Arch," and "Starry Crown" were intended titles of the three movements. These didn't stick, leaving the music absolute and nonpictorial, monumental and personal at once.

At this session, Petrushansky had many ideas that I had not thought of, ideas that went far beyond his usual style of teaching. He was at that moment relating to me as a colleague, more sharing thoughts than teaching, a very different feeling from the many lessons where I tried and physically couldn't replicate what he was doing, tearing up in frustration. Here, finally, the studies had sunken deep enough for me to hold my own, and he immediately sensed and respected this.

I didn't and don't agree with him musically 100 percent of the time. Sometimes I feel that the rhythmic freedoms he favored back then might distort the rhythm and directness of music. Most important in a performance is the pianist's sincerity and depth of intent, and during my studies with Petrushansky, I often found myself so caught up in the intricacies of sound that I forgot the music's overall simplicity and directness. But somehow, over time, things came together. The power of his imagination, the unique beauty of his playing, and the originality of his musicianship had a profound effect on my music-making.

* * *

After playing for Petrushansky in Pine, I was back at the Castello di Galeazza a few days later. I had just finished playing the Schumann Fantasie in C Major, and its ending seemed to be timed perfectly with the ducks waiting in the garden pond. Both they and I remained silent and unmoving while the last chord resounded; only once it had faded completely did the ducks take flight. The audience included the British translator Julia; Clark; Phillipe (a boring pseudo-intellectual); Cecily (a lovely, Jane Austen–style blond from St. Johns College); an infuriating English couple; an Indian girl and her Australian boyfriend; and assorted other Italians.

I still wanted to figure out how to recapture that state of inspiration, fresh out of lessons with Petrushansky, despite the fact that it was ultimately impossible. Inspiration needs to be found anew in performance each time; it cannot be simply replicated from a previous experience. It is like a delicate living creature whose life span lasts only as long as the performance. Coming to Italy, to Petrushansky, had become a personal renaissance. Like Misha, who connected me with the world I came from, Petrushansky helped me recover sound, comfort, passion, and confidence—and use them onstage in a freer, more convincing way.

I slept in my favorite diamond-shaped room next to the library and woke up from a dream of a tsunami. Awake, I realized the terrible heat had subsided, and a cool wind had arrived, conducting an orchestra of trees, heaving and sighing. I dozed off, and when I woke up again, I thought I was still dreaming. I saw a giant red, blue, and yellow hot-air balloon slowly levitate from the castle grounds.

In 2008, Misha and I were married in the castle garden, with fellow musicians and friends from Israel and our closest family around us, along with a leg of prosciutto; homemade fireworks (the police showed up but only to watch); black cats; a musical medley played from a Yamaha grand in the barn; and a group of twenty in their underwear, dancing in the cool fountain like some sort of reenactment of *La Dolce Vita*. A nearby little, family-owned restaurant, cheekily named Quatro Stagione—the Four Seasons, no less!—did the cooking. We wanted paper plates, but the proud owner insisted on tablecloths and silverware: "My food will not be served in this manner!" And the ravioli with

Clark Lawrence attempts to harass me while I sit with Misha before our wedding at the Castello di Galeazza.
Photo by Mark Gurevich

My parents, at the wedding.
Photo by Mark Gurevich

We included a cartoon by Misha in our wedding invitations.

duck sauce, the fresh mozzarella, the tiny pastries, and sculptured ice cream that came out of that tiny kitchen were as much a dream as the rest of the affair.

Four years later, the castle would be destroyed in an earthquake that devastated Emilia Romagna. Clark and his Reading Retreats survived, though he had to move them to Mantua to continue. And so the castle became just a memory for me—like Odessa, the city I had not seen since I was a child.

10

EAT THE WORLD

People often ask what I think about when I play. For me, music frequently evokes images that aren't always literal and can resist description. And for no apparent reason, they may strike you immediately, so suddenly that you feel the hair on your arms stand up. For example, take *"Wild und Lustig"* ("Wild and Funny"), the thirteenth movement of Robert Schumann's *Davidsbündlertänze,* or "Dances of the League of David." In Schumann's whimsical language and imagination, the League of David is a society of those joined by an understanding of and quest for great music with a higher purpose. For the rest of us, I think, this can quite simply mean your friends, those whom you trust, who make you feel at home.

The thirteenth movement is a driven, pulsating gallop. It surges forward and reaches a point of desperation, as if you were forced at great speed to catapult toward a cliff. But instead of falling, you unexpectedly float in the air above the abyss and are propelled forward by the tolling of three bells in B major. And then, a chorus of spirit voices sings a distant march, telling you that at the end of the journey, you will be greeted by those who understand you, who know you. This is the League of David—your most precious memories at the end of life, coming together to embrace you warmly. For a brief moment, you are able to see far back in time.

I am not religious, but this music brings me as close to being a believer as possible. What I describe here is just a guess, a sensation that comes to me with the music if the performance is successful. Schumann wrote this nineteen years before his death. And yet he seemingly knew what it would be like.

After attempting to put into words the experience of making music, I often go back to the piano and discover that things fall flat. Revisiting the images I initially found so inspiring for a given moment in a piece doesn't work. It is as if what happened while I played is too sacred, too private, too strong to be held in place. Perhaps this is why, in the Jewish religion, we cannot say the name of God; doing so shatters the mystery and power of the thing the word refers to.

When I practice, I am following a ritual, communing with something from a different dimension, an alternate world. There are thousands of notes in a given piece. They are like people: Every one is unique in character, in color, in its story, and in its meaning. These notes can come alive as many times as we can remember them and choose to give them life. And when we do, we are suddenly touching something infinitely greater than us, something eternal that will be here long after we are gone, to carry its message and become alive again in each performance, each reincarnation.

* * *

Mr. D was first diagnosed with a nasopharyngeal cancer in the summer of 2009. He told me about it in the hallway of the Music Institute, upbeat as ever: "My brother is an excellent oncologist. He will fix this. I am not even depressed. It's just a little thing." Just a few months later, he had to be moved to a hospice in Cedarburg, Wisconsin, closer to his brothers and sisters.

I'd been preparing for one of my Carnegie Hall recitals under the auspices of the Pro Musicis Foundation. I felt mentally prepared enough to play it for Mr. D and got a flight from New York to Milwaukee. My dad cautioned me, "You are flying to see a dying person. Stay strong." But I didn't see it this way. I hadn't seen Mr. D. very often over the past few years, but he was always with me when I practiced. A person stays alive if you remember them and who they are. And he would always be Mr. D, my teacher. I was nervous to play the program for him and wanted to be ready.

At the entrance to the hospital, I ran into Milton Laufer, the handsome Cuban American pianist who was now the director of the Western Carolina University School of Music. He had studied with Mr. D a generation before me, and his talent and his wild adventures at Eastman were legendary. "The students, they come and go, all day long," said the nurse. There was no piano in Mr. D's room, but she said there was a keyboard I could use, and I asked her to bring it.

Mr. D was sitting up in bed. His hair had started to grow back a bit, postchemo, but it was thin and white. He had suffered a stroke a few weeks before, and his usual smile was lopsided. There was a dish of *sinangag*—Filipino garlic-fried rice—on the counter and a few Chopin CDs, mostly from pianists whose names I didn't know. I picked up one of the discs and recognized Claire. She had been after my time. Her Chopin was wonderful. He pointed at the track listing on the recording—the Sonata no. 3. Still so proud of his students' accomplishments, he remembered what everyone played. I took out a CD of my own playing—Rachmaninoff, Ravel, Boris Pasternak (yes, the one who wrote *Doctor Zhivago*!)—and added it to the stack of recordings. "I hope you like it."

On the keyboard, I played the slow second movement of the Rachmaninoff. (Had I played the first or third movements, I might have knocked the keyboard off its stand.) I also played Schubert and Beethoven. He listened peacefully and, to my relief, winced at a few wrong notes. He was still my teacher.

A few months later, Mr. D had another stroke. Time was of the essence now. I flew to Wisconsin to say goodbye. This time, he was lying in bed with his eyes closed. The nurse said, "I don't think he recognizes anyone anymore." But his eyes opened, and he squeezed my hand with the might of a pianist in his prime. How grateful I was to be able to say goodbye.

Near the end of my first visit to the hospital, I had asked Mr. D whether he wanted to hear any other pieces. "Play Chopin's Barcarolle," he'd said.

This late work of Chopin's had always been his favorite. A barcarolle is a boatman's song, typically in 6/8; the rocking triplets of the accompaniment are supposed to recreate the feeling of being on the water. The opening of the piece makes you hug the world; to play the low, deep C-sharp octave in the basso profundo range, answered by a chord in the upper register, you must open your arms to embrace the entire keyboard. An intimate yet expansive tune, in thirds, it rocks gently. Then the waves get larger, the breathing turns labored, heavy, punctured by sighs—and suddenly, in one of the most surprising middle sections of any Romantic work, we are taken into a dream world, marked sfogato—airy and light, like clouds, like the sugarless ice cream Mr. D loved so much. The middle section of the Barcarolle is a most inward and intense joy, a place where you are left with your innermost thoughts and finally feel at peace.

I'd never played it and have never been more ashamed of not having learned a piece of music. After his death, I flew home and began working on it. I only wish I could have played it for him when he asked.

* * *

The program that I did play for him was the one I'd had to play in one of my Carnegie/Weill Hall recitals as part of the Pro Musicis Foundation Award that I won in 2005. The foundation had originated with Father Eugene Merlet, a Franciscan priest from Paris. The concept was simple: Music is meant to be shared. For every recital in a major venue, whether in Paris, where the foundation originated, or in New York, where the US offices were located, the artist was to play three or four other recitals for audiences who were not typically able to get to a concert hall—in hospitals, schools, jails, hospices. Some of the most wildly imaginative, uninhibited, and personal performances happened in those concerts. As a Pro Musicis artist, you played many concerts in series throughout the world over several years.

Father Merlet had an office on Seventy-Ninth Street, with an organ, a piano, and a murphy bed. He came to New York once a year from Paris; the rest of the time, the apartment served as an office for the foundation's gentle director, John Haag, a man so kind he seemed to come from a fairy tale.

Back in 2005, the year I won the award, the finals were held at Carnegie's Weill Hall, and the famous pianist, chamber musician, and new music force Gilbert Kalish headed the jury. It was all a bit uncomfortable because I had been accepted into his studio at Stony Brook University for my doctor of musical arts degree but was still trying to decide between that and the Manhattan School of Music. I knew the right thing would be to work with Gil, but that also would mean living in Long Island as opposed to being in Manhattan—my dream. I had first played for Gil when he came to Peabody for a few master classes. He had all of Fleisher's musical integrity but none of the imposing grandeur. He treated young musicians like colleagues he respected and never spoke as if from a pedestal. His musical suggestions were often as clear and simple as the soup he brought for lunch in Tupperware containers. They could unlock musical conundrums with a satisfying click. After I

With Gilbert Kalish, on the eve of my final DMA recital at Stony Brook.

played in the final round—some Schumann symphonic etudes, Tchaikovsky's Nocturne, Beethoven's Sonata no. 32—I went to say hello to Gil. "I am sorry I am taking so long. I don't know what to do," I said.

"It's okay," he said. "You are not in my life now, and I am not in yours, and that's fine, and you'll do fine no matter what. But I'd like us to be in each others' lives." At that point, I realized that there was no other way than to get my DMA with this luminous yet down-to-earth musician.

I wanted a doctorate because I thought I had a lot to give—not just as a performer but also as a teacher of young artists like myself. Mr. D would soon be gone. I knew I didn't have his abilities in teaching children—endless patience, first and foremost—but I still wanted to share my artistic experience as intensely as I wanted to keep performing. For this, I had to find a program that was performance-centered and allowed me to continue developing my career. I felt that my experiences thus far could make me a sympathetic mentor to young artists at a high level. And for that, a piece of paper that said, "Doctor," was a necessity. On a bathroom door at Stony Brook, somebody had carved "DMA—Doesn't Mean Anything." On one hand, I believe this to be generally true: Musicians do not save lives. On the other, the degree signifies a deeper commitment to sharing, making, and teaching music. Often, teaching is verbalizing the process of music making in order to help others visualize it. My work with Gil Kalish would help me find equilibrium, using what I had learned from previous teachers while asserting my own voice calmly and confidently.

After I won the Pro Musicis Award, I would occasionally practice in the foundation's office, getting ready for my Weill Hall recital debut, supported by the organization. This was a luxury; finding a piano to practice on in New York, if you don't live there and don't have the money to rent a studio, is as hard as finding an affordable apartment. I was now living in Stony Brook; working on my degree; and renting a small room in a big, spacious country house. While there, I was researching the painter Egon Schiele; studying the music of Schoenberg, Berg, and Webern; practicing for my tours and concerts; and enjoying my lessons with Gil. But I'd take the train into Manhattan as often as I could get away, and every few months, I'd go to Italy, to the Accademia Pianistica.

The house in Stony Brook oppressed me. In addition to the abominable cell phone service, I had a creepy, obsessive-compulsive mathematician housemate, Alexey. He and Olive, the elderly landlady, were a perfect match. Olive had a penchant for leaving bright-pink Post-Its on my door: "Please do not move the tea kettle." "Please do not leave your book on the side table." "Please walk softly up the stairs at night." Alexey's notes were not as pretty, handwritten on crumpled graph paper in craggy Russian: "You touched my pizza box in the fridge and moved it by 5 degrees. Please do not do it again." I was afraid that one night they would be waiting for me by the stairs with an axe.

At that time, Misha and I were not yet married, and we were still doing the long-distance thing. On one of his winter visits from Israel, I wanted to play though the program of my upcoming, first Pro Musicis recital for him and had arranged with John Haag to use the office. As we took the old elevator up to the ninth floor, I played with the key in my pocket, singing to myself, "I have a key to an apartment! With a piano! In New York!" It wasn't my apartment or my piano, but I felt awesome as I took my boyfriend into the office. Misha took off his coat and began to untangle himself from two woolly sweaters. He wasn't used to the New York cold.

He emerged with matted hair and a wrinkled business shirt. "Misha! The shirt is a mess! You can't go like this to a theater!" We had tickets to a Broadway play in three hours. I didn't know where the iron was, nor would I have known how to use it. But I had a better idea. I made him take off the shirt and took it inside the old, tiled bathroom. I turned on the shower, waited for the scalding water to fill the tiny room with steam, hung the shirt up on the towel rack, and closed the bathroom door.

Jet-lagged Misha silently resigned to my machinations, sat at the window next to the wheezing radiator, and may have even dozed off during the gnarly, serious pieces I was forcing on him. Outside, yellow cabs lined up on Amsterdam Avenue, honking as I launched into Schubert's C Minor Sonata, then

Shostakovich's D Minor Prelude and Fugue. My Weill program was very dark and very long.

A knock on the door interrupted the wild, all-obliterating bell sounds at the end of the Fugue. The building superintendent was waving his arms about and yelling something incoherent. I was still in a daze from the music, but I seemed to hear the words *water* and *bathroom*.

The shirt! I had completely forgotten about it. I ran to the bathroom.

The floor was covered in water. During my two-hour practice program, the water had flooded the bathroom and made it down to the floor below. We were looking at thousands of dollars in damage. But the shirt was wrinkle free!

John Haag called moments later. "The super said you are up there with a man without a shirt! I am so disappointed, Inna." Before joining Pro Musicis as its director, John had been a priest. This somehow made the situation more painful.

Explaining what had happened to John, I depicted myself as the annoying girlfriend yelling at her non-American boyfriend for wearing a wrinkled shirt. His sympathy for Misha outweighed his dismay. The story sounded made up, but it was true, and he believed me. John really was the kindest person either of us had ever met. "Inna, calm down. The floor is very old. I am sure the repairs won't cost so much. I can't wait until your concert. Come back anytime. Just be careful next time." John wouldn't accept any money for fixing the floor. He didn't even want the key back.

* * *

A few months after Mr. D's death, in winter of 2011, I was at a Renée Fleming recital at Carnegie Hall with my friend Anna. She and Mark—the Gureviches—were our best friends in New York. They had two kids already and owned an apartment nearby on Riverside Drive. Anna loved me intensely, wanted me to join the mom club, and frequently let me know it. During the intermission, I complained about my many upcoming concert trips. I was trying to balance them with teaching at Northeastern

Illinois University in Chicago—my first official university teaching position. I was flying there roughly every two weeks. I was exhausted, sleepy, and nauseous and looked a wreck. Not even Schumann's *Dichterliebe* song cycle was helping. She raised her shapely eyebrow and gave me a knowing look. "Don't you want kids?" she asked. "How's this travel schedule going to work?"

In fact, I revealed to her, I was expecting one. "But so what? I am still going to perform."

Having kids, in my view, was not going to stop me from being a musician. Being a performer is about transmitting the human experience to an audience. Having more experience makes your emotional vocabulary that much larger, I thought, so having a kid would only help this. Would it be easy? Perhaps not, but it was happening.

When I first told my mom, I didn't get the kind of joy I was expecting. "Are you sure? How do you know?" Her voice shook. Her own experience with childbirth had been harrowing in ways I could never fully imagine. I was born during a hepatitis pandemic, two months premature, in a dirty, understaffed Odessa hospital. There were no supplies. My dad wasn't allowed to see Mom. They were twenty-four at the time and had already lost a child: Four years earlier, my mom had a daughter who died a few days after birth. She didn't know that I knew, and she never spoke to me about it, but the immensity of this trauma must have weighed heavily on her still.

"Mom, please, at least try to act joyful. It's a boy! I will be fine! I just went jogging! There are three inches of snow, but it's not too cold in Central Park. I did my usual route around the reservoir."

Our son Nathaniel was due to be born in early September, and that summer was the hottest I'd ever experienced in New York. My parents were visiting from Chicago, staying with us in our small apartment, walking around with as few clothes as possible and drinking freezing white wine mixed with seltzer. I eyed the wine with envy. I was getting heavier, but I didn't let that stop me from doing things. I was scheduled to perform the Liszt Concerto no. 1 at the Peninsula Music Festival in Wisconsin with Victor Yampolsky conducting. So what if I had to perform this rambunctious and athletic piece a few weeks before my due date? I was doing it, damn it! I was cancelling nothing! That is, until the orchestra management called my manager and politely asked to rebook me to a later season. The nearest hospital was hours away from the festival. It would be safer to focus on the following few summers.

I was not about to start cancelling more concerts. Nathaniel would hate for me to do that, I kept telling myself, as I wobbled over to Brooklyn to play a recital at one of the most magical places on earth: Bargemusic, the floating concert hall. Every New Yorker knows the Barge, which is moored permanently at the Fulton Ferry Landing underneath the Brooklyn Bridge. On gusty days, it can be especially fun to balance on the stage, as the entire venue rocks back and forth. It doesn't matter if you get seasick; the music makes you forget it. I'd been playing there for years and missed the rocking boat after being away for too long. This time, the waves were quite uncooperative. Perhaps if I had chosen something a little bit lighter than *Erlkönig*, Liszt's lavishly difficult virtuoso transcription of Schubert's great song. Set to a Goethe poem, it features four characters—the rider, the child, the evil elf king, and the narrator. When sung or played masterfully, it can be chilling. Playing it eight months' pregnant was perhaps a bit risky, but it also gave me a wonderful feeling of centeredness. I felt like an unmovable tree, solid in front of the instrument, unfurling my branches wide. The waves rocked the boat. I was nauseous and missed some top notes in the galloping melodic section, but my octaves mostly landed. Then, aided by the waves and by Nathaniel in my belly, I played Chopin's Barcarolle. With my larger frame, it was easier to hug the world.

After the concert, we walked across the Brooklyn Bridge, where a biker almost ran me over. Anna's husband, Mark, screamed expletives at him. "Do you see this woman? She is pregnant! You almost fucking ran her over!" I looked around to find the pregnant woman he was talking about because I still couldn't imagine or accept that it was me.

We went to get dessert at an all-night molecular gastronomy restaurant, WD-50, run by the popular chef Wylie Dufresne. If I couldn't drink, I was going to have a four-course dessert dinner that reimagined New York staples like black-and-white cookies and bagels with lox. Dehydrated salmon with chocolate shavings? Pickle jelly? Bring it on!

This was one of our last prebaby New York hurrahs. At midnight, we crossed the bridge back to Brooklyn to see a film premiere in Williamsburg by a friend of a friend. The garage was full of artsy people from all over the world, decked out in outrageous hats, chic asymmetrical coats, colorful tattoos, and sky-high platform shoes. One of them was saying to a group of others, "I am simply addicted to Sotheby's." He was wearing an Armani suit and looked out of place. There were pajamas, too, and lots of weed—the smell of it made me sick, but I wanted to stay.

The film turned out to be a clay animation feature about Wolfie, an adorable toy wolf and his adventures with an owl, a fox, and some other forest creatures. I thought the age of the intended viewers was probably around three. For some reason, everyone cheered and stomped their feet and made speeches as if this was the work of Peter Greenaway or Derek Jarman or Kurosawa. "Go Wolfie! Yeah!" "Oh my god. That was . . . profound. Life-changing. Eat the world. Yeah man." "Sundance is next." "Forget Sundance. I see Palme D'Or." There was clearly some experimental edge that both Misha and I were missing.

Wolfie wanted to "eat the world"—this was the leitmotif of the film, a phrase repeated throughout that was meant to communicate his enthusiasm for adventure and discovery. Each time, I thought of the opening of the Barcarolle and how I had to hug the world at the start. Nathaniel kicked me, and I felt hungry again. At the same time, I was, quite literally, full of life: the boy inside of my belly, the ongoing buzz from the Bargemusic concert, the sugar high from the deconstructed black-and-white cookie, giggling to myself about the unpredictable weirdness of this night in Brooklyn, and wondering what Mr. D would have thought of my *Erlkönig*. Somewhere, somehow, I hope he heard it and gave a small *tsk*.

11

JFK–LAX

After earning my DMA, I had begun teaching piano at Northeastern Illinois University, a small school in Chicago. I had a studio whose windows looked out onto the Bohemian National Cemetery, but I didn't mind. Each time I parked and walked past the flat gravestones, I would remember Marina Tsvetaeva's poem "Stop, Passerby," in which she speaks from the grave to the living. I thought it was rather uplifting, compared to my first exposure to academia from the inside.

By 2011, commuting between Chicago and New York had become difficult, especially while pregnant. But the students made it worthwhile. There was an elderly lady named Jean who had decided to go back for her master's degree in piano; she practiced Ravel's *Valses Nobles and Sentimentales* with a fierce tenacity, forcing her knobby, stiff hands and wrists to mold Ravel's sinuous shapes—and sometimes succeeding! Margaret hailed from Mongolia, where she had been something of a pop star. Exquisitely beautiful, she wore sexy shift dresses and high-heeled boots, turning heads everywhere she went, and had a passionate, tender, and natural way with Chopin that could melt the heart of Genghis Khan. Jim was a stoner obsessed with Glenn Gould; he learned Bach's D Minor Concerto in two days and was slogging his way through the *Goldberg Variations*, despite my protestations that he had to first learn some preludes and fugues and maybe a partita.

That year, I established a concerto competition for the students in the school. The winners would get to play the concerto with the university orchestra. The first winner was Kiyana, a bright and very hard-working student; every sentence she uttered and every phrase she played on the piano was carefully considered, conceived, and delivered with a depth and purpose. One morning, I was overseeing the rehearsal with the orchestra and was dismayed to find the piano open on half-stick in the back of the space. "Isn't this where it goes?" asked the conductor. He was teaching orchestra to students, yet he had no idea where the piano goes onstage in a concerto. I wondered how much longer he would be allowed to show up to work, given that he also hit on female students and made racist remarks.

For her performance, Kiyana's mother, a tea ceremony master, visited from Japan and held a professional one for us. Both Kiyana and I would be dressed in traditional festive kimonos for the performance. Her mother took great care not to wrap me too tightly. The baby bump barely showed. Wound in layers of black, rose, and white silk, I could still move my arms freely, while my posture at the piano was ramrod straight. Kiyana's kimono was ivory, blue, and gold. It forced her to sit up with even more poise than usual, phrasing broadly without getting lost in the grind of the sixteenth notes. After this concert, she would be graduating—and for the first time, I experienced the parental pang of letting a student go. She would be a star that night. But I'd been traveling between New York and Chicago to teach for three years. It was time to move on.

* * *

Nathaniel, a joyful, curly-haired boy, was born in Manhattan on Labor Day. We moved two blocks up from 103rd Street—even closer to the Silver Moon bakery, the first café I ever took him to. We spent long afternoons in Central Park and Riverside Park, and when he slept, I practiced. I was immersed in my project, Music/Words.

I had started Music/Words a few years earlier. It was my answer to being married to the piano, locked in a practice room. I'd carry a book of poetry with me backstage, anywhere I played. Those few lines of Pasternak gave me an extra shot of beauty, a feeling of flight and freedom as I'd make my way toward the piano onstage. How could I translate that feeling into something tangible? I decided to join musical performances with poetry readings; it felt inevitable. I planned four evenings in a gallery in Soho that happened to have an unusually beautiful nine-foot Grotrian piano. It also had gaudy, vaguely risqué art pieces that looked like Dalí copies with glitter purchased outside the Met, but I'd have to overlook this detail. I asked my friend Jesse Ball to be the inaugural poet and to read from his *Parables and Lies*, a book of prose poetry. Friends, friends of friends, and people who read the *Village Voice* and *Time Out New York* showed up and filled the space. Jesse's first poem was called "Coming up Upon a Play" and described walking along a riverbank and coming across a makeshift theater that was about to begin a show. It was perfect as an intro: Jesse's mellow voice and then the opening cascade of Beethoven's *Fantasie*.

I would find participants by going to readings, by subscribing to *Poetry* magazine, by talking to poets about other poets, by taking writing classes at St. Mark's on the Bowery. When we workshopped the poems we'd written the week before, I'd be amazed at how much I didn't get. At an open-mic night in St. Mark's, a tall pixie rocker in a leather miniskirt read a villanelle that only used the words *cum, piss, black, shine,* and *hard*. She had workshopped it in our class the day before, and I couldn't understand how everyone took it so seriously. Even weirder was the fact that her reading was followed that night by a tame, lyrical narrative poem read by Philip Glass.

I had developed a sense of what worked and what didn't and how to pair reading voices with musical ones. I learned to recognize a poetic voice that thought about words musically. Those writers usually would be excited about taking part in the series.

Once, I was playing at Cornelia Street Café in the West Village, following a reading by Sandra Beasley and a vocal performance by Clarice Assad. I'd gotten to the celestial triplet sixteenths of Beethoven's last sonata, no. 32, the part that Daniel Schlosberg danced to with a fork in my practice room at Peabody. This is one of the most magical moments of the piece, the "noodling bit," as my sound engineer Joe Patrych called it when listening to different takes during our recording sessions. As I looked up at the ceiling (Why do we look up when the music gets particularly ethereal and searching? There is nothing there!) during this section, the bartender came up to the piano and shouted, "Hey, I've got to close up your tab. We need to start the next set!" I kept playing while he shouted and didn't stop until the music came to its inevitable end. It was a convincing performance, I thought, but apparently it wasn't actually worth a half-pint of Blue Moon.

For another Words/Music installment, I shattered a whiskey glass on the stage of Le Poisson Rouge, another downtown music club. I hadn't been drinking whiskey; I hate the taste of it. I was using the glass to create sounds inside the piano by scraping it up and down the thick bass strings, as the microtonal composer John Eaton had directed. It was for a premiere of a song cycle with the baritone David Adam Moore. Mark Levine had just read his set of poems and just missed being hit by tiny flecks of glass.

Despite this, or perhaps because of it, Music/Words started to get attention from the press. I produced it as a radio show on WFMT in Chicago and took performances on the road. One memorable show, with the gorgeous poet Deborah Landau, took place at the Poetry Foundation in Chicago under a glass dome and with a packed house. Our entrances onto the stage felt effortless and perfectly timed as we volleyed the readings and music back and forth to each other. That's what it was all about: the feeling we were improvising a story through words and music.

* * *

I had started to travel to Los Angeles years earlier to take part in the LA County Museum of Art's beloved Sundays Live series.

I would stay at the house of Misha's Aunt Tanya, who lived across the street from the UCLA campus. I didn't understand the spotless sunshine and found the palm trees annoying. "We would never live there," I snidely thought each time my plane returned to New York, with the Fata Morgana of Manhattan, our reality, emerging from the clouds.

One snowy morning in 2012, I saw an opening for a tenured professor of piano at UCLA advertised in the *College Music Society Bulletin*. Vitaly Margulis, the revered, legendary Russian piano guru, had passed away, and his position was now open. I asked Misha whether I should apply. He had gotten a new job writing algorithms for a hedge fund, Nathaniel was a half-year old, and the Silver Moon bakery never tasted better. "Do you have any contacts there?" he asked. "Is there any chance you'll get it?"

"None. I'll apply just to get interview practice."

I responded to the lofty job description ("must understand and exemplify the role of the twenty-first-century artist") and reached the Skype interview stage, where the search committee told me they were looking to find a "combination of Einstein, Gertrude Stein, and Artur Rubinstein," no less. When I'd made the finals for the position, I packed my breast pump and flew to LA. I stayed minutes away from Tanya at the UCLA guesthouse, but I didn't want to tell her about this development. What was the point? I was sure I wouldn't get the job.

But the campus beckoned with blooming roses; luscious fig trees; and the majestic, Sienese-looking Royce Hall, the campus's performing arts venue. Schoenberg had taught there, and everyone wanted to use the word *interdisciplinary* in as many sentences as possible. Could this be a perfect match? After the first day of meetings, lunches, performances, and master classes, I collapsed into bed, exhausted. My breasts were sore, swollen, and lumpy; I felt feverish and needed to pump. I rummaged in my suitcase for what felt like an hour and finally had to concede that I'd left a crucial part of the awkward mechanism at home in New York. Getting the milk out by hand would take all night, and I still had to do a lecture about Music/Words in the morning and meet with the dean. Tanya's daughter Anya had just had a baby, so I called Tanya. "Please don't get too excited. I am here for the final round of a UCLA job search. No, I probably won't get it. Can you get me a breast pump?" An hour later, Tanya was at my door. In one arm was the hated breast pump; in the other, a giant vat of borscht.

A month later, I was recording a recital for Yamaha's Disklavier Library in Orange County. I'd record the music of CPE Bach into a MIDI file and then edit it on a computer as though manipulating a detailed map, moving around tiny dots that signified notes and how I had played them. It felt futuristic, oddly satisfying; getting rid of the tiny blemishes was like popping bubble wrap. The work took three days of nonstop listening and adjusting and had sensitized my ears to a point that any hint of audio imperfection caused physical pain. After a few days on the MIDI grid and away from actual life, I checked my messages and found a warm greeting from the chair of the department. I'd been unanimously selected for the position.

"Mom! I don't want to move to LA."

Mom usually was quite conservative when it came to making changes, but then again, she had come to the United States with nothing. When a big decision needed to be made, a step to take with no looking back, she was fearless. "You need to do this. Tenure? At thirty? This is a rare opportunity. And Mr. D would be so proud."

And then she reminded me of the hand-me-down sweatshirt I'd worn to my first audition in Odessa, the one with the UCLA mascot on it. "Remember Ooklah the bear? It came from our Los Angeles relatives." She was right. Here was the chance I was looking for: to share my knowledge and experience on my own terms. This school and department seemed to want me exactly for who I was. They heard my artistic voice and were eager to have me share it with their students. An artist should never sit still. We had to move.

I started to say my goodbyes to New York. We couldn't move immediately, and even once we did, Misha would have to commute from the East Coast for at least the first few years. Initially, using Disklavier remote lesson technology, I taught my UCLA piano students long distance. I would meet with a student on the screen via Skype, and whatever I played on my

Disklavier piano in New York would be reproduced simultane-ously in LA, with every gradation of tone, color, and pedaling preserved. It was surreal, and it was the future. These were the first official remote lessons ever at an institution of higher learn-ing in the United States. And it was just the beginning. Little did the students know that a few years later, videos of these lessons would be viewed hundreds of thousands, if not millions, of times in China, where the dawn of Disklavier technology had not yet begun.

When Misha, Nathaniel, and I finally moved, our first apart-ment's zip code was 90210, just like the show I'd watched as a teenager. Our New York friends invoked Brandon, Dylan, Brenda, and Kelly and made fun of us. We had a white shag rug, a bar, and a Jacuzzi in our small apartment. Jacarandas bloomed outside, and the flowers gracefully descended to the sidewalk, forming a purple carpet. I wondered if Nathaniel would miss the giant rats of his playground on Ninety-Sixth Street in Manhat-tan. We couldn't find bagels we liked yet, and the pizza left a lot to be desired. But we bought a bottle of viognier and shared it on our balcony, admiring the jacarandas.

Our second week in LA, we left Nathaniel with the baby-sitter and took a walk to Wilshire Boulevard, where the Ace Gallery was hosting a concert by the venerable Borodin String

After a recital at UCLA's Wallis Annenberg Center for the Performing Arts, with my students.

Quartet. They were playing the repertoire they were best known for, Shostakovich's last three quartets. This was music of grief, nerve, tragedy—a diary of human suffering. They took their bows, seemingly oblivious to the fact that they were surrounded by an army of twelve-foot-high black-and-white portraits of suggestively posed nude models, the current exhibit. "Welcome to LA," the models screamed in my head.

It was a fascinating time to join UCLA as one of the few women on the music faculty as the department geared up to become the first official School of Music in the California University System. As time went on, my students would become my extended family, and I would be fortunate to have a window into their worlds and learn from them.

* * *

One night, I was at Schoenberg Hall performing *Polonaise-Fantaisie: The Story of a Pianist*, a one-woman show that included a monologue recital of my life story. During the intermission, I was relaxing in the green room when my phone rang. It was Max! I hadn't heard from him in eighteen years. I knew he had gotten married and had a child, but I had not kept up with him, other than being nominal Facebook friends. "Let the past stay in the past," I thought. I didn't take the call.

Another call came in a few days later, just as I was starting to doze off while in line at the Chinese consulate. I had gotten there at dawn, hoping to pick up the visa for my upcoming concert tour and get back to Westwood before traffic thickened. I was still somehow last in line. I took the call, and it was Kevin, one of Alex's high school friends. It had been a while since we'd spoken. He told me that Max had died the previous day. It seemed likely to have been alcohol poisoning.

My first thought: "See, Max? I was right to leave all those years ago! We never should have gotten married. And now, you've drunk yourself to death. You didn't change at all!"

I thanked Kevin for the call and lied that I was with a piano student and couldn't talk. Leaving behind both the unmoving line and my parked car, I began the long walk down Wilshire

Boulevard toward the hills of West LA. "Nobody walks in LA," my friends had warned me when we moved. I had become determined to prove them wrong and pointedly walked everywhere, once getting stuck in a highway construction zone beneath an overpass between Santa Monica and UCLA. Now, I wanted to walk from Koreatown to Westwood, down Wilshire Boulevard like it was Broadway, a vein connecting miniature cities. The news had to be digested. I called my husband, told him what had happened, and reassured him I was okay.

My feet carried me forward on that odd November day, sun leering in the cloudless Los Angeles sky, in the direction of my studio at UCLA. I needed to play something, anything. When I finally got there, I sat down and played Schumann's Symphonic Etudes. The lamentful theme of this piece—one of my mom's favorites—felt warm and comforting under my fingers, and as the passionate, surging music unfolded, it gave me solace. The sounds came effortlessly. Before getting to the triumphant finale, I stopped playing and started crying for a terrifying end to a life that had touched mine so early on, for the mistake of that doomed youthful marriage, for the stupidity and hurt of my first love. Then I called Misha and asked if he could pick me up. It had been a very long walk, and I was tired.

Interlude

MAYA MIRO JOHNSON, "MANUSCRIPTS DON'T BURN"

The Wende Museum in Culver City, California, focuses on art, music, and thought related to the Cold War. When you walk in, you are greeted by a hot-pink porcelain bust of Lenin. There are walls of old Russian books, just like in my grandparents' room in Odessa. You can easily spend hours exploring propaganda posters, the archives of artists who dissented, academic realist paintings, experimental sculptures, drawings by Soviet hippies. It's a magnificent place.

Joes Segal, the museum's curator, and I are hanging out in the storage room. It contains all the things that have not yet been put into themed exhibits but are waiting to be dusted off and showcased. He pulls out a strange untitled painting by Stanislav Molodykh: An authoritative black cat sits in the middle of what appears to be a mixture of a church with a checkered marble floor and a mental institution. It looks like a fantasy on the themes from Bulgakov's *The Master and Margarita*. (In case this hasn't become clear up until this point, I am a tiny bit obsessed with the novel. It's practically been my Bible since childhood, since I carried it through immigration, since Misha found me, since I watched the sunrise from Bulgakov's grave.) And until now, I never knew about this painting! Joes and I brainstorm a program built around the novel for Wende's adventurous, interdisciplinary-minded music series. Generously given an

217

opportunity to commission new pieces for the program, I decide to combine my Music/Words experience with my favorite book. I start to have questions.

Who is Margarita? Is she a really a well-developed character? When I was little, I saw her as the great muse to a persecuted artist: a housewife turned witch, a Moscow society lady turned outlaw lover. Is she a person or an idea of a person? I want to see her in a different light than just the master's muse and savior. I want to understand her as a person in her own right, separate from the master who validates her existence. I feel she deserved her own piece.

I've asked nineteen-year-old Maya Miro Johnson to write a piano piece about Margarita, where I would get to use words from the book in any way other than singing them outright. I first met Maya—a frighteningly mature and intelligent composer, dancer, and conductor—at Young Arts LA when I was artistic director of the week-long program in 2019. She is the only American I have ever met who read *The Master and Margarita* and most of Dostoyevsky before reaching driving age. I gave Maya the most random of assignments for Young Arts, asking her to compose an eleven-minute piece for a collection of performers that included two oboists, a violist, two percussionists, two vocalists, a pianist, and a double bass player. The result was a drama based on Chekhov; it played out powerfully and inevitably.

Maya's piano piece is called "Manuscripts Don't Burn," the most famous phrase in the entire book. In the beginning, I need to perform an act of acrobatic balance: While pedaling quickly with my right foot, I reach inside the piano with both hands and scratch the bass strings, creating the sound of "dry paper burning in the fire." While that's going on, I need to play chords in the high register, piercingly and accurately. These sounds of flames—which are perhaps in Margarita's mind—turn into echoes and lead from one note to the next with irregular rhythm, quiet, demure, searching. A difficult octave passage gallops with "manic jollity," followed by a section that sounds like many cathedral bells, ringing as if heard all over the city, far away. This subtle, rhythmically complex music alternates with the return of the manic octaves until back to the piano strings I go. And then, I begin to speak. I repeat the same quote in different registers while muting strings and hammering at them with my fingernail: "The men in tuxes and the women turned to ashes, the sepulchral air enveloped the hall. The columns fell, the lights went out, all disintegrated, no more fountains, tulips or camelias. Only the modest living room and through the door, ajar, fell a slice of light. Margarita walked in."

Maya has astutely picked the moment when Margarita decides to throw all doubts and fears to the wind and meet the Devil, who has invited her to preside over his ball. He can grant her what she most desires—the return of the master, her lover—but at this point in the novel, we do not know this. We only know that a woman has abandoned the path that was expected of her and taken an unexpected turn. The piece ends with chanting a chorale—lips closed, on an *m* sound—and then whispering the phrase once more. I will later premiere a version of the piece in New York, and an overall positive online review will say, "Faliks echoed and resonated from simple one-note tunes to crazy-fast phrasing. Musically I couldn't judge it. Atmospherically, it was scary."

When I was eighteen years old, right before moving to Baltimore, I played another piece that begins with a crash—Rodion Shchedrin's *Basso Ostinato*—in a master class in Chicago. This short piece has a heavy, energetic ostinato in the left hand and jazzy, pointillist figures in the right. In the big climax, the hands crisscross: The left hand ends up playing on the top part of the keyboard while the right has to reach all the way to the left, to the deepest, darkest bass. As I got to this part, the teacher came up behind me, stood uncomfortably close, and looked down my shirt. After my performance, he explained, "I am always curious to see how women handle this section, with their appendages and all."

The best revenge is living well, so instead of reporting this incident and every other similar incident throughout my career—as I perhaps should have—I simply chose to forge on. It has never been about the discomfort and fear of speaking out in the treacherous, male-dominated, fiercely competitive, frequently random field of classical music. For a long time, I simply didn't know that speaking out was a choice.

I would often hear from others that I "play like a man," especially in my teens and early twenties. I don't want to think of myself as a "woman pianist." I am just a pianist, much in the same way as other musicians don't want to be thought of as "women composers" or "women conductors." We need to get to a place where such qualifiers are no longer used, but that long road takes time and conscious effort.

I haven't composed any music since my teens. Too many times, I had been told it's simply too hard for a woman to be a composer—even harder than being a pianist. But who knows? I may try it again.

12

VOICES OF BEIJING

It was December 2018, and I was halfway through my concert tour of China. I was staying at a lavish, futuristic hotel in Shenzhen. The view from my fortieth-floor suite was 360 degrees, and the floor-to-ceiling windows revealed a scene from *Blade Runner*, minus the flying cars. On the way down to the lobby, I caught a glimpse of the Olympic-size saltwater pool and marble bar, with abstract paintings of English words that made no discernible sense. Birds-of-paradise filled the pine-scented lobby. Ling, the translator assigned to accompany me, ran toward me, grabbed my arm, and shoved me into the SUV outside. "Quick, quick! We are already late!" (How could we be? I barely had enough time to drop off my bag, and I only took ten minutes to take off my coat, put up my hair, and get into my dress.)

When we moved to Chicago, my dad rejoiced at the sight of skyscrapers—to him, they symbolized progress, novelty, hope, and the excitement of starting anew. My mom dismissed them as a "stone jungle," cold and impenetrable. Now, we drove through another stone jungle of giant buildings, their silhouettes like huge, menacing robots against a pinkish-gray, unnatural-looking sky. I asked whether it was going to rain. "No, that's how the sky is. We rarely see blue. Too much pollution."

We arrived at a concert hall that reminded me of a giant mausoleum; the space seated two thousand, with a large platform behind the piano. An enormous video screen had been set up above me to my left, dominating my field of vision. It was about eight times my height and completely overshadowed the piano. I learned that when things got fast and furious, it would light up to show my hands. Not looking at the screen was like ignoring the elephant in the room: The eyes simply gravitated there as it watched unnervingly, waiting for the hands to slip up in real time.

The hall temperature was below freezing. It would take hours to heat the space adequately, but I'd been told that they weren't allowed to turn on the heat until forty-five minutes before the start of the performance, per local government ordinance. I kept my coat on until the last moment. Finally, as in every concert I'd played on this and other tours in China, a model dressed much more extravagantly than me came out and read a long introduction with brio and dramatic pauses. The lights were blinding, and I hoped they would distract me from the giant video screen.

I played Schumann's *Symphonic Etudes* wearing gloves with the fingers cut off. Its C-sharp minor theme is a series of descending legato chords, the top line singing an exhalation of grief. That's difficult to capture when you have just left the very rough backstage bathroom and its lingering aroma follows you onstage like a cloud of flies.

During the concert, people smoked; texted; chatted; took videos of me that would end up on Youku (Chinese YouTube); and shouted at their children, who ran between seats and waved at me. I should have been distracted and annoyed, but isn't this what a concert would have been like two centuries ago, minus the phones? When did we all get so snooty?

In smaller cities in China, audiences are shy to clap because expressing emotions wildly is considered ill-mannered. The scant applause used to bother me, and I'd walk off thinking I had bombed. Then I realized it was simply not the custom. In Beijing, Shanghai, Tianjin, Guangzhou, and other big cultural centers, it had been different, outwardly more warm and enthusiastic. But this shy response had its own special meaning. These people had stayed for the duration of the concert, and every seat was taken.

Backstage in China. I wore fingerless gloves in an attempt to stay warm despite the freezing temperatures.

By the end of the recital, my hands no longer felt like wooden spatulas, and warm blood flowed through my fingers, just in time for the encore, a Chinese folk tune arranged in frilly runs and trills. I'd been handed the score during intermission. The piano was a gorgeous Yamaha, and the quiet, gentle technician had spent nine hours working on it that day in the freezing hall. Such dedication to the instrument's perfection preceded each concert. I would touch the piano and forget about any discomforts or perceived inconvenience that may have annoyed my spoiled, Western sensibilities.

I took my final bows and shook hands with a man who handed me a gargantuan bouquet of pink lilies and an ornate document. Without realizing, I had just accepted a visiting professorship position at this music college where I was performing. I would have to drink to that later, during the banquet. (By the end of my tour, I would master the art of discreetly pouring out clear shots of Baijiu underneath the table and filling my shot glass with water.) While only eleven music schools in China carry the honorary title of "Music Conservatory," thousands of other institutions there dedicate themselves to the study of Western classical music.

After the concert, I sat next to the piano for what could have been hours, like Santa, while threads of students and parents took pictures next to me. I was suddenly exhausted. I still had to go back to the hotel and then attend a lavish banquet with a sweet potato dragon centerpiece surrounded by sea cucumbers with beef sauce, pig ears and ginger, fresh fish in black bean sauce, and Mapo tofu. This was the usual rhythm of touring. After a few hours of sleep, I would be off to the airport for the flight to the next city and concert. Sometimes, there would be a master class in the morning; that meant I could sleep a few extra hours and maybe have a chance to see the city I happened to be in. On tour for weeks, I played in cavernous, unheated winter halls and resonant, warm, wood-paneled conservatory auditoriums; explored the canals of Nanjing; heard the fastest Liszt octaves possible in Tianjin; jogged on the freezing beaches of Tsingtao; marveled at the Terra-Cotta Army in Xi'an; drank fermented yak's milk from a shofar-like horn to celebrate a concert in Inner Mongolia; explored Buddha caves in Hangzhou; read my name on red banners the size of buildings in Zhuhai; and endured the most consistently annoying electronic renditions of Christmas songs available to man, everywhere.

Touring China felt like meeting with a familiar past. The banners, the declamatory long speeches, the inefficient heating systems, the squat toilets with no toilet paper (flowing pants with heels were not advisable concert attire) took me back to my childhood in Odessa. These discomforts were juxtaposed confusingly with the perfect pianos; the lushness of five-star hotels;

Warming up before a recital in the opulent hall in Zhuhai, China.

the mind-boggling dinners; the gleaming, evolving architectural splendor of brand-new cities rising up before my eyes. Each time I looked at the line of eager, young piano students gathered to talk to me after a concert, I thought that I stood face to face not with the past but with the future of classical music.

This tour was my third, and getting to China this time had been no picnic. The schedule was grueling. Every concert and every master class were very closely planned so that I could make the flight connections and play the maximum number of concerts in my two weeks there. Missing a flight would inevitably mean a collapse of the entire schedule. The first performance was in Xi'an. Initially, I was supposed to leave the next morning, but I asked to stay a little longer in order to see the Terra-Cotta Army, the sculptures around the tomb of Qin Shi Huang, the first emperor of China. This meant I needed to fly to Nanjing and play a concert there on the same day, a difficult thing to do. But I was fine with that, if it meant that I would get to see this archeological wonder.

I had flown to China from a concert in Nelson, British Columbia. To get there, one takes off from Vancouver and lands in an airport in the nearby tiny village of Castlegar—nicknamed "Cancelgar" because it is impossible to land a plane there in even the gentlest rain or snow. Nelson itself is a magical sprinkling of old movie theaters, bookstores, cafés, and galleries next to the Kootenay Lake and the Selkirk Mountains. It is home to a boisterous, drug-laden music festival, as well as the Doukhabors, a Russian sect of non-Orthodox Christians that found its way to Canada in the early twentieth century and are famous for their nude protests. If you enjoy a hearty borscht served in a tiny airport, easy access to drugs, or both, then you will love Nelson.

The day of my performance there, the sky looked cloudy. Planes probably couldn't take off, but if I didn't make my flight back to Vancouver and then on to Beijing, then my first concert would not take place as scheduled. The tour was tightly packed, with flights every other day, sometimes with a performance on the same day. If I missed the initial flight to China, then I would miss the concert in Xi'an (and, subsequently, the Terra Cotta Warriors), and my entire tour was likely doomed. So instead of taking the risk of changing the schedule, the Chinese hired a driver to take me over the mountain ranges in the middle of the night, in the heart of a snowstorm, and put me on another flight in Kelowna, a larger city in British Columbia with a bigger airport. Amazingly, I'd gotten on my Vancouver connection and just forty-eight hours later faced the Emperor's Army.

* * *

On my very first trip to China, in 2016, I and a group of UCLA colleagues went to Beijing to play a concert of Chopin, Debussy, Gao Ping, and traditional music that called for a mix of Western and Chinese instruments, such as the sanxian, a three-stringed lute encased in the skin of a male snake. One piece—a trio for cello, piano, and sanxian—was polyrhythmic, hypnotic, and difficult and would take the most rehearsal. I was charged with playing the piano part alongside Antonio Lysy, the cellist, and Shan Cheng, a sanxian virtuoso. Its driving, kinetic character fit oddly well alongside Debussy's cello sonata, a play of subtlety and gesture. The program also included a piano duet by Gao Ping, full of mystical colors and interesting, gnarly polyphony, and a gnarly world premiere by UCLA composer David

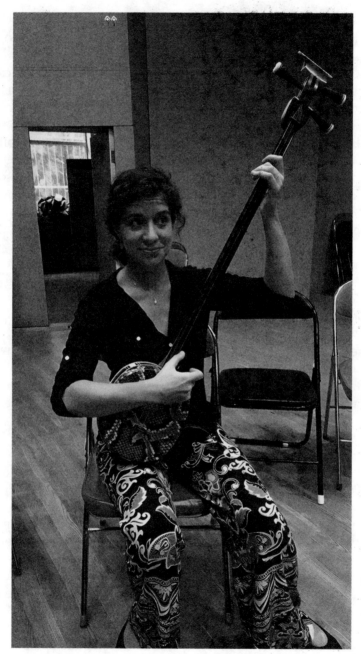

Me on tour in Beijing, taking a lesson on the sanxian.

Lefkowitz for chamber orchestra, piano, and two tenors (Michael Dean sang baritone, and Neal Stulberg conducted) based on Li Bai's famous poem "Drinking Alone under the Moon."

Our first few days in Beijing, Antonio, Michael, and I became inseparable, falling into a summer music camp dynamic as we discovered the city with the help of Gao Ping and Shan Cheng. David and Neal came with their spouses, who were less than thrilled at the rock-hard mattresses in our hotel, the squat toilets, and the chemical smell of the sheets (which I masked by sleeping amid mandarin orange peels). Having grown up in Soviet squalor, I had by now become Western and spoiled. My colleagues and I hadn't realized that the three faculty members hosting us at the college had to share one room among them. We simply wanted better rooms because we could not imagine not having them. So we packed up our stuff and moved to a nicer hotel up the street, paying for the difference in price. David bought a softer mattress and carried it on his back while pushing his voluminous luggage and eliciting furtive glances from passersby.

We wanted to swallow the city whole. After our concert was done, we started at eight in the morning and bolted between narrow historic hutongs; the Temple of Heaven; the new 789 Art District; and—my favorite—Lama Temple, a Buddhist structure with the largest statue of Buddha carved from a single tree, the size of a three-story building, and covered in gold.

Antonio downloaded an app that translated any menu item sign from Mandarin to English, though results, such as "dear donkey silver balls" and "gently sexual hydrangea flower stems," didn't really help. We scaled the Great Wall of China, where Michael broke into a thunderous "Nessun Dorma." We drank Tsingtao beer and ate stinky tofu from the carts in the alleys of Haidan District near the Summer Palace. A generous and polite young man, the boyfriend of a piano student, led us through an overwhelmingly informative tour of the Forbidden City. He must have prepared for weeks because the emperors, concubines, ministers, murders, and intrigues came to vivid life in his stories.

We wanted to feel at home in Beijing, the backdrop to our cozy, crazy camaraderie, so easy and so familiar to musicians who have rehearsed and played a concert together. But despite our adventures, Beijing remained like a hidden monolith to us, the soul of the ancient city invisible behind the landmarks and the Soviet-style buildings, the red stars, the changing of the guard, and the familiar bureaucratic obstacles we faced at every turn. Michael and Antonio wanted to see Mao's mausoleum on Tiananmen Square. I refused vehemently, telling them that my dad would disown me if I put down my hard-earned money for this. I was more interested in seeing anything related to the dissident artist Ai Wei Wei, but his work was impossible to find. Next to Tiananmen Square was the Giant Egg: the National Performing Arts Center, an elongated, shining sphere that changed colors in the dark. I'd be back to perform a recital there in just a few months.

Some mornings, we taught music students at Capital Normal University; it was not China's premiere music school (that was Central Conservatory, where I would end up teaching and performing eventually), but the students were earnest and well prepared. One of them, Shin Lu, played Liszt's "Tarantella" with the smallest hands I'd ever seen, scattering repeated notes like tiny electric sparks. She played the notes with great speed and verve. She needed to work on connectivity, on legato, on making the piano speak with a soft, relaxed hand, as opposed to hiding behind the pedal. And I worked with her to make sure that each instruction of the composer—like *poco meno presto ma sempre con molto brio*: a little less quickly but always with great brilliance—was understood and internalized. The piece came from a volume called *Years of Travel*, I told her; what aspect of Liszt's biography did this refer to?

Finally, I wanted to help her connect to the music with her own emotions and experience. It seemed that she, like many students I would encounter, just needed permission. If in her own life she could find joy, love, shyness, humor—the varied emotional vocabulary any actor needs in order to perform a scene—then she could begin to recognize the character of the music. I wanted her to understand that music could not be separated into two realms, the technical and physical versus the emotional and musical. From the very beginning of learning a piece, one has to first conceive of the character and understand the musical details, the composer's vision, and the directions for realizing it. Then, the fingers begin to do the work. If we first learn the notes and then sprinkle them with musicality, a simulation of emotion, then we get a musical dish with no taste.

On my last day in Beijing, Shan and I went to the National Museum of China. Along with huge paintings depicting the sunny futures of Communist nations—really, they could have been painted in the Soviet Union in the 1930s—I saw an exhibit of Tang dynasty screens and fantastical, animal-shaped porcelain pillows owned by royalty. We came outside to Tiananmen Square in time to see the changing of the guard. Shan eyed the handsome soldiers flirtatiously while I battled Soviet PTSD, reminded of the endless propaganda that had made up the theater of our daily lives in the Soviet Union. It brought forth a mixture of sarcasm at the sadly comical surrealism; anger (How could anyone take this seriously, given the history of lives and families destroyed, of the blood of millions? Do they not know what had happened?); gratitude at having been taken out of that world; and a strange, bitter nostalgia for childhood. I tried to engage Shan on the subject of Mao and Stalin, but it was a no-go. She was Westernized in this way: Where many young women would live at home before inevitably getting married, she was an accomplished musician, a hip and attractive single mom, living alone and dating an award-winning Chinese chef who cooked for the French Embassy. She was confident in her sexuality and open-minded in her societal views, but politically, she would not open up.

"China is a big country. And Mao did some important things." That was the end of it.

Shan took me to a small fish restaurant in the hutongs behind the square, where you could pick the sauce; she chose peppercorn and garlic black bean. The pugnacious peppers set my eyes and mouth aflame, my lips tingled pleasantly, and my throat felt numb at first and then throbbed. I drank warm tea and immediately wanted to repeat the sensation—the start of what became my addiction to the Szechuan peppercorn. After dinner, we left the old part of town and walked between the faceless,

identical rows of tall apartment buildings. Five highways inter-
sected above us. I didn't like this part of Beijing—so cold, and
everything looked the same, with no personality. And then I
saw a man on stilts, with a long-nosed papier-mâché mask and
in a silken red robe, was practicing tai chi in a clearing between
two apartment buildings. He lifted his arm behind his head in
an arc, wide sleeve billowing in the evening breeze, lifting the
opposite leg on a stilt at the same time. A group of about thirty
people in four rows mimicked him in silence. The cars on the
highway whizzed above them as they moved silently, absorbed
in the gradual movements, as though living through a piece by
the experimental composer Morton Feldman. I took a few steps
forward and joined the last row. At that moment, I thought that
maybe I'd gotten the spirit of Beijing.

* * *

The following year, I was at the Xinghai Conservatory in Guangzhou, a big city in the South of China that smells of the sea. One
of the most respected Chinese music schools, its old, intimate,
wood-paneled auditorium felt like Stony Brook, and I'd played
my heart out. The next morning in the master class, a student
named Deng Zhao performed Robert Schumann's *Fantasie* with
the focused passion, darkness, and depth of an old soul. Still, I
pushed her further: Where could there be more layers of color?
How could a phrase speak like a human voice, where no two
notes are exactly alike? What does Schumann mean when he
asks to play softer and softer and softer or faster and faster and
faster without telling us where or how to stop? We spoke of Flo-
restan and Eusibius—the yin and yang figures in Schumann's
fanciful musical imagination—and Beethoven—his statue in
Bonn, his Sonata no. 28 and its connection to the *Fantasie*. She
understood me before could finish a sentence. Her classmates
filled every seat, once again, and after the master class ended,
they stayed for more than an hour, asking questions.

I found the passion and work ethic of Chinese music students staggering, and likewise, the dedication of audiences,
evident, as every seat at every performance, regardless of the

city, was always taken. Reverence for Beethoven, Chopin, Tchaikovsky, and Schumann seemed universal.

In the Soviet Union, musicians sent to win international competitions came back as artists of national distinction but also, in many ways, pawns of the Soviet state. Being labeled a great artist meant you were now representing the Soviet Union globally. Anything that translated to national prestige and/or hard currency for the benefit of the state—be it Olympic sports, chess, classical music, or space exploration—was promoted and supported. In the Soviet Union, classical music as a whole, and the weighty tradition of Russian music specifically, was viewed as the height of European culture, and the Soviets used artists to present a picture of cultural supremacy to the rest of the world. There is a definite similarity in the intensity and passion for the study and performance of classical music, especially piano, in China. To whatever extent this is intentionally encouraged by state cultural policy, all I can say is that the enthusiasm of the audiences and the devotion of the students seemed completely genuine and spontaneous.

Living Chinese composers, such as Du Yun, Gao Ping, and Zhou Long, combine the most current trends in new music with Chinese tradition. Sixty-five percent of my students at UCLA are Chinese or Chinese American. Pianists from China, after graduating from the best music schools in Europe and the United States, return home to pass on classical music traditions in their own distinct ways. This musical exchange is exponentially growing. As concert halls remain half-filled in our nation's capitals, especially when the music is performed by anyone who is not a household name, in China, a Beethoven-Chopin program is neither boring nor unhip. Chinese audiences are hungry for more, be it music old or new—especially piano music.

As a child, I was trained with an intensity familiar to Chinese piano students, and upon arriving in the States, my musical nerdiness set me apart in junior high. Being into Mozart was decidedly uncool. But in China, where Western classical music has gained a foothold only relatively recently, the opposite is true. Every music student dreams of studying in Europe or the States, and when they arrive there, they often become the stars of the music department. As a teacher, I can vouch for this. Yet it is endlessly frustrating for me that many liberal, open-minded institutions of higher learning present seemingly insurmountable academic and bureaucratic obstacles for students who would like to come from China for graduate work in piano. Not the least of these are unrealistic requirements for the doctor of musical arts programs at top American universities. If more is not done to ease the way for talented, bright, creative young artists to come here, then there may come a point when they will no longer want to do it.

Within the echelons of the classical piano world, one will often hear a xenophobic sentiment—from competition judges, teachers, audience members—that Chinese students' interpretations of Western music are anchored by technical brilliance but lack emotional depth and understanding of context. This stereotype is as reprehensible as the ideas about gender that are still prevalent in the music profession. I first became familiar with this as a newcomer to Mr. D's studio, where the non-Asian parents complained about the "Orientals who play fast with no feeling."

Chinese pianists are known for their rigid discipline from the earliest age. There are occasions in the early stages when a focus on virtuosic technique eclipses the development of a more personal sensibility. Often, this has to do with a culture of humility and emotional restraint. As Shan had explained to me, "In our culture, we are taught early on to respect our elders and mentors. It is not about us or our emotion. We learn with modesty." Even if this suggests a suppression of natural instincts or desires, this is exactly when an excellent mentor can help shape a young artist and point them in the needed direction. The freedom that technical ability allows is a must for any performer who hopes to have a career in music—and it is difficult to catch up on this aspect later in life. But to say an entire people lacks feeling or understanding is a racist trope. It also exposes the unwillingness or inability of a piano teacher from the West to inspire a student from a different background.

Music students in China, while living in a restricted, undemocratic society, are eager to embrace music from the West and make it their own. Young Chinese pianists strive to be like Lang Lang and Yuja Wang, two high-powered names whose career successes have paralleled China's emergence as a global power and who in many ways help drive the global classical music economy.

Among China's endless paradoxes, Western influences go hand in hand with an ancient cultural heritage, ironclad politics, and the nation's blindingly fast economic rise. This brew is unlike any other, and young classical musicians coming up in this extraordinary landscape are bringing an entirely new energy to the art.

* * *

Harbin is the capital of Heilongjiang, the northernmost province in China, and it sits along the Russian border. In the late nineteenth century, Russian engineers worked on the construction of the trans-Siberian railroad there. This explains the agate-green Russian orthodox church Santa Sophia, the matryoshka dolls on display in souvenir shops, and the borscht served in restaurants. I bundled up and walked around in the unfathomable cold, dazed by the collage of images from my childhood and from China. Finding Russian food here felt as surprising as in British Columbia. It was as if I had traveled around the world to come back to the same place. It was ten degrees below zero, and I bought a sweet potato on the street from an old lady in a dark kerchief who baked them in a portable oven. I snapped a photo of a mall with the sign "Manhattan." Underneath, a yellow cab had stopped, and its Mongolian driver was having a smoke—or, perhaps, it was just his breath ascending in ringlets. Was I in Manhattan? Brighton Beach? Russia? Ukraine? China? Wherever I was, it was freezing, and I had a concert to play.

We drove along the river, past the famous ice sculpture festival. The new Harbin Performing Art Center emerged in the distance like an enormous, primordial snail. The piano onstage was freshly tuned and voiced, impeccably colorful, immediate in its responsiveness. When I took out my handkerchief to wipe the keys, the stagehand ran toward me. "No!" He took out another cloth, dustier and thicker. "We only can use this to wipe the keys."

At the airport check-in counter when I was on my way home, I saw a familiar face looking down from an enormous ad for bathroom tiles. Past security at the gate, there he was again, this time with a glass of baijiu. Lang Lang was everywhere, and what other country can boast a true classical music celebrity like him? Where else does a classical musician get to advertise tiles and alcohol? At first glance, the ads were joltingly tacky, but I also found them to be thrilling and hopeful. Classical music is alive and beloved in China. Its audiences are young and eager; its performance halls, new, architecturally stunning, and full.

13

ALONE, A WHITE SAIL GLEAMS

For the first time in their lives, my parents were flying overseas in business class. My dad helped my mom recline, urging her to eat something. The food was better in this part of the plane, he tried to tell her. She weighed ninety-seven pounds, and eating caused her pain. Thirty-two years before, in the air between Rome and New York, she tried to convince me to eat hot bits of chicken from a foil container. That flight had taken her to a new life, while this one was taking her back to Europe: Switzerland, where she would be able to die with dignity.

They landed in Zurich, and two days later, she was given a liquid barbiturate by an attending physician. She drank it herself and fell asleep quickly. Her heart stopped beating a half hour later. It would, of course, have been much easier if my father did not have to take her there, if she had been allowed to choose this at home, in Chicago. But unfortunately, medically assisted suicide is not legal there.

In May 2020, we didn't yet know Mom had brain cancer. As life came to a standstill during the coronavirus pandemic, she was making soft, colorful masks that said "World's Best Grandpa" out of my kids' old burp cloths and learning how to teach piano over Zoom. One evening, she got up from a nap and hobbled over to my father in his office, her face twisted to one side, her foot dragging. At the hospital, the doctors performed

Amid the pandemic and Mom's declining health, I tried to keep performing through a series of "Corona Friday" concerts livestreamed over Facebook and Instagram.

emergency brain surgery to deal with the huge hemorrhage that had left her paralyzed and speechless.

On Mom's third day out of neurosurgery, a diligent nurse established a three-way Zoom connection between the ICU, Los Angeles, and my parents' home in the Chicago suburb of Highland Park. In a small square, I saw a grainy image of Mom in the hospital bed, smiling at me with the left side of her face, her green eyes full of life. I brought a giant, white orchid up to the screen. "Mom, I haven't watered it in a month!" She raised her brow in surprise—a familiar expression. For the next few weeks, the orchid would be a ritual, a marker of her gradually improving cognition. I would call in; Dad would already be there, telling his inimitable Odessa jokes. I would proudly lift the orchid to the computer screen; watch for a reaction; and then, switching between English and Russian, ask if I should play for her. I played music she had learned in childhood: Tchaikovsky's *The Seasons*, Schumann's *Kinderszenen*, old Soviet songs. She would half-smile with the left side and doze off while I played. Zoom was not created for music. It speeds up and slows down unpredictably, the metallic pings and echoes forming a one-of-a-kind, pandemic-tinted experience. I probably tired her out with the wobbly sound of virtual Tchaikovsky.

A month later, I put on three masks; fashioned a dress out of a garbage bag so that I could immediately throw it out after exiting the airport; and, resembling Darth Vader, flew to Chicago. My dad and I were finally being allowed into the hospital to be trained for Mom's home care. I asked her if she remembered the orchid, and her eyes filled with tears. She had understood everything. Day after day, I watched Mom retrain her mouth to make shapes that would eventually lead to sounds. She had started moving gradually, then walking. The loss of dignity she experienced—she had always been so elegant, in control, articulate—was eased only by the therapists insisting that partial recovery was possible. One day, we sat in a circle, the speech therapist slowly forming an *ah* sound with her mouth, and we heard my mom's voice echoing it. Next came more vowels and, finally, a garbled but recognizable "Happy Birzday." Dad and I, both in tears, called everyone we knew. "Irene finally spoke!"

When it was finally time to go home from the hospital, I rolled her wheelchair out of her room, as proud as a new mother, and her nurses and therapists gathered at the exit and rang little bells together in celebration of her, a chorus of Campanellas. We indulged ourselves in something that would sustain us for eight months of the pandemic quarantine—the luxury of hope. "Hope is a thing with feathers," said Emily Dickinson, but I disagree; hope is the peach ice cream from Homer's that we had together at home.

Back at home in Highland Park, we were learning how to take care of a severely disabled stroke patient. Almost on autopilot, I was learning the vocabulary of stroke: how to clean feeding tubes, the complicated mechanics of swallowing. How many different types of gauze can there be? And all the varieties of tape: One kind would stick to the skin of her caved-in belly, and the other one wouldn't. If I didn't use the correct one, then the tube inadvertently moved when she went to bed, and she would cry out in pain. But gradually, she ate, spoke, moved better. Soon, she had banished the wheelchair to the garage and refused to wear the barbaric black boot intended to help her straighten her right foot. The only thing still completely immobile was her right hand. I imagined that it was like a piece of clay left out in the cold; it would become malleable and warm with time, ready for any musical phrase Mom wanted to play. For now, we focused on naming notes and rhythms.

Helping Mom relearn how to speak, I read her *The Master and Margarita*. She smiled dreamily at the familiar words, closing her eyes and imagining Margarita's flight on a broom, invisible and free. "Mom, this word has six consonants. Where should I put the accent?" After a little while, we broke Russian words into syllables and said them by memory. I gave her the same piano lessons she had given me when I was five—patiently and slowly, fingers asleep on the keys and then, like spiders, awake and ready to scamper. Rainbows drawn with the hand, from octave to octave, from the key, up to the air, and back to the next key. The fingers of the left hand slowly remembering; the fingers of the right swollen, purple, immovable. Her posture was intact, ramrod-straight, as always, her features slender and expressive, all thoughts vibrantly alive on her face. The words in her mind took longer to form, each one carefully sculpted. We breathed deeply, slowly, focusing on the shapes of letters inside her mouth. We used consonants to sing the opening of Beethoven's Fifth, clearly, forcefully: "Pa-pa-pa *pa!*" That's how Fleisher would teach the energy of various rhythms: "Would you use *Pa* or *Ga* or *Ha* on this?"

As my dad gave her the crushed pills (she could not swallow a whole one yet), I sat next to them at the piano, playing the middle section of the Brahms B Major Trio's scherzo movement, the kindest of waltzes lilting gingerly yet generously, as though breathing warm air onto a tiny, frozen flower. Music was her air and mine; it was the love that connected us.

Only when I felt that Dad was set up with help and a routine and that Mom was steadily making progress did I return home to LA in midsummer. When I got home, my phone rang. It was Mom. *"Ya-te-bia-lyu-blyu*, Innochka"—"I love you," spoken syllable by syllable. I shook from head to toe. I knew my mother loved me. But this was the first time I had ever heard her say it. All her life, she had been inhibited, rigid like a piano string. The stroke took away all those restraints. For the next year, she would say it to me every day.

I took a day off at the beach with Misha; Nathaniel; and our daughter, five-year-old Frida, who had been born three years after Nathaniel and who managed to get whacked between her eyes with a heavy boomerang on this beach trip. Seeing my child covered in blood, I heard myself scream hysterically but only for a moment. I'd learned how to be in emergency nurse mode in Chicago, and the instinct kicked in. Delighted to ride in an ambulance, Frida flirted with the police officer who accompanied us to the ER and demanded ice cream after surgery. After two sets of stitches and weeks of recovery, she would be just fine. Like her grandma, she was a tough cookie. We were lucky; she didn't lose an eye, and the scar would fade. This was the first of the "war stories" she would love to regale others with. Most

Frida and Nathaniel, 2019.

recently, she was accosted by a giant orange iguana on a trip to Costa Rica. The creature stole her banana as she napped, and it nibbled on her ponytail a little. Frida woke up, looked him in the eyes, and said, "I do not appreciate this. Please don't do it again."

As a wave of Zoom fatigue set in at the start of the academic year, my mom was frustrated at the seemingly slowed progress of her improvement. Something was not quite right. When I try to imagine the exact moment the tissue in my mom's brain met a sneaky, malignant cancer cell, I picture the sea floor, the darkness, the tentacle reaching out. To me, the very word *glioblastoma* embodies those childhood monsters: an amorphous cephalopod; a shape-shifting tanuki; a slimy, starfish-like creature. At which moment did it decide to nest and grow in her shapely, immaculately coiffed head? And why didn't we know about it when we needed to? It turned out that the cancer had caused Mom's stroke and was missed during the postoperation biopsy. Eight months after the stroke, the dapper, avuncular neurosurgeon had to get in there again.

While it was happening, I was recording Beethoven's *Appassionata* for a concert series at St. James Church in Los Angeles, to be broadcast on YouTube a few days later. Had I not known the piece for many years—I had played it on my Japan tour as a teenager and in my college auditions—it would have been hard to get through. I had probably performed it more than any other Beethoven sonata. In the cavernous, freezing, starkly beautiful church, the fateful opening arpeggios transported me into a tragic world. The tessellations of sound coursed through the space, each note with a ten-second life span, even without the pedal, thanks to the church's acoustics. I thought of Dame Myra Hess playing the piece in wartime London: its loving, proud second theme and its shattering ending; Londoners and the falling bombs. Now, it was my companion for the night.

After I finished recording, Misha and I went to see six large paintings by Gerhardt Richter at the Gagosian Gallery. Five at first glance looked like playful musings on the stripping of paint from wood. The sixth reminded me of Ondine the water nymph—it was impossible to look away from it, like staring at the ocean. It illuminated the others, engaging them in a quiet exchange. New shapes and colors were released. It all looked like pain and silver linings and a bit of hopeful light.

The next morning, the call came. It was a malignant tumor. Glioblastoma kills in eighteen months on average, shutting down body functions until the person is reduced to a near-vegetative state. Mom had gone through ten months already. This time, the *Appassionata* heralded the beginning of the end.

The hardest part is not death itself. It is the knowledge of it and the experience of inevitable and total suffering as one progresses toward it. Mom decided quite soon after the diagnosis that she wanted to leave life on her terms, with the help of the Dignitas Foundation in Switzerland. We understood this. My graceful pianist mother couldn't imagine herself losing more functions, one by one, after the stroke and the recovery. Every moment of her existence was filled with suffering, and her decision gave her hope to leave lightly.

To humor my dad and show a fighting spirit, she faced the endless parade of doctors and nurses and put herself through chemo and radiation. Then, she chose to stop. As Mom approached death, she did it with the same staunch discipline with which she helped me become a pianist and composer in Odessa. In this discipline, she retained her quiet dignity until the last moment.

Their days were strictly regimented. In the mornings, my dad would make her oatmeal. She would oversee every detail and stir the pot with her left hand. Mom was always a little obsessive-compulsive about cleaning, but now it seemed as though any crumb on the floor or on the stove caused her actual pain. So Dad would calmly clean wherever she was pointing, even at the risk of burning his fingers on the still-hot stove. She hated eating with the stubbornness of a child, fearing the pain any given combination of ingredients could cause her. Dad, who had never ventured beyond cooking an egg, suddenly had the run of the kitchen—and did it calmly, neatly, as though all was as it was supposed to be. He made an art out of retaining equilibrium. He diced kiwis one day and mixed blueberries with plain yogurt and cinnamon the next. He baked sweet potatoes and

Even in her last days, Mom practiced the piano every morning. No longer able to control her wrist or the fingers of her right hand, she did exercises in the hopes of gaining mobility.

peeled and cooked beets. He would take out the recycled paper and refill the compost and water the flowers, trying to hold on to a sense of normalcy in the midst of hell.

After breakfast, they would sit at the large table at which they used to host their friends. It now was covered with a plethora of objects that, to an outsider, might have looked like a whimsical children's game. A glass container filled with colorful, puffy, little cotton balls. A jar of change. A long rubber band and two long foam rollers. A tower made of empty Chobani containers. Frida's pink toy volleyball. At first, Mom and Dad would stand six feet apart, he would throw the ball to her, and she would throw it back, thirty-two times. After the sit-ups, the stretches Dad helped her do, and the exercises with the foam roller came the truly tortuous part. Sitting at the table, she needed to first take out the colorful puffs from the container and then put them back, with her right hand. With a healthy arm this would take twenty seconds at most. It often took her thirty minutes, every motion pained, deliberate, angular, slow, and filling her with endless torment. A similar exercise, even more difficult, involved pennies strewn about the table. These exercises had been in her regimen since the stroke, and she would not give up on them until the end. When I visited, I oversaw the exercises, giving my dad a few moments to himself. I still dream about those terrifying, colorful balls.

After the exercises, Mom would go over to the piano and practice. I had brought her Czerny etudes and the second movement of the Bach F Minor Concerto transcribed for the left hand by Hiroyuki Tanaka. While Dad allowed himself a short moment to take a breath, she would play scales, arpeggios, Czerny, and Bach—autumnal music, transcendent and even more painful because of the major key. More often than not, I could not stay in the room to listen. I would hide in the bedroom, choking on tears.

After practicing, it was time for a walk. My parents went on three walks a day, often covering more than fifteen thousand steps daily. They had nicknames for their different lush, green parks. One of them, the Larry Fink Memorial Park on Clavey Road, was the lake park, as it consisted of a long path around a softball field and a mossy green lake. Sometimes I would go for an early-morning jog around the lake, aiming to return before Mom woke up. One morning, I saw a black tortoise, like a giant flying saucer that had landed in the middle of the field. It filled me with a ridiculous, giddy joy, as if it was a sign of some sort, a message from the heavens that turned pomegranate in the sunrise.

My favorite was Rosewood Beach. You would park in a lot next to a large, green field overlooking Lake Michigan. It was one of the most beautiful sights imaginable: the opal blue of the water peering out from the wild branches of acacia and oak trees, the stratus clouds playfully changing shapes in the wind. We would walk down an overgrown path, next to a stream and wildflowers and, in the crux of summer, ripe wild blackberries. My dad held Mom's hand, and they volleyed poetry in Russian, back and forth. This was part of her speech therapy, but it was also the dialogue of rhymes and rhythms I grew up with. "*Beleyet parus odinokii*," he would begin. "*V tumane morya golubom*," she would answer. Alone, a white sail gleams in the blue fog of the sea. This poem, by Mikhail Lermontov—who, like Pushkin, had died obscenely young in a duel—was also the source of the title of Valentin Kataev's novel about Odessa, *Alone, A White Sail Gleams*, one of my parents' favorites.

The poems were endless. My dad seemed to have one stored for every moment of the day, and he read them breathily, his voice caught between tenderness and pain. As we would walk down to the water, Mom's face would open into an almost-full smile as she looked onto Lake Michigan. She always felt at home next to the water. I stayed behind a bit, watching them, and they looked young, as though on a first date, holding hands gently.

After the walks, Dad and I scrambled to make lunch and dinner that Mom might be willing to eat; the options waned with each of my visits. Her favorite was avocado on toast. She could finish a half-slice of sprouted-grain bread and a soft-boiled egg if we pressed her. As crickets began their nightly show, Dad would turn up Venice Classic Radio or the Beatles. One night, he put on "Let It Be" and then picked her up from her chair and whirled her around the kitchen in a slow dance. He knew how to find beauty and joy in small moments; it is a gift he had throughout his life, and he desperately tried to share it with

Mom. Afterward, we would go downstairs to watch the news and perhaps a Russian film. Mom's English after the stroke was no longer fluent, and she wanted to watch what she remembered from her youth in the Soviet Union.

Each visit, I would take Mom for a pedicure in a salon a block from their house. Never one to indulge in that luxury, she was suddenly frequenting the salon each of these numbered months. She could not do her own nails now, but she had to have them neatly shaped and colored on a regular basis. On my last trip, I watched her pick out a bright blue color, the hue of Lake Michigan, of a cloudless sky. As mothers and daughters around us chitchatted and giggled, we stared ahead silently from our spa chairs, her eyes fixed on the Kate Hudson and Adam Sandler romantic comedy on the flat-screen television. She was far away.

In the morning, I would climb into her bed and hold her bony frame in my arms, her once-lush hair just a wisp of curls on her skull. By then, Dad would be up, going through the macabre email exchanges and preparing documents that would enable her trip to Switzerland. His last gift to her, this trip, was to set her free.

* * *

While their plane flew through darkness to Switzerland, I sank into our sofa with my two kids in West LA and watched the Disney movie *Luca*. "*Silenzio*, Bruno!" is a cry made up by one of the characters to combat his inner fear as the boys race into the sea on a makeshift Vespa. Bruno was as reasonable a name for one's fears as any. My mom and dad silenced them when they left everything behind and traveled to a dreamland where their Jewish daughter could become a concert pianist. They silenced it when they filled out the exhaustive, painful paperwork marked with the eerie name *Dignitas*; when they flew to face her death in a small, blue building in Switzerland; as she fell asleep forever, listening to Chopin Nocturnes played by Artur Rubinstein, with him holding her hand.

As the pandemic gradually lifted its grip, I found myself preparing to be onstage again. Practicing Tchaikovsky's and

Chopin First Piano Concertos, the very pieces she had accompanied for me in competitions when I was a teenager, I would also take respite in Bach's F Minor Concerto, the last piece she ever played on the piano, just hours before boarding the plane. It was the very first concerto I had ever learned. I first performed it, with her at the second piano, in Odessa. The dark gait of the first movement gave way to the transcendent second and the lilting third. I could not believe that my muscles could still remember. But such is the resilience of the human brain. Perhaps it was time to bring the piece back into my hands and my heart.

Postlude

YELLOW AND BLUE

I am crouching in the corner of a giant, cold dressing room in a long blue and yellow dress, straining to find the few bars of cell phone reception available in Frost Auditorium's backstage labyrinth. Tonight's fundraiser for Ukraine—a combined effort of Culver City Unified School District, the Wende Museum, LA's cutting-edge Jacaranda Music Series, and multiple other organizations—aims to raise money for medical supplies to help Ukraine following the Russian invasion; by the end of the night, it will have raised more than $100,000. But right now I desperately need to find the email with the event's program order. Do I play *The Great Gate of Kiev* before Silvestrov's *The Messenger* or after?

"Inna, you need to be onstage!" My friend Patrick, the heart of and mastermind behind Jacaranda Music, pops his head in the door. His socks are blue, and his funky geometric glasses, bright yellow. He seems nervous and exasperated. That's odd. I already had my warm-up session at the piano, and I thought I have plenty of time before the actual performances commences.

"You are singing the national anthem!"

"I am *what*?"

"Did we not discuss this?"

"I said I wanted to sing in the chorus. I have not sung solo onstage since *The Cat's House* opera days."

"Inna, you sing beautifully, and nobody else here can read Ukrainian. Please, just go and do it. The students from the orchestra just got here. We have ten minutes to rehearse. Here's the sheet music."

"Patrick, we need to bring this down a third lower! I cannot do a high B-flat! I am a mezzo!"

"We have to do it as is. They can't transpose. They are in high school."

There is no use arguing with Patrick. I quickly speak through the words. The third stanza, clearly printed from Wikipedia, gives me pause.

"Patrick, I cannot sing this out loud. This is about Bohdan Khmelnytskyi. It does not serve us well." Khmelnytskyi was the Cossack hetman who, in 1648 and 1649, not only aligned the Ukrainians with the Russian tsar but also simultaneously led the Cossack massacre of thousands of Ukrainian Jews.

But that was then. And now, Volodymyr Zelensky is the young, bold Ukrainian Jewish president of a nation violently, immorally attacked by what I had always considered to be its blood brother. Russian is what I grew up speaking. And now, it is the language of war. We agree that I will simply sing the first stanza three times, with the refrain.

The war has shocked me and shaken me to my core. It has not clarified my identity one way or the other, but my identity is not important in the face of a historic tragedy. When the war first started, I recorded a video, playing Beethoven's *Appassionata* for Odessa. Years ago, after a couple seasons of Music/ Words, I was asked by Chicago's International Music Foundation to join Leslie Nicol (a.k.a., Mrs. Patmore of *Downton Abbey*) in my first foray into theater, as the pianist in the play *Admission: One Shilling*. It tells the story of the great British pianist Dame Myra Hess, who was known for staying in London during the Blitz and performing concerts in the National Gallery to keep up public morale. One of Hess's most famous performances at the National Gallery had been of Beethoven's *Appassionata* sonata, as the city around her went up in smoke.

Playing the tragic, fateful falling-thirds motif, I had felt profoundly inadequate. I wore my mom's cream-colored Ukrainian

Playing for friends, still holding the weight in my fingertips.
Courtesy Alexey Steele

vyshyvanka shirt, with its billowy sleeves and red, woven flow-ers. I also wore her bloodred beaded necklace; Dad had recently brought all her jewelry and most of her clothes for me to sort through. Had she felt Ukrainian? Not especially, but she felt Odessan, like feeling Barcelonian rather than Spanish or Mar-seillaise rather than French. She loved the tasty, idiomatic expressions of the Ukrainian language and was proud of her *vyshyvankas*. Did I feel Ukrainian? What did this mean to me? Suddenly everyone wanted to know, and I had no idea how to answer. I have always dreamed of going back to beautiful, ele-gant, funny, gritty, and culturally bubbling Odessa to perform. But I have never been back. I have pictured the homecoming thousands of times: I'd climb the Potemkin steps and kiss the Duc de Richelieu and cry and go back to our tiny old apartment building and hug Anastasia, my childhood best friend with whom I'd put on a vaudeville at the summer house on the Black Sea. I've only seen her as an adult on Facebook.

In my piano competition years, my name would often appear in the program next to a tiny yellow-and-blue flag, listing me as "Ukrainian American pianist Inna Faliks." I rarely encountered the flag, otherwise. Now, the blue and yellow is everywhere, including a "Ukraine" flavor at a Los Angeles ice cream shop that was just vanilla with food coloring. Being from Ukraine is not a commodity, it is not hip or fun, and it is not an identity to be performed. This is about families destroyed, people dying, and a power of pure evil seeping into the larger world.

I feel helpless. My place of birth is being erased off the face of the planet. Will it disappear like the Soviet Union, like the castle where Misha and I were married? Like my mom? What can I do? I begin the anthem. My high B-flat is wobbly, but I hit it and keep on singing. And the audience joins in.

INDEX

253